Why Should Jews Survive?

Why Should Jews Survive?

Looking Past the Holocaust toward a Jewish Future

MICHAEL GOLDBERG

New York   Oxford
OXFORD UNIVERSITY PRESS
1995

Oxford University Press

Oxford   New York
Athens   Auckland   Bangkok
Calcutta   Cape Town   Dar es Salaam   Delhi
Florence   Hong Kong   Istanbul   Karachi
Kuala Lumpur   Madras   Madrid   Melbourne
Mexico City   Nairobi   Paris   Singapore
Taipei   Tokyo   Toronto

and associated companies in
Berlin   Ibadan

Copyright © 1995 by Michael Goldberg

Published by Oxford University Press, Inc.
200 Madison Avenue, New York, New York 10016

Library of Congress Cataloging-in-Publication Data
Goldberg, Michael, 1950–
Why should Jews survive? / by Michael Goldberg.
p.   cm.   Includes index.
ISBN 0-19-509109-4
1. Jews—Identity.
2. Judaism—20th century.
3. Holocaust, Jewish (1939–1945)—Influence.
4. Holocaust (Jewish theology)
5. Exodus, The—History of doctrines.
I. Title.   DS143.G573   1995   296.3'11—dc20   94-36969

9 8 7 6 5 4 3 2 1

Printed in the United States of America
on acid-free paper

To my father,
in memory,
To my sons,
in hope,
To my God,
in thanks.

I shall not die, but live to tell
the story of the Lord's deeds.
Psalm 118:17

Preface

This book will provoke many people. It is meant to.

But the provocation is not for provocation's sake. It is for God's sake and for the sake of the Jewish People, his people. This book means to provoke, to spark passionate discussion among that people about what it means to be God's people. For part of what this book claims is that unless we are such a people, there is in the end precious little to talk about—and even less worth listening to. Instead, the air will be filled with chatter about "Jewish identity," "Jewish values," and that old chestnut, "Jewish survival."

Clearly, such topics are important to most Jews, especially post-Holocaust. But why they should be important to anybody else is far from clear. And yet we Jews have generally never been content to have our conversation stop at the borders of our own community. Something about us, we have been wont to say, is not merely significant, but *vital* for the rest of the world to hear. Once, it was word of our God, who was not our God only, but the world's own true Lord. Now, following the Holocaust, many Jews would change that word to warning, not from God's chosen people, but from history's preferred victim: "This could happen to you! We will let it happen to us never again!" That word, however, seems to be reaching an ever-shrinking audience, even among Jews—witness the ever-soaring intermarriage rate. Ironically, word of the Holocaust absent word of God may subvert Jewish survival instead of sustain it.

Provocative books sometimes provoke readers to read them carelessly and thus attribute to them positions they do not hold. Here are some positions not taken by this book:

First, the book most definitely does *not* take the position that the Holocaust never happened. In all its awful brutality, it surely did happen. This book does not dispute the fact of the Holocaust—only its significance for the Jewish People.

Furthermore, the book's position is not "anti-Israel." It is, however, *anti* any position that would have us view the State of Israel like any other nation-state and that would fail to see its establishment as both a God-given opportunity and trust with wider implications for the rest of the nation-states on earth.

Moreover, the book does not take any position that could or should be labeled "Orthodox," "Conservative," or "Reform." In the 1990s, the world witnessed the collapse of the greatest ideology it has ever known. Hence, it hardly seems worth the effort as we approach the twenty-first century to champion ideologies from the nineteenth that are little more than Jewish versions of German philosophical mistakes.

Finally, the book's position is not liberal, nor is it conservative; these stances, too, represent contemporary holdovers from another century's flawed philosophical ideals. The editors of the liberal *Tikkun* and the conservative *Commentary* have more in common, respectively, with Jesse Jackson and Ronald Reagan than either of them has with Maimonides—or with me. If one party says that two plus two equals six, and another party replies that two plus two equals eight, the correct response is not that two plus two equals seven. In the language of this book, today's Jewish liberals and conservatives are inhabitants of the same "master story." This book asks them to enter a different story.

So if all these are positions the book does not take, what positions does it finally espouse? If that question were answered in the Preface, what need would there be to read—or to have written—the rest of the book?

This book could not possibly have been written or brought to publication without the help of many other people: Louis Bernstein, Barry Cytron, David DeCosse, Lilian Furst, Peter Hellman, Martin Kahn, Wendy Lipkind, James McClendon, Julie Magilen, Nancey Murphy, Margie Rashti, Hal Rast, Barbara and Dan Shellist, Theophus Smith, Dick Snider, Susan Stern, and Marc Wilson. I particularly want to thank both Cynthia Read of Oxford University Press for her exceptionally insightful editorial suggestions and Rosemary Wellner for her first-rate copyediting. The counsel of all these people proved not simply beneficial, but crucial. If this book does indeed provoke controversy, let it be said that while the views expressed are mine, the courage and commitment reflected are theirs. It has been and remains a blessing to know them, and I thank God for them.

Finally, I thank God for God: *Baruch ata Adonai, Eloheynu Melech HaOlam, sheasah li nes bamakom hazeh.* "You are to be praised, Adonai, our God, King of the World, for having performed a miracle for me in this place."

Erev Yom Kippur, 5755   M.G.
September 14, 1994

Contents

Why Should Jews Survive?

Chapter 1

A Tale of Two Stories:
Exodus vs. Holocaust

A survey of the American Jewish community, reported in both Jewish and non-Jewish media, shows that fully 57% of all Jewish marriages are now intermarriages involving a non-Jewish partner who has not converted to Judaism. In addition, the overall Jewish birthrate in the United States remains so low that demographers warn that American Jewry may not be able to replace its own numbers.

In Russia, the ultra-nationalist Vladimir Zhirinovsky wins 25% of the vote in the parliament's lower house, and, according to a fund-raising letter by the Simon Wiesenthal Center, "unleashes a rash of vicious antisemitic and xenophobic rhetoric, vowing, 'I'll act as Hitler did in 1932.' "

As Israel and the Palestinians embark on the first phase of their historic treaty with Israeli troops pulling out of Gaza and Jericho, Yasser Arafat, according to news reports, tells an audience that this is just the first step of a "jihad" or holy war for Jerusalem.

Jews' interest in these stories is not "current events": it's *survival*. The first story reflects Jewish anxiety over the survival of American Jewry, the second over the survival of Jews around the world, and the third over the survival of the State of Israel. In sum, all these stories touch in Jews the same raw-nerve issue—the survival of the Jewish People.

But what specifically is *Jewish* survival? Furthermore, are there any limits to the kinds of actions Jews may take to ensure their survival? Last, and most important, why should the Jewish People

survive? My central contention is that although each of these questions can be answered convincingly from the perspective of the story
of the Jews' Exodus from Egypt, none of them can even be raised
meaningfully from the standpoint of the kind of story Jews today tell
about the Holocaust.

We hear the word "story," and we tend to think almost immediately of something that is false by definition—a fiction, a fable, a
fairy tale. But we need to remember that other kinds of stories also
claim to render true accounts of our experience as human beings:
news stories, life stories, histories. Indeed, the work of journalists,
psychotherapists, and historians hinges on their ability to link together disparate facts, events, and persons into some sort of narrative account that makes sense of them and thereby shows their true
significance. As human beings, we live in a story-shaped world.

Jews seem to have realized this from the very first. The Torah
directs Jewish parents to explain their people's Passover practices in
light of the story of their Exodus from Egypt: "And you shall give an
account to your child on that day saying, 'It is because of what the
Lord did for me when I went out of Egypt' " (Exodus 13:8). The
Hebrew word translated as "give an account" comes from the root
hgd, meaning "tell" or "narrate." Strikingly, that very same root
appears in Haggadah, the paradigmatic telling of Israel's story at the
Passover seder. From the vantage point of Jewish scripture and tradition, explaining the survival of the Jewish People and the meaning
of its practices requires telling a story, and, for most of Jewish history, that story has been the saga of the Exodus.

But in the last half of the twentieth century, a rival story has
emerged, telling of the Holocaust, in Hebrew shoah—"catastrophe."
For many Jews today, that story has supplanted the Exodus as an
explanation of the nature and meaning of Jewish survival. American Jews, while largely content to acquaint their children with the
Exodus story by perfunctorily reciting it at their seders, have by
contrast vigorously supported the introduction of Holocaust courses
into public school curricula so that new generations "may not forget
the lessons of the past." Additionally, many Jews today who consider the numerous Exodus-based practices surrounding Passover as
archaic nuisances, nevertheless display wholehearted devotion in
their fund-raising for Israel, spurred by the memory of the Holocaust
and the motto "Never again!" Finally, virtually every Jewish community of any size is assured a turnout at its annual Holocaust observance that easily dwarfs synagogue attendance on Passover.

On one level, the Exodus and Holocaust seem to tell the same story: The Jewish People, having suffered slave labor and genocide at the hands of a maniacal tyrant and his all-too-willing people, nevertheless survive while their oppressors go down to ignominious defeat. Themes of oppression, deliverance, and liberation course through both narratives. But there the similarities end. The Exodus narrative would have us see Israel's outliving Egyptian persecution as evidence of a powerful God who makes and keeps generation-spanning covenants. But if we view Jewish existence through the perspectives of a Holocaust-shaped narrative, neither God nor covenant worked to save the Jewish People from Hitler: If Jews survived, it was simply because the gas chambers failed to work quickly enough to kill them all. For the Israelites, deliverance meant more than merely getting out of Egypt; freed from Egyptian servitude, they were free to enlist in God's service as a "kingdom of priests and a holy nation" (Ex. 19:6). By contrast, for those rescued from Auschwitz and Bergen-Belsen, there was no goal beyond getting out alive. For such as these, survival itself became not a means to an end, but instead an end, a mission, in and of itself. And while the land of Israel beckoned the fugitives from Egypt as a place of promise where building a people could go hand-in-hand with fashioning the kingdom of Heaven on earth, for those who lived through the camps, the land fundamentally represented a place of protection—a haven for refugees, a stronghold for their defense, in other words, a sanctuary in which to observe their most sacred Jewish rite: survival.

At first glance, Jewish survival seems to be the sort of thing whose value is virtually self-evident. But closer scrutiny uncovers a string of questions we dare not overlook—the very questions I raised earlier about the nature, limits, and purpose of Jewish survival. If I am right that we cannot even begin to raise such questions meaningfully from the vantage point of the Holocaust, then the real threat posed to Jews by the Holocaust did not die with Hitler in a Berlin bunker. Instead, it still imperils the Jewish People today in the form of a story that mutilates Jewish self-understanding. Within the context of that Holocaust-framed story, there are no positive reasons Jews can give for remaining Jewish. At most, they can only point to their enduring determination to exist in spite of their enemies' enduring desire to eradicate them. But over the long run and against sometimes even longer odds, the sustenance such a bitter story provides is thin, unappetizing gruel, insufficient to nourish a people— or its children. The challenge to Jews today is not outliving Hitler and the Nazis but overcoming the life-threatening story created in their aftermath.

I call the kind of narratives exemplified by the Exodus and the Holocaust "master stories." For the communities in which master stories are told and heard, they are meant to provide models for understanding the world and guides for acting in it. Every master story could well begin, "Life is like this . . . ." Because master stories thus form as well as inform us, they mold our understanding of the world and our life in it. Such narratives supply the background context within which a community's core convictions about itself and the world gain their sense and significance.

When set against the backdrop of these rival narratives, Exodus and Holocaust, what happens to the Jewish community's convictions about God, Torah, and the people Israel? These three, after all, have historically been the focal points of Jewish identity. And what of that other, more recent focal point of communal attention— the survivor? What convictions should Jews have concerning the role, status, and significance of the survivors among them? In our day, "survivor" has become a term used to refer to everything from enduring the camps and eluding the crematoria to getting through a bad day at the office. It may well be that because "survivor"—like "Holocaust"—has become so elastic in use and reference, Jews have correspondingly become so obsessed about insisting on the Holocaust's "uniqueness" so that its meaning might not be trivialized. But if an event's meaning is ultimately story-dependent, then I submit that the Holocaust's true significance—like the Jewish People's true purpose—can only come clearly into focus through the powerful corrective lens afforded by the master story of the Exodus.

Whatever else happens as a result of what I have written, I hope that it will at least get people to start taking seriously (again) the stories that we tell each other—and our children. The stories embedded in religious traditions, once vibrant and sharp, seem particularly susceptible of being turned into sappy platitudes. Virtually every Jew who has had any religious education knows the rabbinic tale explaining the reason for taking out a drop of wine from the seder cup as each of the ten plagues is recited. The drops, say the rabbis, represent the tears God shed as the Egyptians, his children every bit as much as the Israelites, were drowning in the Sea. Over the years, the "point" of the story—that we share a common humanity even with our tormentors—has become dulled as the story's annual recitation has turned into a "mere ritual." But what if we were to try to restore the story's edge, its bite, by extending it to say that God's tears were shed not only for Egyptians drowning at the Sea, but also for Nazis freezing at Stalingrad—and for Palestinians shot and killed on the Temple Mount at Jerusalem? If such things are hard to say, the story has done its job anew: It has gotten us to think hard about the kind of life story we Jews are enacting as individuals, the kind of history we are creating as a people.

Once, there was a forest, and in it lived rabbits, lions, and monkeys. Everyone was happy, until one day, something terrible happened. Some creatures came into the forest with a big net and took away the rabbits. The monkeys saw this, but didn't do anything, saying there were too many rabbits anyway, and anyway, the monkeys weren't rabbits. Things returned to normal for awhile in the forest, until later, those with the big net returned and took away the lions. This the monkeys also saw, but as before, they didn't do anything, saying the lions were a danger to the monkeys anyway, and anyway, the monkeys weren't lions. Things once more returned to normal in the forest, even better than normal for the monkeys, because now they had it all to themselves, free of the detested rabbits and lions. The monkeys were doing just dandy, until one day, those with the big net returned and . . . .[1]

In various forms, the tale above may be quite familiar. It is the kind told about the Holocaust whose "moral" seems so obvious as to be almost a cliché: Because we just may share a common fate, we must show solidarity with all who are oppressed, and thus speak out against anybody's oppression anywhere we find it. But that is not the only possible moral to draw from the fable—or from the Holocaust. For there is another moral of the story—a far different lesson from the Holocaust—lurking in the background, and it is a chilling one: Just make sure you get yourself a net—a net bigger than anybody else's!

A people's story involves more than just an ethos; it also involves an ethic. An ethic deals with much more than the narrow constraints of a people's mere existence, because in it lie a people's larger ideals and aspirations. That is why we cannot let ourselves be lured on by stories that promise survival only. If a story is to be truly life-sustaining, then it must also tell of dreams and hopes. For Jews living at the end of the twentieth century—near the close of the fourth millennium of Jewish existence—the choice of stories at this time is critical. For today, something is more endangered than the Jewish People's survival: its soul.

Master Stories—The Stories on Which We Stake Our Lives

Each of us is the author of a story—our own individual life story. We tell that story to those whom we want to know us for the people we truly are: lovers, friends, children, . . . therapists. As human beings, we have no more basic way of giving voice to our identity through time than by rendering it in story form.

But we are not merely authors of a story; we are each heir to some story, too. As we grow up in a society, we hear of its storied past, recounting from its most distant origins how it came to be the community it most distinctly is. Eventually, that narrative—that master story—winds its way down to its current chapter, in which we learn that we, too, now figure as a character in our community's continually unfolding saga.

How does a community tell its master story? Sometimes, it commits the story to writing, line-by-line, perhaps even chapter-and-verse. More often, however, it transmits the story orally and re-enacts it ritually. Consider, for example, something we might call "the American story." Internalized by American children as they grow up, it takes a form called by professional historians "consensus history." In short-story version, it goes like this: The American story is fundamentally a story about a quest for freedom. Indeed, it begins with tales about Pilgrims who set out in search of freedom. Later, the story reaches its climax with chronicles of revolutionaries who struggled for their independence. Afterwards, it continues with an epic about a civil war waged to liberate all those within the nation's borders. The American story next moves forward with legends about rugged individualists who pioneered those hard-won liberties in uncharted new frontiers. And throughout the story as a whole, we repeatedly hear of American men and women willing to fight and, if necessary, die to defend their cherished freedoms.

To learn the American story, neither our children nor we turn to some sort of sacred scripture that lays it out in a single, authoritative fashion for all to read. Instead, we take the story to heart in another, more basic way. Year after year, that American freedom story is retold through communal rites like the Fourth of July, Thanksgiving, and other such national holiday observances. These public rituals, with all their attendant acts (speeches, parades, fireworks) and symbols (turkey, cornucopia, Pilgrim hats), train Americans to envision life's meaning in terms of their freedom, especially the freedom to break free of the past and thus move toward a future full of unbounded opportunity. Certainly, that storied vision has guided generations of immigrants to America's shores, from nineteenth-century Germans to twentieth-century Asians. Moreover, it's not too much to say that the vision of life generated by that story is reflected in *the* American rite of passage—a teenager's passing a driver's license test. How better to dramatically re-enact the crucial storied connection between having the ability to get up and go and having the capacity to attain life's promise? Without such communal rites and practices, a master story remains "just a story."

Clearly, the stories that the Exodus and the Holocaust have to tell are given voice through Jewish communal rites. At the Passover seder, the Exodus is recounted through the seder's key observance— the Haggadah, the narration of Israel's going out from Egypt. Meanwhile, the day set aside for communal Holocaust observance— known in Hebrew as *Yom Hashoah*—articulates the story Jews would relate about that terrible episode in their history. What are each story's crucial themes, and what are their implications for the life— that is, the survival—of the Jewish People?

In the first place, both narratives announce early on that they are indeed to be taken as master stories, as accounts that have earth-shaking, world-shaping consequences. In its opening few passages, the Exodus informs us that at the beginning of their sojourn in Egypt, "the Israelites were fertile and prolific; they multiplied and increased very greatly so that the land was filled with them" (Ex. 1:7). Words such as "fertile," "prolific," and "multiplied" call to mind another story—the one in Genesis recounting the creation of the world and all life in it. Thus, the Jews' story is linked to a larger, world-encompassing story for which it may well bear meaning.

The Holocaust, too, has master-story aspirations. Yom Hashoah observances typically begin with proclamations made by prominent non-Jews, such as politicians and other civic leaders. In that way, those holding the observance announce that the Holocaust calls for attention not only from Jews, but also from the world. Accordingly, President Reagan closed his 1981 Yom Hashoah proclamation, saying

The hope of a ceremony such as this is that even a tortured past holds promise *if we learn its lessons. . . . It is up to us to ensure that we never live it again.* (Italics added)

Like the traditional telling of the Exodus story at the seder, Holocaust observances do more than invoke the memory of some bygone
event. Instead, they call on people to take notice of certain "lessons"
of the past that bear meaning for the present and future. Just what
those lessons are remains to be explored.

For now, though, it is enough to notice another initial similar-
ity shared by the narratives framing the Exodus and Holocaust.
However much the Exodus and Holocaust "storylines" may diverge
in the end, they at first run on track together. Whether we hear of
the Jews' persecution in Egypt or in Germany, the policies that led
to Jewish suffering sprang from the same source. As the Exodus
narrative tells it,

A new king arose over Egypt. . . . And he said to his people, "Look, the
Israelite people are much too numerous for us". . . . So they set taskmasters
over them to oppress them with forced labor. . . . But the more they were
oppressed, the more they increased and spread out, so that the [Egyptians]
came to dread the Israelites. (Ex. 1:8–12)

Apparently, nothing more than Israel's fruitfulness brings on the
king's suspicion and his people's dread. But why should Israel's mere
fertility strike such terror? After all, God had promised Israel's ancestor, Abraham, to make his descendants "a great nation" (Gen. 12:2).
Even more basically, God had commanded *all* life at creation: "Be
fertile and increase" (Gen. 1:22, 28).

Notice, then, what drives Egypt's fear: "And the king said to
his people, ". . . The Israelite people are much too numerous for us.
Let us . . . deal shrewdly with them, lest they increase, and in the
event of war, join our enemies in fighting against us.' " Apparently, Egyptian alarm is based on a perception of difference between the two peoples, between "us" and "them." Israel's oppression, in other words, seems to stem from nothing more than its
perceived "otherness."

Likewise, Nazi persecution of Jews was part of a long-standing
German fear of the purported threat of Jewish otherness to German
society. In the late nineteenth century, for instance, the German
historian Heinrich von Treitschke lamented that "the Jews are our
misfortune." In fact, to account both for Jews' differentness and their
own attitude toward it, Germans had by 1879 coined a new, scientific-
sounding word: anti-Semitism. Discrimination against Jews could
now be robed in the mantle of science, thereby justifying their exclu-

sion from the German body politic. Or, as an eminent German scholar, Paul de Lagarde, declared in 1886, Jews were

aliens [and] nothing but carriers of decomposition. . . . [With such] trichinae and bacilli, one does not negotiate. . . . They are exterminated as quickly and thoroughly as possible.[2]

Eerily, the Germans' effort to get rid of their "alien" Jewish element pursued a course of action similar to the one the Egyptians had followed over 3,000 years before: first came slave labor, then attempted genocide.

"But the more they were oppressed, the more they increased." From the beginning, the Exodus narrative signals us that the Egyptian plan to eliminate the Jewish People from its midst is doomed to failure—as are all such extermination schemes. Ultimately, they run up against God's grand design for the world, a world in which he has deemed all life "very good" (Gen. 1:31). Creation is so good, in fact, that God has given all in it the same prime directive: "Be fruitful and multiply." Hence, to divide that creation into two irreconcilable camps of "us" and "them," and then to try and snuff out the spark of life in "them" is to attempt to establish an entirely different kind of world. More than that, it is to tell an entirely different master story. The Exodus narrative reminds us that at stake in the issue of Jewish survival is more than just the survival of the Jews. At stake also is the survival of a storied plan bearing hope for the whole world.

A long time after that, the king of Egypt died. The Israelites were groaning under the bondage and cried out; and their cry for help from the bondage rose up to God. God heard their groaning, and God remembered his covenant with Abraham and Isaac and Jacob. God looked upon the Israelites, and God knew what to do. (Ex. 2:23–25)

No matter how congruently the Exodus and Holocaust storylines may have started out, they soon enough break off in opposite directions. In the process, they begin to school Jews about the source and extent of help they can rightfully expect in times of crisis. In the Exodus narrative, the Israelites, "groaning under the bondage," finally cry out to God for help. Earlier, when the oppression began, the people perhaps viewed it as the freak policy of a crazed ruler, which would presumably die when he did. But when "the king of Egypt died," and his policy nevertheless continued under his successor, they

seem to have been moved in desperation to call out to God to come to
their rescue.

Thus, for the first time in the story, God enters to take an active
part by setting in motion the chain of events that will eventually
lead to Israel's deliverance. But we need to stop and ask: Why should
God intervene *now*? Answers the narrative, "God remembered his
covenant with Abraham and Isaac and Jacob." In other words, God
comes into the story at this point to deliver his people, because it's
precisely at this point in the story that his people call on him to
deliver on his covenantal promises to their ancestors. What moves
God to intervene on the Jews' behalf is neither pity nor indignation.
Rather, what draws God to Israel's rescue are the binding obligations
of the covenant he made. According to the Exodus master story, if
Jewish survival hinges on any one thing, it is on God's fidelity to his
covenant with the Jewish People.

And what outside aid did the Jews of Europe receive in their
desperate hour? Significantly, when the Israeli Knesset inaugurated
the observance of Yom Hashoah in 1951, it formally named the commemoration "Holocaust and Ghetto Uprising Remembrance Day."
Not only that, but it also assigned the commemoration a date in the
Hebrew month of *Nisan*, the very month in which the Warsaw
Ghetto Uprising began in 1943, during Passover. That uprising was
the first civilian revolt against the Nazis in all of occupied Europe.
Thus, commemorating it on Yom Hashoah recalls heroic Jewish courage and resistance. But it ultimately also recalls something else: In
the end, the ghetto fighters received assistance from no other quarter, neither from outside Gentile resistance groups, nor from allied
bombers, nor even, for that matter, from God . . . even though it was
Passover. Despite all the heroism and courage displayed, the revolt
was ruthlessly put down.

Against this backdrop of unspeakable slaughter engulfing a silent God, what Holocaust-based themes emerge for Jewish survival?
The Simon Wiesenthal Center, in a guide for creating Yom Hashoah
observances, lists twenty-four themes that might serve "as the center-
piece of a Holocaust memorial program." Strikingly, of the twenty-
four suggested, only five have any ostensible religious connection—
a fact particularly remarkable since the Wiesenthal Center is generally identified with Orthodox Judaism. Of the other themes suggested by the Center, the list includes "Anti-semitism: Past, Present,
and Future"; "The Passivity of the World to the Plight of Jews"; "The
Resistance Fighters"; and "From the Holocaust to the Establishment
of the State of Israel." What is the most basic theme running through-

out the list? In the end, just this: Jews are ultimately alone in the world and hence cannot look to God or other human beings for help; in the last analysis, whether for aid or rescue, the Jewish People can rely only on itself.

For the Exodus narrative, nothing could be further from the truth. From that story's standpoint, Israel's deliverance from Egypt is literally unimaginable without a Deliverer. Indeed, it is precisely Israel's deliverance that makes its deliverer known *as God.* Hence, prior to the advent of the plagues, God sums up for Moses the whole point of the Exodus, the whole meaning of Israel's surviving Egypt:

I will harden Pharaoh's heart that I may multiply my signs and wonders in the land of Egypt. When Pharaoh will not listen to you, I will lay my hand upon Egypt and bring out my ranks, my people, the Israelites from the land of Egypt by great acts of judgment. *Then the Egyptians will know that I am the Lord* when I stretch out my hand over Egypt and *bring out the Israelites from their midst.* (Ex. 7:3–5)

The continued presence of the Jewish People in the world is the best evidence of the continued presence of God in the world.

That story-based linkage between Israel and God gets even stronger as the deadly tenth plague approaches. The people are told to mark the doorposts of their houses "as a sign" so that their homes will be "passed over" when the plague strikes. Without taking such action, the first-born of Israel would be every bit as much at risk as Egyptian first-born. Thus, to be saved, Israel has to identify itself to the world as a people identified with God. That theme resonates even louder as God sends word to Pharaoh of the terrible event to come:

Toward midnight I will go forth among the Egyptians, and every first-born in the land of Egypt shall die. . . . And there will be a loud cry in all the land of Egypt . . . but not a dog shall snarl at any of the Israelites . . . in order that you may know that the Lord makes a distinction between Egypt and Israel. (Ex. 11:4–7)

By making that distinction between the Israelites and the rest of the population, God distinctively shows his power to Pharaoh and his people. Thus, the most revealing indicator of God's power on earth is the Jewish People's power to survive against any and all powers that would destroy it.

But if Jews' experience in the Exodus reveals God's powerful

presence on earth, then what they underwent during the Holocaust
may reflect either his impotence or his absence—or both. In *Night*, a
work in which Elie Wiesel draws on his childhood experience in
Nazi concentration camps, there is an episode describing his arrival
as a fourteen-year-old boy at Auschwitz in the middle of the night:

Never shall I forget that night, the first night in the camp, which has turned
my life into one long night, sevens times cursed and seven times sealed.
Never shall I forget that smoke. Never shall I forget the little faces of the
children, whose bodies I saw turned into wreaths of smoke beneath a silent
blue sky.
    Never shall I forget those flames which consumed my faith.[3]

Whereas in the Exodus, adults are instructed to tell children about
the great deliverance they have beheld in Egypt, in the aftermath of
the Holocaust, a shocking reversal takes place: Children now testify
to adults about the mass murder they have witnessed in the ghettos
and camps of Europe.

The Jews' rescue in Egypt crucially depended on their displaying
their identity. But in Europe, it was the *revealing* of that identity
that could seal Jews' fate such that the Angel of Death would no
longer pass over them, but instead swoop down with a vengeance. In
a paean still sung daily in most synagogues, the survivors of that
momentous night in Egypt and of the subsequent timely crossing of
the Sea testified to what—and Whom—they had witnessed: "Who is
like you, Lord, among the mighty? Who is like you, majestically
holy, splendorously awesome, working wonders?" And what testimony do the survivors of the Nazi attempt to murder the Jewish
People have to give? No doubt, their accounts of death and destruction are quite diverse. Even so, there is one death to which they like
many, perhaps most, post-Holocaust Jews would attest with unanim-
ity: God's.

By contrast, as the Exodus narrative reaches its literal and figu-
rative high point at Sinai, God reminds the newly liberated Israelites
that they have been eyewitnesses to an altogether different state of
affairs: "You have seen what I did to the Egyptians, how I bore you
on eagles' wings and brought you to me." Because the Israelites have
personally seen and experienced the way God has kept his life-
bearing covenantal promise, they should now be willing to trust him
to fulfill the terms of the broader, more far-reaching covenant he
extends to them:

The Lord called to [Moses] from the mountain, saying, "Thus you shall say to the house of Jacob and declare to the children of Israel . . .' Now then, if you will keep my covenant, you shall be my treasured possession among all the peoples. Indeed, all the earth is mine, but you shall be to me a kingdom of priests and a holy nation.' " (Ex. 19:2–6)

What is it that God is offering those at the foot of the mountain? First, it is a covenant different from the pact he made with their ancestors. Unlike his covenant with the patriarchs, this one (as the story relates a little later on) contains numerous detailed practices to be observed—for example, keeping the Sabbath, honoring parents, eschewing idolatry. By committing to these practices, the Israelites will be committing to the Lord, and because of the nature of the practices themselves—no stealing, no murdering, no coveting— committing to one another in the process. By inaugurating such practices as these and the covenant that goes with them, a new community will also be launched. Up to this point, the Israelites have been at best the kin group of some long-dead ancestor and at worst a rag-tag band of recently freed rabble. But the covenant at Sinai holds out a new possibility: the opportunity to become a people.

However, God is offering something more than just a people-creating covenant. He is giving Israel the chance to be not just any people, but "a kingdom of priests and a holy nation." What is the fundamental nature of the kind of sacred service all priests perform regardless of their respective religious traditions? They minister to the deity by ministering to those who would draw near it. Such is the model for the holy service Israel will be called upon to do: She is to serve the Lord by enabling others to serve him also, thereby bringing the whole world into his service.

Earlier, we saw that a Holocaust-framed story could lead to stunning reversals vis-à-vis certain elements in the Exodus narrative. Another victim of such reversals is Israel's eventful rendezvous at Sinai amid fire and smoke, emblems of God's holy presence. In "The Scroll of Happenings," a text specifically created for Yom Hashoah, these two traditional symbols of God's warm, life-giving power undergo a breathtaking change of meaning as part of a new, Holocaust-rooted "sacred scripture":

And it came to pass when Moshe descended from the Mount that a pillar of fire consumed the tribes of Israel that stood at the foot of the mountain. And six million of the children of Israel went up in smoke. And all that remained

was a pillar of smoke that ascended to the uppermost heaven and can be
seen to this very day.[4]

Within the framework of this Holocaust-centered story, fire and
smoke no longer testify to the presence of God, but to ever-present
death, at large in the camps. More basically, this chilling rewrite of
so central an episode in the Exodus master story as God's revelation
at Sinai suggests that the historical evidence provided by the Holocaust requires nothing more nor less than the radical revision of our
understanding of Jewish history itself. In the last analysis, such evidence testifies to a profound denial of any affirmations stemming
from the Exodus narrative. Hence, if such testimony is justified—if
it more truly reflects the reality of Jewish experience—the Holocaust, not the Exodus, lays rightful claim to the title of Jewish master story.
      According to the Exodus story, for the Jews to live as a people,
they need to live by a covenant whose practices form the basis of
their life together, a community in which even God himself is a
member. But for a Holocaust-oriented view of Jewish life, the observance of Judaism's traditional covenantal practices is not so much
wrong as beside the point. Consider, for instance, the story-formed
vision displayed by a song often used to close Yom Hashoah com-
memorations; written by Hirsch Glick, it is called in Yiddish *"Zog
Nit Keinmol"* and known in English as "The Song of the Partisans."

> Never say that this is the last road, the final way,
> Though darkened skies blot out the light of day,
> The longed-for hour shall come,
> O never fear!
> Our tread drums for the tidings—
> We are here!
>
> From greenest, palm-land to the land of whitest snow,
> We are present with our pain and our woe.
> And there where every drop of blood was shed,
> There will our courage lift its head. . . .
>
> We wrote this song in blood for all to sing.
> It is not the carol of a gay bird on the wing.
> But amidst crashing walls and fiercely flaming brands,
> We sang it holding grenades in our hands. . . .

From the viewpoint of the Exodus master story, what enabled
the Jewish People to outlive Egyptian servitude was God's own bond

to the covenant he made with the patriarchs. However, from the perspective of the Holocaust-based master story lyricized in "The Song of the Partisans," what can ultimately ensure the Jewish People's survival is neither a powerful God, nor an empowering covenant, but instead an indispensable practice exercised by one key party: "holding grenades in our hands." From that perspective, the Holocaust's lesson for Jewish survival is unmistakable. If the Jewish People is to survive, such survival rests in its own hands and in its own armed hands alone.

At Sinai, Jews are offered the chance to be a people who serve God by being in service to the world. Hence, the Exodus narrative ultimately bears a world-encompassing hope. By contrast, what the Holocaust holds out to both Jews and world is a hope-less story. The public proclamation read at the outset of the observance implied that the Holocaust should command not only Jews' attention, but also that of the world. But if all that story can promise is a future of endless struggle between the world's unyielding hatred and the Jews' unyielding resistance, it is not at all clear why either the world or the Jews—and especially young Jews—would ever wish to even hear so bleak a tale in the first place, much less build a life on it. According to that grim story, neither the world, nor the Jews, can ever expect redemption or transformation.

What, then, are the deeper implications of these Exodus and Holocaust master stories, not only for Jewish life, but for the life of the rest of the world? Answering that question requires that we give more sustained attention to crucial issues only briefly touched on in this chapter. In light of each story's vision, how are Jews to envision God? The covenant? The Jewish People itself? And, finally, what of that most fundamental question of all? Though both the Exodus and the Holocaust have held out to us a "how" for Jewish survival, neither story has yet given us the "why."

Notes

1. Cf. Eve Bunting, *Terrible Things* (New York: Harper & Row, 1980).
2. Robert Jay Lifton, *The Nazi Doctors* (New York: Basic Books, 1986), p. 478.
3. Elie Wiesel, *Night*, trans. Stella Rodway (New York: Avon, 1969), p. 44.
4. Balfour Brickner, "A Sabbath Service for Yom HaShoah" creative service, New York, 1984.

Chapter 2

Surviving the Holocaust: What Survived? How? And *Nu . . . ?*

On April 8, 1992, a plane carrying Yasser Arafat disappears from radar and goes down somewhere over the Libyan desert. For hours, there is no word about the plane's fate or that of its passengers: Arafat is presumed dead. But just when all seems lost, he miraculously reappears. He is not severely hurt or injured. Reporters covering the story recount how, once again, Arafat has cheated death. Without a trace of irony, they go on to characterize him as a "survivor."

And why not? We live in a culture in which "survivor" has become a term so elastic in meaning that it can refer to anything from outlasting a bad marriage to lasting through a corporate takeover. But while such experiences may suffice for a guest spot on *Oprah* or *Donahue*, they hardly qualify for even a spot at the table with those who were inmates of Treblinka and Auschwitz. Perhaps no one has tried harder than Elie Wiesel to make sure that at the dais of victims of this century's horrors, the seat of honor is reserved for survivors of the Holocaust. Indeed, in Wiesel's eyes, the Jews are the world's quintessential survivors:

If all the nations, in the long course of history, have taken bitter pains to trample on the Jews, it is perhaps because they wished to know that strange people who, more than any other possess the secret of survival.[1]

For Wiesel, the Jew *is* history's survivor. But the Jew is more than the paradigmatic survivor of history. From its beginning, the Jewish People has also been history's witness. If nothing else, that people is in unrivaled position to testify about the history it has endured. In Wiesel's words, "Whoever survives a test . . . must tell the story."[2]

But is there a single story Holocaust survivors tell? As the old adage reminds us, "Two Jews, three views." Hence, if we truly listen to survivors, we will find that they have different stories to tell us, not only about what they survived and who among them survived, but also about how they survived and, in the end, what of them survived. And something else may differ from story to story: the response sought from each tale's audience—its implication, that is, *for us.* In the process, we will likely learn that there is no single, self-evident, or inevitable "lesson of the Holocaust."

Who Is a Survivor?

> If . . . we are going to be whole, we have got to tell our own stories, relay our own accounts of our sufferings.
>
> Joseph Amato[3]

When confronted with evil as monstrous and as seemingly irrational as the Holocaust, we instinctively grab for something to restore reason and order to chaos. Desperately, we reach for something fixed, logical, and precise. It is as though we believe that if we could somehow define the core of survivors' experience in a uniform manner, we could render it meaningful to all human beings everywhere. Thus we imagine that we could start to construct a world of common values, ensuring that Nazi-like insanity would break out "never again."

That, more or less, is the strategy Terrence Des Pres pursues in his book, *The Survivor.*[4] In search of a common "structure" to survival, Des Pres surveys the testimony of survivors not only from the Holocaust, but also from such other twentieth-century kingdoms of death as the gulags and the killing fields. And what does his exploration of these dark realms yield but—Voila!—an all-purpose definition of "survivor." The survivor, declares Des Pres, "is anyone who manages to stay alive in body and in spirit, enduring dread and hopelessness without the loss of will to carry on in human ways. That is all" (6).

But is it? What precisely does it mean to speak of carrying on in "human ways"? At times, Des Pres speaks of "human ways" as "forms of social bonding and interchange, of collective resistance, of keeping dignity and moral sense active" (vii). Elsewhere, however, he speaks of survival depending on things beyond survivors' control, such as chance and even, perhaps, some innate "biological imperative" (90, 202). Ultimately, Des Pres is forced to admit that "plainly, there is more than one way to survive" (18). He continues by acknowledging that there is

a point after which the heroism of survival turns into its opposite. The distinction is between those who live at any price, and those who suffer whatever they must in order to live humanly. (18)

A definition so continually in need of *re*definition cannot help appearing suspicious.

Still, some may feel that Des Pres's attempt at definition might be salvaged by finding some higher-order criterion to pull all the parts together. Who better to enlist in such an enterprise than Raul Hilberg, the premier historian of the Holocaust and one of the most disciplined minds around when it comes to bringing some coherence to a mass of loosely connected data. In his book, *Perpetrators, Victims, Bystanders: The Jewish Catastrophe, 1933–1945,*[5] Hilberg searches for common traits among those who survived in the camps and forests under the most extreme conditions. He concludes that such survivors tended to be young, in good health at their ordeal's beginning, and practitioners of certain "useful" professions and trades, such as medicine and carpentry. But more important according to Hilberg than the survivors' physical or social traits was their psychological profile: They were realists capable of making rapid decisions in their tenacious struggle to remain alive (188). As for the element of chance, Hilberg, ever the master of understatement, nicely sums things up by noting: "They were lucky *after* they had tried to save themselves" (190).

Now that Hilberg has aided us in seeing more clearly the key factors leading to survival, can he help us determine more accurately who might justifiably be designated a survivor? Instead of trying to discover a hard and fast definition like Des Pres, Hilberg views the term "survivor" as spanning a broad spectrum of experiences:

No ironclad definition of the term Jewish survivor was fashioned during the postwar period. The concept had no distinct boundaries. Yet there is an unmistakable rank order among the Jews who lived through the wartime Nazi years. In this hierarchy, the decisive criteria are exposure to risk and depth of suffering. Members of communities that were left intact and people who continued to live in their own homes are hardly considered survivors at all. At the other end of this scale, individuals who emerged from the woods or the camps are the survivors. (187)

By envisaging survivors' experiences as existing along a continuum, Hilberg can discern various kinds of suffering among survivors that would likely escape Des Pres's attention. Hilberg tells, for instance, of Jews who, though fortunate enough to have escaped to Britain, were nevertheless forced into circumstances no less demeaning than wearing a yellow star: a surgeon reduced to washing corpses in a morgue, a radiologist to repairing radios, a bacteriologist to selling baking soda (122).

Yet, despite his sensitivity, on occasion Hilberg too seems more interested in the general phenomenon of human suffering than in the individual humans who suffered. Granted, he describes children in the Kaunas Ghetto playing grave digging, execution, and funeral, and he reports a refugee constrained to become a domestic, sharing with two dogs not only a room, but also their food (149, 123). But what more does he tell us of the singular men, women, and children who underwent such horror and hardships? For Hilberg as for Des Pres, the victims' individuality, *their particularity*, has been left behind in favor of some abstracted inference or implication. What, then, has been left of the individual human being except a cipher? But, if so, we will never be able to answer at least one very basic question about the survivors: precisely *who* survived? Only by answering that question can we answer another more ultimate, more potentially disturbing one: Exactly *what* survived?

To answer those two questions in all their individuality and detail, we have no choice but to listen to survivors' stories. It is through a story, especially a life story, that we can obtain the richest, the most revealing, and, quite possibly, the most truthful account of an individual human being's cumulative experience. It is just such a narrative that depicts an individual's distinctive identity through time. Des Pres tellingly misses the various story contexts from which his abstract generalizations have been abstracted. Crucially, it is within the context of a life story that the diverse facts and the disparate experiences of a life come together to gain their coherence and significance. No assessment of survivors and their experiences could therefore be more wrongheaded than Des Pres's: "Through survivors a vast body of literature has . . . come into being —diaries, novels, documentary reports, simple lists and fragments, books in many languages, which all tell one story."[6] To see just how wrong Des Pres is, we need but listen to a few survivor stories.

Night and *The Painted Bird:* Is the Holocaust the Exception or the Rule?

> " 'How could it possibly happen?' . . . is the wrong question. Given what people are, the question is 'Why doesn't it happen more often?' "
>
> Max Von Sydow in *Hannah and Her Sisters*

Elie Wiesel's *Night* may be the best-known Holocaust story penned by a survivor. It should be read in tandem with *The Painted Bird*, a story by Jerzy Kosinski, another survivor. Together, the two accounts stand as a striking refutation of the view that survivors all have the same tale to tell. Though the two narratives share a common storyline about a child in peril during the Holocaust, they offer very different portrayals of the evil survived and of the human being who survived it.

Night begins in Wiesel's home town, the Transylvanian village of Sighet, where the twelve-year-old Eliezer is already well on his way to becoming a devout Jew. He studies Talmud, he yearns to learn the mystical secrets of the Kabbalah, and when asked why he prays, is astounded by the question: "Why did I pray? . . . Why did I live? Why did I breathe?"[7] Besides the warmth given him by his father, mother, and little sister, Eliezer receives spiritual nurture from Moche the Beadle.

One day in 1942, Hungarian police come to deport Moche and several other foreign Jews. Though there are tears all around, the local Jews characterize the deportation as one of the unfortunate, but predictable, by-products of war. Soon, the deportees are forgotten, and life returns to normal in Sighet. Several months later, however, Moche reappears with ominous news. At the Polish frontier, Gestapo troops had taken control of the train and forced the Jews into waiting trucks. The trucks were driven to a forest, where the Jews were compelled to dig a mass grave. The Gestapo then systematically executed all the Jewish men, women, and children; according to Moche, the Germans even threw babies into the air to use for target practice! Wounded in the leg, Moche was taken for dead and so eventually managed to escape. But as Moche tells the story of what he has witnessed, Eliezer realizes that something had been wounded besides Moche's leg:

Moche had changed. There was no longer any joy in his eyes. He no longer sang. He no longer talked to me of God . . . but only of what he had seen. People refused not only to believe his stories but even to listen to them. (16)

The traditional world of Moche had been shattered. In its place, a Holocaust-shaped world had begun to take form with seemingly no place in it for the Jew, the witness, or the storyteller.

For the next two years, the Jews of Sighet do everything in their power to ignore the tremors all around them that signal the impending collapse of their world. Even after the Germans arrive in Sighet in the spring of 1944 and herd the Jews into a ghetto, disbelief and denial still abound: "It was neither German nor Jew who ruled the ghetto—it was illusion" (21). Reality about the new world only begins to be accepted, to be *felt*, as the Jews of Sighet, like Moche before them, are loaded onto waiting cattle cars to be deported. After spending days in transit without food or water, they arrive at midnight at Birkenau, reception center for Auschwitz, a world in which there is only night. In a matter of minutes, Eliezer's mother and baby sister are "selected" for death while he and his father are spared—for the moment:

Never shall I forget that nocturnal silence which deprived me, for all eternity, of the desire to live. Never shall I forget those moments which murdered my God and my soul and turned my dreams to dust. Never shall I forget these things, even if I am condemned to live as long as God Himself. Never. (44)

Like his spiritual mentor, Moche, Eliezer has undergone a profound spiritual transformation. No longer does his life story bear witness to the living God of the Jews, but to that time "which consumed my faith."

No story more vividly testifies to Eliezer's experience of the death of God than *Night's* famous episode in which a little boy is hanged with two adults in reprisal for an act of sabotage. Because the child weighs so little, his death is slow, taking a full half hour to come. All the while, the camp's inmates are forced to witness the child's anguish. Eliezer hears a man behind him ask, "Where is God now?" Inside himself, he hears a voice reply, "Here He is—He is hanging here on this gallows" (76). A young boy's faith has been killed in an instant.

The destruction of a child's heart takes a bit longer to accomplish. When the initial selection at Birkenau marked his mother and sister for death, Eliezer desperately clung to his father's arm with only one thought in mind—"not to lose him." But as their situation in the camps, first at Auschwitz, then at Buna, grows increasingly brutal, the relationship between the son and the father is brutalized as well. On three separate occasions, Eliezer seeks to escape his father rather than stay with him. First, as he sees his father beaten by a crazed kapo, Eliezer can think only of two things: how to avoid the blows himself and how angry he is with his father for *not* knowing how to avoid them (66). Later, when the two become separated, Eliezer searches for his father while thinking all the time, "If only I could get rid of this dead weight . . . I could use all my strength to struggle for my own survival" (118). Although the two are eventually reunited, Eliezer's father dies soon afterwards of fever. Before dying, he repeatedly calls out to his son for water. Though Eliezer fails to respond to him, a Nazi guard does, pummeling the dying man again and again to make him be quiet. And the boy's reaction?

His last word was my name. A summons, to which I did not respond.

I did not weep, and it pained me that I could not weep. But I had no more tears. And, in the depths of my being, in the recesses of my weakened conscience, could I have searched it, I might have found something like— free at last! (124)

Perhaps the most striking feature of Wiesel's story is the way in which a boy raised with traditional Jewish values is so transformed by his sojourn on "planet Auschwitz." Wiesel has written that "to be a Jew today . . . means: to testify. To bear witness to *what is*, and to *what is no longer*."[8] *Night* testifies eloquently to "what is no longer"—the warm, traditional, religious world inhabited by Wiesel and other Eastern European Jews before the Nazi onslaught. *Night* derives much of its poignancy by telling not merely of murdered Jews, but also of those Jews' murdered world. In our post-Holocaust era, a time when so many take the death of God for granted, testi-

mony like Wiesel's about the destruction of a faith and a way of life
is commonly greeted with a yawn and a patronizing look that says,
"Welcome to the real world." Ironically, *that* world, one with no use
for God or Jewish tradition and focused almost exclusively on the
use of power, is one in which the Nazis might feel quite at home.

After Eliezer is at last liberated from Buchenwald, he falls sick
with food poisoning and for two weeks languishes in the hospital
between life and death. He eventually recovers enough strength to
get up and look at himself in a mirror, something he has not done
since leaving the ghetto. What resemblance does he bear "to what is
no longer"? What witness does his reflection bear "to what is"? Precisely who—exactly what—has survived?

From the depths of the mirror, a corpse gazed back at me. The look in his
eyes, as they stared into mine, has never left me.[9]

What stares back at Eliezer, the survivor, is an unrecognizable human being, an individual with virtually no discernible identity. No
wonder that an attempt such as Des Pres's to give survivors some
fixed, definitive identity seems so unconvincing.

If Wiesel's *Night* cautions us against formulating facile generalizations about who and what survived, Jerzy Kosinski's semi-
autobiographical novel, *The Painted Bird*,[10] warns us against sweep-
ing statements about how survival was possible. Like Wiesel's Eliezer,
Kosinski's protagonist is modeled on his own childhood wartime
experience. At age six, Kosinski lost most of his family to the Holocaust. The protagonist of *The Painted Bird*, the Boy, is often perceived as—and persecuted as—a Jew or a gypsy. Whether we speak
of Kosinski's own childhood or of the childhood depicted in Kosinski's novel, Wiesel would ascribe such horrible treatment to the evil
of the Holocaust. Not so Kosinski. He would chalk it up instead to
the evil of the everyday world itself. In such a world, the Holocaust
is at most a sideshow.

Kosinski sets his story in a remote part of Eastern Europe that
"had been neglected for centuries" and which is, as a result, gov-
erned largely by "the traditional right of the stronger and the wealth-
ier over the weaker and the poorer." The area's dire economic condi-
tion, its poor soil and severe climate, make its inhabitants "brutal,
though not by choice" (2; italics mine). The dominant moral conditions are not the result of the intrusion of the Holocaust, or of conscious, explicit choice, but simply a consequence of the way the
world is by nature.

In perhaps the most gruesome episode of a book filled with gruesome episodes, the brutality embedded in such a world is made manifest. A jealous miller imagines that a green plowboy is having sexual encounters with his lascivious wife. One night following dinner, the miller attacks the plowboy, kneeing him in the stomach, while pinning him against a wall, his arm pressed against the youth's throat. The miller then grabs a spoon and plunges it deep into one of the boy's eye sockets:

The eye sprang out of his face like a yolk from a broken egg and rolled down the miller's hand onto the floor. The plowboy howled and shrieked. . . . Then the blood-covered spoon plunged into the other eye, which sprang out even faster. For a moment the eye rested on the boy's cheek as if uncertain what to do next; then it finally tumbled down his shirt onto the floor.

. . . The eyeballs lay on the floor. . . . [Cats] . . . began to play with [them] as if they were balls of thread. (37–38)

For Kosinski, even animals participate in the world's brutality and derive satisfaction from it. From the perspective of this survivor story, there is no difference between human beings and animals. All are brutes in an uncaring, even hostile, world.

Nothing attracts the hostility of a such a world more than being different. Again, even animals demonstrate that. The novel's title alludes to an incident involving another savage peasant whose passion breeds violence. The peasant, Lekh, traps and sells birds, and he advises the boy that "a man should always watch birds . . . carefully and draw conclusions from their behavior" (49). Lekh lusts for Stupid Ludmilla, a half-crazed village outcast who lives somewhere in the forest. Whenever his lust for her goes unfulfilled for any length of time, he gives vent to his frustrated passion in a bizarre ritual in which he covers his captive birds with different color paints. On one such occasion, he paints a captured raven red, green, and blue. Then, as other ravens fly overhead, he releases the painted bird to rejoin them. But the moment the differently colored raven tries to reunite with the others,

a desperate battle began. The changeling was attacked from all sides. Black, red, green, blue feathers began to drop. . . . Suddenly the painted raven plummeted to the fresh-plowed soil. It was still alive, opening its beak and vainly trying to move its wings. Its eyes had been pecked out, and fresh blood streamed over its painted feathers. (50–51)

If Lekh is correct that a person can draw conclusions from the behavior of birds, what lesson is there for the boy—and for us—about the relationship of differentness to danger?

Whatever lesson it is, it most certainly is not some survivor's high-minded "lesson of the Holocaust" calling for greater tolerance, pluralism, and education. According to Kosinski's survivor testimony, the often deadly tie between danger and difference is ineradicable. Just as there are differences that are natural, so, too, is hostility to difference: It is just the way the world *is*. Thus, the boy's black eyes always evoke the suspicions—and fear—of the blue-eyed or gray-eyed peasants among whom he lives and for whom his dark eyes mark him as a Jew or a gypsy.[11] The peasants associate dark eyes with the evil eye, a power to be feared, and, if possible, destroyed. Their attempts to kill the boy are not part of a well-developed ideology like Nazism or an elaborate scheme like the "Final Solution." Instead, their acts of violence are spontaneous, visceral expressions of ignorance and superstition, tokens of the peasants' —and the world's—natural disposition. Dozing, the boy dreams that he could invent a fuse which, when lighted, would instantly change skin, hair, and eye color. His invention would also have another miraculous feature. It would ward off the "evil eye" so that nobody would need to fear him, thereby making his life "easier and more pleasant." Recognizing his musings as only idle daydreams, the boy turns his thoughts back to the Germans, the war, and the real world:

The Germans puzzled me. What a waste. Was such a destitute, cruel world worth ruling? (94)

From the vantage point of the survivor story told in *The Painted Bird*, no matter who rules the world, whether the Nazis or somebody else, the world remains *the world*.

Survival in such a world depends on nothing more nor less than having the power to survive. At one point, the boy overhears an old priest telling a parishioner about the power of prayer. According to the priest, God grants a certain number of indulgences in exchange for a certain number of prayers. The formula is simple: the more prayers recited, the more reward received, the fewer prayers offered, the more punishment incurred. The boy imagines "unending heavenly pastures full of bins" where each person's indulgences are stored up according to the number of prayers said. The boy immediately begins spending all his time praying in hopes of acquiring as many indulgences as possible. But he hides his praying from the brutish peasant to whose

"tender mercies" he has been entrusted; he readily admits fearing that
the peasant, "as a Christian of older standing . . . [might] use his
influence in heaven to nullify my prayers or . . . divert . . . them to
his own undoubtedly empty bin." (132–33)

The boy begins to doubt the power of prayer and the power of
God when he loses the power of speech after being attacked by a mob
of peasants on a Christian holy day. Dragooned into serving as an
altar boy (a circumstance he initially views with favor—"At last
someone up there had noticed me!"), he proves too small to handle
the missal. He drops it, and, in the ensuing commotion, a group of
worshippers picks him up, takes him outside, and casts him into a
huge manure pit. After finally managing to climb out of the pit, he
flees into the forest. Covered with sun-baked manure and his own
vomit, he discovers that his voice has left him. His conclusion?

Some greater force, with which I had not yet managed to communicate,
commanded my destiny. I began to doubt that it could be God or one of His
saints. With my credit secured by vast numbers of prayers, my days of
indulgence must have been innumerable; God had no reason to inflict such
terrible punishment on me. I had probably incurred the wrath of some other
forces, which spread their tentacles over those God had abandoned for some
reason or other. (147)

For Wiesel's protagonist, the death of his faith in God is a tragedy to
which he as a survivor must give voice. For Kosinski's lead character, belief in God has been a mistake he is lucky to have survived.
At the very least, it has been a miscalculation of such disastrous
proportions as to have left him speechless—a significant disability
for any who would offer survivor testimony.

Having given up on prayer to God as "the governing principle of
the world," the boy turns in succession to other possible sources of
world-dominating power. First, he considers allying with those
known as the "Evil Ones," thought to be, like the Germans, in league
with the Devil (158–59). Next, he hangs on to a necktie used in a
suicide, because "it was common belief that the rope of a suicide
brings good luck" (180). He later throws in with the Communist
Party, which, he has been informed, knows "the right paths and the
right destination" (205).

But by story's end, the boy has given up on all these would-be
wellsprings of power in favor of one overriding truth. He watches an
educated man kneeling in morning prayer and is filled with con-
tempt for the man for failing to see that "he was alone in the world

and could expect no assistance from anyone." The boy thinks to himself that the sooner human beings realize the truth that everyone is expendable, the better off everybody will be. He does not, however, communicate this truth to the kneeling man. He is, after all, still speechless. But so what? "It mattered little if one was mute; people did not understand one another anyway" (249).

How then does this survivor give his testimony? He does so through the vicious deeds of the grotesque creature into which he has been transformed by his experiences. That creature is just as beastly as any he has encountered during his wanderings. Wiesel's character also undergoes a moral transformation—more accurately, a moral degeneration—but he still retains enough humanity within him to feel the pangs of conscience after he has wished his father dead: "Immediately I felt ashamed of myself, ashamed forever."[12] Not so Kosinski's child. In *Night*, the German defeat and the concentration camps' liberation bring a sense of relief and even of redemption. The prisoners satisfy their craving for bread and sex, but as for any itch for revenge, there is "not a sign" (127). The child in *The Painted Bird*, however, feels no sense of liberation when the Germans appear to be on the verge of defeat. On the contrary, he feels "somehow disappointed; the war seemed to be over."[13]

Moreover, if Wiesel's Eliezer could have had any wish granted, it would surely have been to be reunited with his family. By contrast, Kosinski's child, upon being reunited with his parents, experiences no joy or exaltation, but only a feeling of "being smothered by their love and protection" (242). When he arrives home—by now he is twelve—he finds that his parents have adopted an orphaned four year old. When the tike annoys him, he grabs its arm and squeezes it so hard it breaks (243). He now routinely has violent outbursts in which he finds that his "hands [have] acquired a life of their own and [cannot] be torn away from an opponent" (226). In such vicious acts as these, he does not so much recite some "lesson of survival" as demonstrate it:

A person should take revenge for every wrong or humiliation. . . . Only the conviction that one was as strong as the enemy and that one could pay him back double, enabled people to survive. (227)

Some may think the moral transformation of Kosinski's child too fantastic, the boy's prescription for survival overstated. And yet, near the beginning of 1994, an Israeli settler on the West Bank, Dr. Baruch Goldstein, killed at least 30 Arab men and boys at prayer in the Cave of the Patriarchs in Hebron. The news reports showed footage of Goldstein during earlier interviews in which he was dressed in the mock garb of a Jewish concentration camp inmate. Goldstein and the Arabs whom he shot make the prescription for survival given by Kosinski's child seem anything but make-believe.

Wiesel and Kosinski stand as rebuttals to Des Pres or any other theorist who would have us believe that all survivors "tell one story." Through Wiesel, what ultimately has survived the Holocaust is a message of warning—and thus, by implication, also one of hope that such horror can be avoided in the future. But from Kosinski, by contrast, we receive a bleak message about a world beyond hope and about what it takes to survive in a place so utterly irredeemable.

Responding to Survivors' Stories

Because there is no single survivor story, there is no one necessary "lesson" or response to be derived from all Holocaust accounts. *Schindler's List*, an otherwise superb film, shows what happens if we ignore this crucial point. In our attempt to wrench from a survivor story a "lesson" or audience response untrue to it, we may not only distort the story but also manipulate its hearers in the process.

Winner of the 1994 Oscar for Best Picture and almost universally hailed by critics and audiences alike, *Schindler's List* gets much of its dramatic wallop from Steven Spielberg's sheer talent as a filmmaker. The film is full of unforgettable images: Nazis going through the "liquidated" Cracow Ghetto with stethoscopes to detect any Jews concealed behind walls or under floors; a concentration camp commandant taking target practice at Jewish prisoners from his balcony, shooting them at whim; a little boy hiding *in* a latrine to avoid a selection. Moreover, in a film photographed mainly in black and white, its few color shots are particularly powerful, whether of the flames of Shabbat candles snuffed out at the film's beginning or of a little girl's red coat on an otherwise gray, ashen pile of victims' clothing. No motion picture better depicts the story of the Nazis' progressive victimization of Eastern European Jewry: economic disenfranchisement, ghettoization, deportation, forced labor, extermination.

Schindler's List was originally a 1982 book by Thomas Kenneally. It told the amazing story of a non-Jewish German businessman, Oskar Schindler, whose ingenuity and courage enabled over 1,000 Jews to

survive the worst the Third Reich could throw at them, including
Auschwitz. The story of how the book came to be written is itself
astounding. After the war, one of "Schlinder's Jews," Leopold Pfef-
ferberg, opened a luggage store in Beverly Hills. He had vowed that he
would do everything possible to ensure that this unique survival story
would some day be written and published. Whenever he came across
customers who were writers, he would tell the story in the hope of
interesting them in it. One day, Thomas Kenneally walked into the
shop to look for a briefcase—and found the beginnings of the book
that led to Spielberg's film.

As the story opens, Oskar Schindler is a German entrepreneur
who has come to occupied Poland in search of a business opportunity
to exploit. When we first see him, he is getting dressed as if he were
going out for a night on the town. But Schindler is not looking for
entertainment; instead, he is seeking high-ranking German officers
looking for entertainment. When he finds them, he sends them a
bottle of champagne with his compliments, and, by evening's end, is
partying with them as if they had been classmates at the same military school.

In short order, Schindler is awarded a contract to produce war
materiel with the aid of Jews' forced labor. Because he needs sufficient capital to open and run his plant, he turns to the Jews for
investors since what money they have left, they cannot otherwise
easily spend. One cannot help being struck by Schindler's oblivious-
ness to the perversity of the arrangement: he will literally profit
from the Jews' persecution and enslavement. What can the man be
thinking? He seems not so much immoral—he is not another rabid
Nazi anti-Semite—as amoral.

We meet Schindler later as he is out riding on horseback with one
of his many mistresses. The pair abruptly comes to a ridge overlooking
the ghetto—just as it is being "liquidated." They can see the tumult in
the streets and hear the sounds of gunfire. The slightest trace of uneasi-
ness comes across Schindler's face. For the first time, he may be comprehending what the Jews have been suffering at the Nazis' hands.
More than that, however, we cannot say. *For Schindler himself does
not say, either here or later, what has gone through his mind.* All we
can do is follow him through the rest of the film as he puts his entrepre-
neurial talent to work to save "his" Jews from death. To rescue them
from Auschwitz's ovens, he ends up spending on bribes to Nazi officials all the profits he has made.

Part of what is so intriguing about Schindler's story is its enig-
matic quality. What moved this man to act in the way he did? What

we know of the real Schindler's life story following his wartime experience sheds no more light on that puzzling question. He engaged in countless failed business enterprises while continuing to be a womanizer. Thus, before the war, he had been a hustler and a rake, and after the war, a hustler and a rake he remained. Yet as the film moves toward conclusion, Spielberg seems increasingly uncomfortable with the truth of that part of Schindler's story and all the ambiguity it implies. Significantly, as Spielberg lets go of such ambiguous truth(s) and reaches for a more straightforward "lesson," he ceases to be a filmmaker who artfully engages his audience and becomes instead one who artificially manipulates it.

As the movie winds down, the Germans have been defeated, and Schindler's Jews have been liberated. They fashion a gold ring from an inmate's filling and present it to Schindler in gratitude for his having saved their lives. He erupts into tears and berates himself for not having saved more lives. The outburst, however, is completely out of character for the Schindler whose story has been depicted to this point. It is also untrue to the rest of Schindler's story, since after the war he pawned the ring to help finance one of his unsuccessful business ventures. If Spielberg has begun to lapse into melodrama here, it may well be the result of his starting to be false to Schindler's story.

As the film draws closer to its finale, Spielberg's account rings even falser while growing ever more manipulative. The movie goes from black and white to color as the actual survivors saved by Schindler walk down a hillside in Israel. Accompanied by the actors who respectively portrayed them, the survivors place stones on Schindler's grave, an act of commemoration among Jews somewhat comparable to Christians' placing flowers at a gravesite. In the background, we hear the strains of *Yerushalayim shel Zahav*—"Jerusalem of Gold." Written in the aftermath of the Six-Day War in 1967, the song, celebrating Israel's historic recovery of the ancient city, has become a virtual anthem. Now as we hear that song being sung, we are shown Schindler's Jews, framed in golden sunlight, coming over a ridge in the Promised Land. Spielberg, whose direction to this point has largely been so sure-handed, here seems heavy-handed, bent on wresting one particular emotional response from us: unallayed support for the State of Israel.

But surely, given what has come earlier in the film, other responses would have been more appropriate, such as, for instance, wonder at the mysterious presence of goodness in the world of those on Oskar Schindler's list—especially when it met them in the person

of an Oskar Schindler. In light of the Holocaust, and given the entire, often grisly story of humankind, the presence of evil in the
world, even of world-class Nazi evil, ought not to surprise us. We
ought not to be astonished by how few non-Jews tried to rescue Jews,
but that any at all did—particularly one like Oskar Schindler. The
ending Spielberg has given *Schindler's List* appears forced, even
"schmaltzy," precisely because it contrasts so sharply with the ambiguous, more complex truth of much of the story that has come
before.

Part of the truth surrounding the Holocaust is that there is no
self-evident truth, no clear-cut inference, that necessarily follows
from it—not even the necessity of a Jewish state to protect Jews'
lives. After the Holocaust, some survivors drew the conclusion that
the best way to protect their lives and those of their children was to
cover up their Jewishness through conversion and assimilation. The
results are still out on both these survival strategies—although it's a
safe bet that over the last five decades, more Jews have been killed
for being Israelis than for becoming Episcopalians. At any rate, just
as there is no one survival story, there is no one response, no single
universal "lesson" entailed by the Holocaust.

Corroborative Witnesses for Whom?

The Holocaust is not the first catastrophe in Jewish history for which
we have survivor testimony. Of course, for many Jews caught up in
modernity's story, prior Jewish history counts for nothing. For modernity is the story that says we are part of no previous story that
matters. Not for nothing do teachers in American high schools and
colleges complain that, when it comes to history, their students
more and more know less and less.

Thus, American Jews such as Deborah Lipstadt, author of *Denying the Holocaust: The Growing Assault on Truth and Memory*,[14]
should not be scandalized by Americans' lack of knowledge about
the Holocaust: it's nothing personal. It is not, for example, yet one
more instance of "the world's indifference to Jewish suffering." Lots
of Americans, particularly younger Americans, do not even know
their own history; why should they know anybody else's? Indeed, to
the extent that American Jewish fundraisers for such organizations
as UJA and Israel Bonds have treated recent Jewish history as if it
were the only kind that mattered, they can hardly object when

young American Jews, for their part, treat the Holocaust and the establishment of the State of Israel as ancient history. Both events are, after all, now almost half a century old —older, in other words, than nearly two-thirds of the current American Jewish population![15]

Ironically, certain aspects of previous Jewish history are not as remote from our experience as some would have us believe. For instance, certain pieces of survivor testimony from earlier periods parallel some from our own. Psalm 137 was composed by a survivor of the fall of Jerusalem in 586 B.C.E.; along with most of the rest of the Jewish People, he (or she) was carried off into exile in Babylonia, and the resulting psalm testifies not only to the forlornness of the captives, but also to the cruelty of their captors:

> By the rivers of Babylon,
> there we sat,
> sat and wept,
> as we thought of Zion.
>
> There on the poplars
> we hung up our lyres,
> for our captors
> asked us there
> for songs,
> our tormentors, for amusement,
> "Sing us one of the songs of Zion."
> How can we sing a song of the Lord
> on alien soil? (Ps. 137:1–4; NJPS)

Next, after the famous vow to remember Jerusalem—"If I forget you, O Jerusalem, let my right hand wither!"—the psalmist-survivor lets fly a not-so-well-known malediction:

> Fair Babylon, you predator,
> a blessing on him who repays you in kind
> what you inflicted on us;
> a blessing on him who seizes your babies
> and dashes them against the rocks! (Ps. 137:8–9)

The Nazis were apparently not the first to brutally murder Jewish infants, nor is the psalmist's ferocious desire to pay back the Babylonians in kind the last such sentiment to be expressed by Jews. Thus, one Holocaust survivor, bearing witness for those who perished in the camps, told Israeli students, "The one injunction left . . . by the victims . . . was revenge, revenge, revenge."[16]

But as with the Holocaust, so, too, with the Babylonian exile, there are other bits of testimony to be heard—and other possible "lessons" to learned. The prophet Jeremiah roots his witness in the Jewish People's first survival experience—the Exodus from Egypt. He recalls how "the people escaped from the sword [and] found favor in the wilderness" (Jer. 31:2). Memory of the Exodus, the Jews' paradigmatic survival story, enables even such a "prophet of doom" as Jeremiah to deliver a message of hope. Thus, in delivering that message, God's message, he hearkens back to the time when, with timbrel and dance, Miriam and the other women celebrated Israel's survival at the Sea after it had narrowly escaped the pursuing Egyptian host:[17]

> I will build you firmly again,
> O Maiden Israel!
> Again, you shall take up your timbrels
> And go forth to the rhythm of the dancers. . . .
>
> For thus said the Lord:
> Cry out in joy for Jacob,
> Shout at the crossroads of the nations!
> Sing aloud in praise, and say:
> Save, O Lord, Your People,
> The remnant of Israel.
> I will bring them in from the northland,
> Gather them from the ends of the earth. . . .
>
> Hear the word of the Lord, O nations,
> And tell it to the isles afar.
> Say:
> He who scattered Israel will gather them. . . .
>
> They shall return from the enemy's land.
> And there is hope for your future
> —declares the Lord. . . . (Jer. 31:4,7–8,10,16–17; NJPS)

Through Jeremiah, the Lord assures the people that just as the Jews survived Egypt, they shall likewise survive Babylonia and Exile. As important, they shall live to tell the story of their survival, a story not only theirs, but God's.

For God is the chief survivor of the Babylonians' victory over Judah. In the ancient world, when a people was conquered, its deity was considered similarly vanquished, and when a people was exiled from its land, its deity's power was thought correspondingly uprooted. The death of the kingdom of Judah should have spelled the death of God. It clearly should have spelled the death of the Jews. *But it spelled neither: both God and Israel survived.* Each's survival depended on the other's. Ezekiel, another witness offering testimony, interprets the brevity of the exile in just this light. Israel's survival and restoration to its land is God's remedy for an unexpected—and unacceptable—consequence of his decision to exile Israel among the nations. As Ezekiel explains on God's behalf:

When [the Jews] came to those nations, they caused My holy name to be profaned, in that it was said of them, "These are the people of the Lord, yet they had to leave His land." Therefore, I am concerned for My holy name, which the House of Israel have caused to be profaned among the nations to which they have come.

Say to the House of Israel: Thus said the Lord God: Not for your sake will I act, O House of Israel, but for My holy name. . . . I will sanctify My great name which has been profaned among the nations—among whom you have caused it to be profaned. *And the nations shall know that I am the Lord . . . when I manifest My holiness before their eyes through you. I will take you from among the nations and gather you from all the countries, and I will bring you back to your own land.* (Ez. 36:20–24)

For the sake of the survival of his reputation as God—a reputation built through the saving, powerful acts he displayed on Israel's behalf in Egypt—God must come to the Jewish People's rescue again to make sure they survive Babylonia. As for the Jews, their continued survival rests precisely on God's surviving as their Lord; they dare not award Marduk or some other Babylonian deity that title. The exilic prophet Isaiah, yet another witness to be heard from, sums up this survival plan best when, through him, God says to the Jewish People:

All the nations assemble as one,
The peoples gather. . . .
Let them produce their witnesses and be vindicated,
That people, hearing them, may say, "It is true [that the other
    nations' gods are real.]"

But My witnesses are *you* . . .
My servant, whom I have chosen.
To the end that [they] may take thought,
And believe in Me,
And understand that I am He:
Before Me no god was formed,
And after me, none shall exist—
None but me, the Lord. . . .

So you are My witnesses
　　　　—declares the Lord—
And I am God. (Is. 43:9–12; cf. NJPS)

The word *midrash* comes from a root meaning "to draw out," and a rabbinic midrash on this verse does exactly that, drawing out the significance of Jews' testimony about God: "When you are my witnesses, I am God, and when you are not my witnesses, I am, as it were, not God."[18] Jews are not to be merely eyewitnesses to disaster, but corroborative witnesses to the One who enables the Jewish People to live on despite disaster.

Since there is no single survivor story of the Holocaust, no uniform witness to it, neither can there be any necessary, obvious "lesson" to be drawn from that grim time in Jewish history. Hence, even though many Jews infer from the Holocaust that the Jewish People is alone in the world and/or that the State of Israel is indispensable to Jewish survival, at least one altogether different conclusion remains a distinct possibility—namely, that there is a God who sees to the survival of his people, knowing that his own depends on it. That conclusion may represent in fact more than a mere possibility, for the Jewish People has survived to bear witness to the truth of that storied inference for over three millennia—originally in Egypt, recently in Europe.

And yet, suppose God does disappear from the survivor testimony Jews would give, that he drops out of the story they would tell. To what, then, would Jews' story witness?

Notes

1. Elie Wiesel, *The Town Beyond the Wall*, trans. Stephen Becker (New York: Atheneum, 1964), pp. 67–68.
2. Elie Wiesel, *One Generation After*, trans. Lily Edelman and Elie Wiesel (New York: Avon Books, 1970), pp. 184, 224.
3. Joseph Amato, *Victims and Values: A History and Theory of Suffering*, foreword by Eugen Weber (New York: Greenwood Press, 1990), p. 191.
4. Terrence Des Pres, *The Survivor: An Anatomy of Life in the Death Camps* (New York: Oxford University Press, 1976).
5. Raul Hilberg, *Perpetrators, Victims, Bystanders: The Jewish Catastrophe, 1933–1945* (New York: Harper Collins, 1992).
6. Des Pres, p. 30; italics mine.
7. Elie Wiesel, *Night*, with a foreword by Francois Mauriac, trans. Stella Rodway (New York: Avon Books, 1960), p. 13.

8. Wiesel, *One Generation After*, p. 224; italics mine.

9. Wiesel, *Night*, p. 127.

10. Jerzy Kosinski, *The Painted Bird* (New York: Bantam Books, 1978). Recently, a controversy has arisen concerning the actuality of the events depicted in the book. See James Park Sloan, "Kosinski's War," *The New Yorker*. October 10, 1994. In a November 1994 phone conversation with me, Kosinski's widow, Kiki, explained that her late husband thought of the work as "autofiction." Kosinski himself wrote that "as an actor playing Hamlet is neither Hamlet nor merely an actor, but, rather, an actor as Hamlet, so is a fictive event neither an actual event nor totally a created fiction with no base in experience; *it is an event as fiction*" (Jerzy Kosinski, *Passing By: Selected Essays, 1962–1991* [New York: Random House, 1992], pp. 201–202).

11. But to the peasants, it really does not matter which, and, hence, Kosinski leaves the boy's true identity ambiguous.

12. Wiesel, *Night*, p. 118.

13. Kosinski, p. 191.

14. Deborah E. Lipstadt, *Denying the Holocaust: The Growing Assault on Truth and Memory* (New York: The Free Press, 1993).

15. See Barry A. Kosmin et al., *Highlights of the CJF 1990 National Jewish Population Survey* (n.p.: Council of Jewish Federations, [n.d.]), p.15.

16. Tom Segev, *The Seventh Million: The Israelis and the Holocaust*, trans. Haim Watzman (New York: Hill and Wang, 1993), p. 500.

17. Cf. Ex. 15:20–21.

18. Midrash Tehillim on Ps. 123:1.

Chapter 3

The Holocaust Cult

On the march to work, limping in our large wooden shoes on the icy snow, we exchanged a few words . . . [Resnyk] told me his story. . . . [It] was certainly a sorrowful, cruel, and moving story; because so are all our stories, hundreds of thousands of stories, all different and all full of a tragic, disturbing necessity. We tell them to each other in the evening, and they . . . are simple and incomprehensible like the stories in the Bible. But are they not themselves stories of a new Bible?

Primo Levi[1]

As the Holocaust has become many contemporary Jews' master story, so, too, its perpetual observance has become their paramount Jewish practice, its veneration their religion. And as with any organized church, this Holocaust cult has its own tenets of faith, rites, and shrines.[2]

Even the word *holocaust* has religious roots. It stems from the Greek translation of the Hebrew Bible's oft-repeated word *olah*, which means "burnt offering." In fact, the English word "victim" initially referred to just such an offering, and, up until a few centuries ago, it signified any "living creature killed and offered as a sacrifice to some deity or supernatural power."[3] The phrase "holocaust victim" in its original sense is therefore bitterly ironic. For it easily brings to mind the kind of deity that Jewishly ignorant Christians have always ascribed to the "Old Testament," a god whose fiery, all-consuming wrath must be appeased.

Is there a name for what happened to European Jewry that is religiously less problematic? Ultraorthodox Jews call it "the third *churban*." They see it as the third great act of destruction in Jewish

history, the razing of the First and Second Temples being the other
two. By rights, then, this latest *churban* should be commemorated
on *Tisha' Be'av*, alongside its two predecessors.[4] Yet what if one
believes that the third *churban* so surpassed the other two on some
"Richter Scale of Ruin" that it requires its own separate day of remembrance? Besides, *Tisha' Be'av* calls on Jews to display abject
humility and contrition before God so that he will save them from
affliction in the future. In remembering the third *churban*, however,
Jews are called on to manifest a steely resolve that *they* will "never
let it happen again."

    Is there any way to refer to the murder of Europe's Jews that is
free of religious baggage? *Shoah*, a term already in use in Israel and
increasingly gaining favor in America, might fill the bill. It literally
means "catastrophe" and commonly covers a whole range of disas-
ters; people speak, for example, of an economic *shoah*, an ecological
shoah, a moral *shoah*.[5] But as with many words in the Hebrew
language—and as with the People whose holy tongue that language
has been—religious underpinnings are never far from the surface.
Thus God, via the prophet Isaiah, warns of an impending *shoah* if
the people fail to change their sinful ways:

Ha!
Those who write out evil writs
And compose iniquitous documents,
To subvert the cause of the poor,
To rob of their rights the needy of My people:
That widows may be their spoil,
And fatherless children their booty!
What will you do on the day of punishment,
When the catastrophe [i.e., *hashoah*] comes from afar . . . ? (Isaiah 10:1–3)

No matter what the Jewish People calls the Nazis' attempt to exterminate it—"Holocaust," "Churban," "Shoah"—it cannot entirely
mute all possible religious overtones. Instead, it can only determine
which religious chords will be struck—and to whom hymns of praise
will be offered.

Tenets of the Faith

Just as we would be wrong to think that somebody who shouts
"Goddammit!" while stuck in traffic must be a theist, we would also

be mistaken to believe that someone who denies God's existence must have no religion whatsoever. This chapter's title, "The Holocaust Cult," is not chosen rashly. As the Latin root, *cultus*, reminds us, and as its derivative, *cultivate*, makes clear, at the center of a cult is what people care about or cherish. That's why Paul Tillich's celebrated characterization of religion as a person's "ultimate concern" rings so true. We see someone who devotes every waking moment to expanding his company's market share; who devoutly studies each day's sales report; who cloisters himself away from family and friends at certain set times (e.g., before the annual shareholders' meeting); and who treats Standard & Poor's as his Bible. Of such a person, we can say without hyperbole that his business is his religion, because moneymaking is what he worships.

The social scientist Robert Bellah applied a similar functional understanding of religion to the realm of secular society and politics. In 1967, he coined the term "civil religion" to refer to the stories, ideals, and practices that modern polities endow with a sense of transcendence so that their citizens will treat the state with a sense of reverence.[6] Over the years, Bellah's idea has proved intriguing to observers of the State of Israel. Tom Segev, for example, has characterized the Holocaust as the civil religion of Israel.[7] In an extended analysis, Charles Liebman and Eliezer Don-Yehiya have argued that Israel has actually had different civil religions at different times in its history. They point out, however, that a Jewish state is particularly ripe for a civil religion because of its deep roots in a traditional one—Judaism. Thus, with the rise of a Jewish civil religion and the corresponding decline of its traditional counterpart, the secular state of Israel had little trouble appropriating the authority—and the allegiance—that once belonged to God.[8]

Israelis are by no means the only adherents of a Jewish civil religion. They have plenty of co-religionists in America who share their fundamental faith in the Jewish State. How else to account for the truth in Jonathan Woocher's shrewd observation that "American Judaism recognizes only one heresy which subjects the perpetrator to immediate excommunication: denial of support to the State of Israel"?[9] In all, Woocher lists seven "major tenets" in the credo of American Jews:

1. The unity of the Jewish People.
2. Mutual responsibility.
3. Jewish survival in a threatening world.
4. The centrality of the State of Israel.

    5. The enduring value of Jewish tradition.
    6. *Tzedakah*: philanthropy and social justice.
    7. Americanness as a virtue.

Taken together, these tenets constitute the core of what Woocher aptly dubs "civil Judaism."[10]

    At first glance, most of civil Judaism's central tenets appear virtually identical with those found at the heart of traditional Judaism. What could be more Jewish than dedication to the Jewish People's unity or commitment to the practice of *tzedakah*? After all, civil Judaism's power stems, in part, from its ability to draw on the themes, in some cases the very language, of Jewish tradition—a tradition whose "enduring value" it explicitly affirms in its credo.

    And yet, what civil Judaism does with the concept of Jewish tradition is anything but traditional. For instance, during the General Assembly of Jewish Federations and Welfare Funds, when thousands of Jewish professional and lay leaders come together for civil Judaism's yearly version of a revival meeting, Sabbath services are routinely offered. Offered—but not mandated as among the traditional Ten Commandments or, for that matter, even proposed as among the "ten suggestions" for living a "better" Jewish life. Civil Judaism, despite its roots in traditional Judaism, is more plainly an offshoot of another tradition altogether: Western liberalism. For from liberalism's perspective, all religious observance is solely a private matter of individual preference. Says Woocher,

Defining the scope and content of . . . tradition beyond those elements which are clearly functional in the communal context is a task in which civil Judaism *has no stake or interest*.[11]

Rather than merely transforming Jewish tradition, civil Judaism guts it.

    Although civil Judaism's other basic tenets do not reflect the kind of radical makeover given Jewish tradition, their complexion has nonetheless been changed. For example, civil Judaism's minister-fundraisers constantly invoke the need for Jews to bear "mutual responsibility." As support, they often trot out a favorite maxim from the Talmud: "All Israel is responsible for one another." Hence, Jews in America must not turn their backs on needy Jews in Israel or Russia as though those Jews' plight were no concern of theirs. Instead, traditional Judaism posits a clear-cut obligation to assist fellow Jews in distress.

Crucially, however, civil Judaism's idea of Jews' moral responsibility for one another extends no further than an arm's length reach into a wallet—certainly not to the trigger finger of a West Bank Jewish settler who has murdered an Arab child. As part of the traditional Yom Kippur liturgy seeking God's forgiveness, Jews are required to confess in unison: *"We* have committed violence." But civil Judaism is absolutely silent as to what, if any, communal responsibility Jews bear for such savage outbreaks, let alone how Jews should atone for them.[12] Civil Judaism's understanding of "communal responsibility" is as malformed as Woody and Mia's notion of "family."

Along with its emphasis on the centrality of Israel and Jews' mutual responsibility, civil Judaism stresses the unity of the Jewish People among its cardinal tenets. Its devotion to that doctrine is shown by its seemingly eternal attachment to one of the UJA's old campaign slogans: "We are One." Given the frequency and the fervor with which civil Judaism intones that slogan, the phrase could easily serve as its mantra. But when it comes to another kind of "oneness," civil Judaism has seemingly taken a vow of silence. It has nothing to say about the singularity Jews traditionally claimed as "the Chosen People." To be sure, civil Judaism can serve up a dish of "chosenness lite." It can coax—remember: it dare not command!—Jews to exemplify various "Jewish values" that one day might be observed by humanity as a whole. But as Woocher quickly points out, such values are little more than "general principles of moral behavior."[13] They are, more precisely, the moral imperatives that classical liberalism preaches can be discerned by all rational beings, regardless of religious background. In its most unobjectionable—and least interesting—form, civil Judaism's version of Jews' uniqueness would do any university's multicultural program proud: "Of course, the Jews are unique, but, so, too, is every other ethnic group. Isn't diversity wonderful?!"

If, under civil Judaism's influence, many Jews have relinquished their People's traditional claim to uniqueness, have they nevertheless, with its blessing, staked a claim to uniqueness elsewhere, namely, within the sacred precincts of the Holocaust? For it surely seems that as a key article of faith, many Jews at least insist on the Holocaust's uniqueness. But in what does its uniqueness lie?

As if killing chickens, [the Khmer Rouge] executioners had grasped [the babies] by their heels and slung them against the banyan. Their aim had been very exact; a six-inch section of bark was still bloodied and broken.

> . . . *Elie Wiesel, the Nobelist and Auschwitz survivor,*
> *[was] asked how the Cambodian holocaust compared with the*
> *one he had endured. "Different," he had said.*
>   Robert Sam Anson, "Crazy in Cambodia"[14]

Perhaps no one has devoted more time and sustained attention to the subject of the Holocaust's uniqueness than Steven Katz; his magisterial study, *The Holocaust in Historical Context*, is to be a three-volume treatise on it. The first volume alone, *The Holocaust and Mass Death before the Modern Age*,[15] runs to over 700 pages and at times resembles a law review, displaying more notes than text. In excruciating detail, Katz compares the Holocaust with one appalling historical event after another in order to mark it off as crucially different. In an article written in the 1980s for a popular audience,[16] Katz previewed some of his thinking on the issue. In that essay, he cautions that we must distinguish between genocide and ethnicide. He characterizes ethnicide as the intent to destroy a group's national, religious, or ethnic identity—but not necessarily the physical bearers of that identity. Had Hitler aimed only at destroying Judaism—and not all Jewish individuals in the world—the Holocaust, in Katz's view, would not have been unique:

The world historical record is replete with examples of attempts to eliminate "identities" of various sorts, ranging from the resettlement policy of the Assyrians which created the Lost Tribes of Israel, to the resettlement and cultural mandates of Stalin.[17]

Katz explodes the claim that the Holocaust must be judged one-of-a-kind simply in sheer numerical terms. He convincingly shows that the percentage of American Indians killed by whites roughly equals the proportion of Jews murdered by Hitler. Consequently, he concludes, "If numbers alone constitute uniqueness, then the Jewish experience under Hitler was not unique."[18] Is there any way, then, in which the Holocaust *can* be considered unique?

"Yes," answers Katz. From the vantage point of years of research, he unequivocally affirms that

the Holocaust is phenomenologically unique by virtue of the fact that never before has a state set out, as a matter of intentional principle and actualized policy, to annihilate physically every man, woman, and child belonging to a specific people.[19]

The practitioners of Nazi genocide considered utterly fatuous Jews' individual attempts to disassociate their physical being from their "group identity." Conversion, assimilation, and the like were thus beside the point. The inevitable, inexorable goal of Nazism was a *Judenrein* world. In terms of duration, scope, and single-mindedness of purpose, the Holocaust, declares Katz, was—and still is— definitely unique.

Katz's impressive scholarship leaves virtually no room for doubt that the question of the Holocaust's uniqueness has once and for all been answered. Another, more basic question, though, remains un-answered: *So what?* In a variety of ways, that question was repeat-edly put to Katz at a scholarly meeting a few months before his book's publication.[20] After he articulated his central thesis that "the Holocaust illumines Nazism and not the other way around,"[21] some-one perceptively asked, "But, Professor Katz, what if you're not inter-ested in Nazism?" Katz seemed truly stunned by the question, and his response was feeble: "The imperative of scholarship is under-standing." When the interrogator followed up by asking "Under-standing of *what?*" Katz could only lamely reply, "Of, for instance, the fact that technology is a servant."

To understand *that* fact does not require a decade of research or even the Holocaust itself. We could learn it from Love Canal, Chernobyl, and countless other historical instances where our tech-nology has served us poorly. Does that mean, therefore, that the Holocaust is, as an example of the same phenomenon, unimportant or insignificant? No—only that it is not unique. Simply because we can learn something equally well from two different sources does not logically entail that we should discard either one of them.

Katz would likely counter here that the Holocaust is important because it provides our only source for understanding Nazism prop-erly. But how is that different from saying that the American colo-nies' discontent with British rule provides our only source for under-standing the American Revolution? Who would dare argue that a better source for understanding it would be, for example, the French populace's displeasure with Louis XVI and Marie Antoinette? The main point stands: it is understanding that is important—*not* unique-ness. Katz is not guilty of bad scholarship, but of misplaced emphasis.

Given a mind as keen as Katz's, how to account for such an error, such obsession with uniqueness? Once more, his remarks at the meeting are revealing. He advised his audience that in establishing the Holocaust's uniqueness, "We must separate the historical from the theological and, for now, bracket off the theological." From his book, it appears that "for now" could well mean "forever." The Holocaust's singularity, Katz believes, is compatible with any number of differing theological views, none of them preferable to any other.[22] From civil Judaism's perspective, Katz's move is not merely wise, but welcome: Put to one side all the unresolvable, potentially divisive theological questions and pay attention only to the questions that can be answered by the facts.

But the question of why the Holocaust's uniqueness is at all significant is not something decided solely by the facts, no matter how many facts—or footnotes—we might bring. Perhaps that explains why Katz seemed so taken aback by his interrogator's first question: Katz had just assumed that everybody must be interested in the Holocaust and Nazism. Clearly, we may view a person who isn't interested as naive or even callous. But such a person reminds us of at least one crucial fact: Caring about the Holocaust is not something determined by "the facts" alone. Civil Judaism's belief in the Holocaust's uniqueness as being ultimately significant per se is neither self-evidently true nor convincingly argued. It thus epitomizes the type of belief for which religious faith is both famous and infamous—a dogma. And like all such dogmatic beliefs, the more it is challenged, the fiercer the faithful become in its defense. For them, the first of the Ten Commandments has been revised: "The Holocaust is a jealous God; thou shalt draw no parallels to it."[23]

For history, uniqueness cannot be what matters. Many, including Katz, have seen that every historical event is unique in a trivial sense by virtue of its "irrepeatability." As Yosef Hayim Yerushalmi has reminded us, that's what makes an event historical: "Not history, as is commonly supposed, but only mythic time repeats itself."[24] Because no two historical events ever stand on all fours with one another, we necessarily reason by analogy when comparing one historical event with another. To look for historical identities is therefore misguided or perverse—as should be made clear by the bloodshed in Bosnia. When some observers started to compare the Serbs' actions against the Muslims to the Nazis' against the Jews— for example, "ethnic cleansing," concentration camps, torture, and execution—some Jews began to complain that what has happened in Bosnia is not the same as what happened during the Holocaust. Of course not. Again, no two historical events can ever be the same. But can they be in relevant ways similar? If not, why not? If, in case after case, we Jews keep insisting there are no relevant similarities— How many instances of genocidal Hitlerian intent are we ever likely to encounter anyway?—then whether we subscribe to traditional

Judaism or to its civil counterfeit, we will have committed sacrilege. For in saying that there are no significant similarities that matter, we will be saying in effect that the Holocaust lacks any real significance beyond itself, that in the end, it was only an historical oddity. And what could more profane the memory of what happened to European Jewry than that? We will have turned the Holocaust into some sort of religious relic locked away in a case, safely out of touch from any who might want to examine it more closely to learn what historical import it might contain.

What are we to make of civil Judaism's fixation on "oneness," that is, its pious devotion to the uniqueness of the Holocaust, its unending hosannas to the unity of the Jewish People? Such professions of oneness as these almost seem like a kind of compensation that is at once both psychological and theological. It is as though civil Judaism has a guilty conscience over its total silence about another type of oneness, the very oneness the Jewish People historically proclaimed to the world: "Hear, O Israel, the Lord is our God, the Lord is One!"[25] Strikingly, of civil Judaism's seven tenets, *not one has anything to do with God*. The word "God" does not even appear. Woocher made a similarly startling discovery after having perused countless documents authored by civil Judaism's "clergy" and "laity."[26] According to him, even when reference to God is made, "and especially in the vast majority of instances where it is not," the role which God plays in civil Judaism is "thoroughly insignificant."[27] To avoid antagonizing any of its constituencies, civil Judaism remains largely silent about God's specific activity in human life. After all, as Woocher once more reminds us, "The watchword of civil Judaism is unity."[28] The Jewish People's watchword used to be the *Shema*.

What has replaced God as civil Judaism's center of devotion? For those who worship at the Holocaust cult, the object of veneration can be but one thing: survival. Woocher puts it perfectly when he says that for American Jewry, "Commitment to Jewish survival is an unqualified demand of its civil religion."[29] So while talk of God has all but disappeared from the various pronouncements of civil Judaism's leaders, "survival" has become their shibboleth. Once again, civil Judaism has transformed—some might say deformed—traditional Judaism. By making survival Jews' "consuming passion,"[30] it has altered Judaism's most fundamental precept: "And you shall love survival with all your heart, and all your soul, and all your might."

Of course, civil Judaism, in its zeal to preserve "Jewish unity," keeps its talk about survival, like its discourse about God, highly abstract and generalized. Jewish survival has come to refer to everything from buying Jews out of Russia to ensuring U.S. aid to Israel to building a bigger health and fitness facility at the Jewish community center.[31] One issue, however, does not figure in civil Judaism's concerns about survival—the time when Jews' survival need be a concern no longer. The Jewish People, according to the faith of civil Judaism, will always live in a world hostile to it. It is therefore a world in which Jews will never outlive the necessity of fretting about their survival. Not surprisingly, "Jewish continuity" has become the current talisman of civil Judaism's faithful, whose vision is fixed on—and transfixed by—a Holocaust-dominated past. Continuity, survival, mere existence—what else is there for such Jews to hope for in the future? They certainly cannot hope for a future that realizes Jews' chief hope through the ages: the establishment of the kingdom of Heaven on earth. Instead, civil Judaism counsels survival for survival's sake, continuity for continuity's sake, in an altogether different kind of world, one without even the possibility, much less the prospect, for such a kingdom's coming. For civil Judaism and its worshippers of the Holocaust cult, it truly is "a world without end." Amen.

Rites

What a cult worships is best seen through how it worships. Its rites, rituals, and ceremonies are all enactments of its fundamental values, beliefs, and stories. The Holocaust cult is no different.

In both Israel and the Diaspora, the Holocaust is remembered ritually through the observance of Yom Hashoah. Indeed, in the whole of the Jewish liturgical year, it may be the most communally remembered of all days. Whether Jews share a memory of the Holocaust is debatable; that they share the experience of commemoration is not. In Israel, just as the shofar sounded in ancient times to signal a time of national alarm, on Yom Hashoah the blare of an air-raid siren brings the whole country to a standstill. In America, where many Jewish communities are riven the rest of the year by internecine warfare among Orthodox, Conservative, and Reform Jews, Yom Hashoah observances mark a one-day truce when all the rabbis in a community can be found sharing a common *bimah* in a common *shul*. Any reality inhering in civil Judaism's alleluia of "We Are One" manifests itself ritually on Yom Hashoah, Catastrophe Day.

As we saw in Chapter 1, the Knesset's selection of the twenty-seventh of *Nisan* for commemorating the Holocaust gave a new twist

to the old story of the Exodus. The Knesset placed Yom Hashoah
between Passover and the Warsaw Ghetto Rebellion on the one side
and Israel's Independence Day on the other.[32] As James Young explains, a radically new storyline emerged:

This period [can] be seen as commencing with God's deliverance of the Jews
[in Egypt] and concluding with the Jews' deliverance of themselves in Israel.
In this sequence, biblical and modern returns to the land of Israel are recalled; God's deliverance of the Jews . . . is doubled by the Jews' attempted
deliverance of themselves in Warsaw; the heroes and martyrs of the Shoah
are remembered side by side (and implicitly equated) with the fighters who
fell in Israel's modern war of liberation: and all lead inexorably to the birth
of the state.[33]

With its creation of a new sacred calendar, the Knesset likewise
fashioned a new sacred narrative. Through its invention—and
ordering—of a novel set of holydays, the Knesset had, says Young,
"emplotted the entire story of Israel's national rebirth."[34]

*At a United Jewish Appeal big givers' dinner in St. Louis in
the early 1970s, the UJA's Executive Director, Rabbi Herbert
Friedman, arises from his seat on the dais to ascend the podium.
Behind him is a huge banner picturing an automobile with that
year's GM's advertising slogan emblazoned under it: "Buick—
Something to Believe In!" Turning slowly toward the banner with
arm outstretched, Friedman bellows to the audience, "that, ladies
and gentlemen, is what America gives you to believe in—a piece
of junk designed to be obsolete in five years. But what I give you
to believe in are Israel and the Jewish People, a legacy of three
thousand years!"*
A huge sum of money is raised that night.[35]

Like several of its tenets, many of civil Judaism's practices be-
speak a traditional background that is reflected in their very names
as well as the other language they employ. Through rites such as the
"mission" and "retreat," the elect of civil Judaism can experience a
sense of mystical "renewal."
No ritual of civil Judaism is more powerful than the UJA or
Federation mission, an intense, often overwhelming journey to
Israel—and to a particular understanding of Jewish history and identity. Devised in the wake of the Six-Day War, these missions were

the brainchild of the UJA's Herbert Friedman, a chief rabbi of civil
Judaism if ever there was one.[36] At the same time he conceived the
missions, Friedman also inaugurated the UJA's "Young Leadership
Cabinet," composed by and large of successful businessmen under
forty. Part of the mission's role was to make such young(ish) Jews as
these converts to the cause of the survival of Israel and the Jewish
People. Besides increasing their own "gifts" to UJA, these new disciples were expected to recruit other young souls for the mission/
pilgrimage and, hence, for the true faith.

On a typical mission, the participants, sometimes numbering in
the thousands, trace the Holocaust cult's equivalent of the stations
of the cross. Marching under the banner of the mission's credo,
"From Holocaust to Rebirth," the pilgrims typically begin at the
cult's most sacred shrine, Yad Vashem.[37] From there, they move on
to other holy sites. At a border settlement, they vicariously experience the threat to Israel's security; at a government office or military base, they get a high-level briefing as privileged recipients of a
saving *gnosis*; at the sacrosanct ruins of Masada, they hear of Israel's
ancient heroism and modern determination; at an "absorption center" for new immigrants, they see the "good works" their donations
have accomplished.[38] Finally, all those on the mission receive "the
call"; individually or collectively, they are solicited for their "commitments." Civil Judaism's story of the Jewish People in the last half
century has now become their story. The Jewish People, once close
to death, is now alive again. The participants' own Jewish identity,
perhaps previously also close to dying, is now revitalized, thanks to
the mission and its rite of passage. As the founding of the State of
Israel renewed the Jewish People's will to survive, the mission has
renewed the participants' commitment to make sure that that People indeed survives. Woocher nicely captures the essence of what
makes the mission so powerful a rite:

The emotional impact of such . . . [missions has] proved, not surprisingly, to
be enormous. Here, normal successful American Jews [are] made to feel as
helpless as the victims of Nazi murder and as powerful (albeit besieged) as
the Israeli army officers from whom they received private briefings. Having
personally experienced the mythic journey of the Jewish people in our time,
how could they fail to identify, how could they fail to respond?[39]

In as little as the week to ten days a typical mission lasts, Jews can
have a life-shaping transformation as dramatic as Paul's on the road
to Damascus.

For those who lack the time (and money) to spend on a full-blown overseas mission, the weekend retreat represents an attractive alternative. Incorporating some of the mission's elements and overtones, it, too, promises a potent religious experience. By removing participants from their workaday world, the retreat immerses them into a new reality, characterized by entry into a new fellowship full of new insight and new commitment.[40] Like born-again Christians, Jews who have undergone the experience are still able years later to speak in rapture of the moment when their lives were personally, powerfully transformed, as they made an irreversible commitment to dedicate their lives to the service of Israel and the Jewish People.

Crucially, however, born-again Christians usually speak of dedicating their lives to the service of God; the sense of intimate contact with God's presence in the person of Jesus Christ provides the touchstone for their faith. For the initiates of the mission and retreat, the decision to commit their lives to Jewish survival depends on having contact with an entirely different presence: the Holocaust's. As Woocher succinctly puts it, "the [Holocaust's] power . . . lies in its capacity to provoke an absolutely predictable response on the part of American Jews."[41] Virtually corroborating that observation, Samuel Belzberg, the main financial backer of a Los Angeles Holocaust memorial, once told a reporter, "It's a sad fact that Israel and Jewish education and all the other familiar buzzwords no longer seem to rally Jews behind the community. The Holocaust, though, works every time."[42] Although Jews' observance may have lapsed in such areas as *Shabbat*, *kashrut*, and *talmud Torah*, their scrupulosity in maintaining the Holocaust cult remains steadfast and enduring.

Shrines

> *The idols of the nations are silver and gold,*
> *the work of men's hands.*
> *They have mouths, but cannot speak;*
> *they have eyes, but cannot see;*
> *they have ears, but cannot hear,*
> *nor is their breath in their mouths.*
> *Those who fashion them,*
> *all who trust in them,*
> *shall become like them. (Psalm 135:15–18)*

*There's an old saying: "Be careful what you worship, because
you will become what you worship."*

Derek Bok

Since World War II, thousands of monuments and at least one hundred museums have been erected in Europe, Israel, and the United
States to enshrine the memory of the Holocaust. The wealth lavished
on their construction and upkeep testifies as much as any ancient
Buddhist temple or medieval Catholic church to their adherents' devotion to the cult. As many people now make pilgrimage to these Holocaust shrines each year as died during the Holocaust itself![43]

Ironically, throughout most of their history, Jews traditionally
eschewed shrines, particularly, shrines to the dead. They viewed
them as *goyisch*, and historically, at least, they were right. As early
as the first century, Christians started building "martyriums" honoring martyrs' graves or sites of death.[44] In contrast, Jews turned not so
much to sacred places, but to sacred times to recall individual or
communal tragedies. Fast days and *yizkor* could be put in the service
of sacred memory through special prayers of consolation, *yahrzeit*
through special donations to *tzedakah*.

Lately, however, Jews seem to be trying to play catch-up with
Christians in building monuments to the martyred dead. Like watch-
ing TV, erecting shrines to Jewish suffering appears to have taken on
a life of its own, with no goal other than to produce more of the same
behavior. As if the local temples to the Holocaust in New York and
Los Angeles were insufficient to pay it proper homage, $167 million
was raised to build a U. S. Holocaust Memorial Museum in Washington, D.C. Constructed on the Mall, America's acropolis, the museum
opened in April 1993. Michael Berenbaum, the museum's director,
argued for its need by saying that "telling the story of the Holocaust
depends on what vantage point you tell it from; a museum in America will be different from one in Jerusalem."[45] But Young notes that
the storylines of the U.S. museum and Yad Vashem run remarkably
close together:

Like the museum narratives in Israel, where lives were rebuilt after the
Holocaust, this [American] exhibit . . . end[s] with the "return to life." For
this is the story of an ideal shared by America and Israel: both see themselves as lands of refuge and freedom.[46]

The two museums differ not so much in their story as in their storytelling. The U.S. Holocaust Museum is to Yad Vashem as Disneyworld

is to Disneyland—a lot of the same themes and vistas, but a whole lot more high-tech.

But even if the U.S. Museum replicated Yad Vashem in every detail, Berenbaum would still deem its construction justified. In his view, part of the museum's goal is the "Americanization of the Holocaust." By being located on the Mall near the monuments to Lincoln and Jefferson, the museum serves, in Berenbaum's view, as a "counterweight" to American ideals, a kind of "countermemorial" indicating what it means to be American by vividly displaying what it means *not* to be American.

There is another way that the museum's location can serve to "Americanize the Holocaust." The museum stands as a grim reminder that for all its purported ideals, America nevertheless turned its back on Jews fleeing Hitler. During that period, the only American values the nation can be said to have practiced were "pluralism" and "equality" as it, with diverse countries around the world, likewise looked on while Jews were being murdered.[47] Hence, the museum's recalling what happened to Jews in the past may move Americans and their national policymakers in Washington to support Israel in the present, lest in the future, the same fate lie in store for Jews again—and the same moral failure await Americans once more. Regardless, Berenbaum looks upon "Americanizing the Holocaust" as "an honorable task provided that the story told is faithful to the historical event." The challenge, he believes, is to tell that story

in such a way that it [will] resonate not only with the survivor in New York and his children in Houston or San Francisco, but with a black leader from Atlanta, a midwestern farmer, or a northeastern industrialist. Millions of Americans make pilgrimages to Washington; the Holocaust Museum must take them back in time, transport them to another continent, and inform their current reality.[48]

But telling the story "faithfully" is not as simple as stringing together a bunch of assorted facts. Which facts to include and in what order to string them, constitutes no straightforward task. As Berenbaum's comment implicitly acknowledges, much of the story narrated depends on its tellers and its hearers.

A class of non-Jewish schoolchildren visits the U.S. Holocaust Museum in Washington. They come to a case filled with religious artifacts of the victims. Their teacher points to some of the objects and explains, "There's a prayerbook, and there are some

candlesticks, and . . . ." hesitating for a moment when his gaze
falls upon a talit, "there's a tablecloth."

A little later, the class comes to a screen running some old
Nazi film of the medical experiments performed on Jewish
concentration camp inmates. One of the students blurts out, "Oh!
Gross!" Another student instantly responds, "Yeah, neat!"[49]

The common wisdom says that by making sure the story of the Holocaust is never forgotten, we can help ensure sure it will never happen again. But why suppose that to be true? Why should we imagine
that after having seen museum exhibits that graphically display
violent acts and their aftermath, visitors will then deplore the use of
violence? Critics complain that teenagers, who constitute the largest
audience for "slasher films," get desensitized by such gory goings-on,
making it therefore less likely that these adolescents will refrain
from engaging in violent acts themselves.

Even more basically, why assume that Americans, of all people,
will identify with the victims? Americans are notorious for identifying with winners—sports teams, Horatio Alger types, political cam-
paigns with momentum. Although Americans are also famous for
supporting underdogs, that support does not extend to those whom
they consider "losers," especially while such people are in the midst
of losing—as Bosnia's Muslims have learned to their chagrin. And
here's where the usual train of moral argument for Holocaust memorials may ultimately derail. As Young perceptively puts the matter,
"Imagining oneself as a *past* victim is not the same as imagining
oneself—or another person—as a potential victim, the kind of leap
necessary to prevent other 'holocausts.'"[50]

Again, witness the American response—or lack of it—to the
plight of the Bosnian Muslims. President Clinton toured the U.S.
Holocaust Museum at its opening and learned of the inaction of his
predecessors in saving Jews from the ovens. Months later, one of the
museum's officials was addressing an audience when he wondered
aloud, "Did the museum affect the President? I don't know."[51] The
subsequent months of butchery in Bosnia would *prima facie*, at
least, seem to provide an answer. Not that President Clinton may
not have been moved by the Museum. He was just not moved
enough to act, such as, for example, by ordering the bombing of the
bridges over which the Serbs carried arms and supplies into Bosnia.
In this, he was like another American president half a century ago
who, though perhaps moved by the Jews' suffering, nevertheless re-

fused to authorize air attacks on the railway lines leading into Auschwitz because of some allegedly larger, more complex strategic considerations.[52] In the thirties and forties, if the Nazis had not invaded other countries but had been content to exterminate every last Jew in Germany, the rest of the world likely would have been satisfied to stand by passively and watch. Today, the world, America included, seems once more ready to be an onlooker to mass murder, first in Bosnia, then in Rwanda, and who-knows-where next. Clearly, there may be great costs to stopping the wholesale slaughter of civilian populations—higher taxes for greater military spending, perhaps even larger standing armies necessitating the reinstituion of a peacetime draft. But the moral cost for failing to try to stop such murder may be even higher as our indifference encourages not only callousness but ever more numerous outbreaks of genocide. In any case, if the U.S. Holocaust Museum's goal is to spur America's conscience so that "it never happens again," so far, it seems, it's been a $167 million bust.

Even if the museum should rouse Americans to moral action, its cost to Jews may still prove too high, for in their efforts to Americanize the Holocaust story, they may have de-Judaized their own story. As Young insightfully notes, "A Jewish memorial to the Shoah is one thing, a civic monument to the Holocaust another."[53] Because the U.S. Holocaust Memorial Museum sits on public land, it can have, by law, no specific religious orientation. Initially, therefore, the museum was to stay open all year round—except for Christmas, which in America, of course, is only a "cultural" holiday. Only later was it decided, as a virtual afterthought, that the museum should probably be closed on Yom Kippur, too, as though that might make it "neutral as between religions." Small homage—and small comfort—to the Jewish victims of the Holocaust, who were largely from Eastern Europe and, unlike their American cousins, faithful practitioners of traditional Judaism rather than its pale civil imitation.

For those Jews, the de-Judaized story the "nonsectarian" museum tells could not possibly be more disturbing. It is a story that has no room, that by law can have no room, for their Exodus master story's key character: God. Thus, God is missing not only from the story the museum relates, but from the museum itself. To be sure, as a temple to civil Judaism, the museum manifests a certain religiosity akin to Yad Vashem's. Yad Vashem has an *Ohel Yizkor*, a tabernacle of remembrance, its name reminiscent of the Jews' tabernacle in the desert and of many similarly-named synagogues. But as Tom Segev indicates, *Ohel Yizkor* is not a synagogue. . . . There is a synagogue in one wing of the museum, but it is not used for prayer services; it is a memorial to the demolished synagogues of Europe. Yad Vashem does not employ a rabbi.[54]

The U.S. Holocaust Museum likewise has a Hall of Remembrance; it is the room visitors come to at the end of their tour. An inscription on one of its walls serves as a parting reminder: "For the dead and for the living, we must bear witness." The Hall's other walls also carry inscriptions. They are a series of biblical passages stressing the importance of remembrance:

Your brothers' blood cries out. . . . (Gen. 4:10)

Take utmost care and watch yourselves scrupulously, so that you do not forget the things that you saw with your own eyes. . . . (Dt. 4:9)

I call heaven and earth to witness against you this day: I have put before you life and death, blessing and curse. Choose life—if you and your offspring would live. . . . (Dt. 30:19)

You are my witnesses. . . . (Is. 43:12)

But what exactly do these inscriptions imply we should remember?

As presented in the Hall of Remembrance, all these biblical passages seemingly refer to the victims. They charge the museum's departing visitors to go out and witness to what happened to those victims and thereby to sustain their memory as well as the Holocaust's. But in their biblical context, every one of these verses is either spoken by God or spoken of him. We recall that the Isaiah passage in fact does both: "You are my witnesses, and I am God."[55] But we would never know that the verse had anything at all to do with God if all we had was the museum's wall to go on. This passage, like the others etched into the walls, has been cut off mid-verse, and thus, God has been cut out. For all their insistence on the importance of faithful remembrance and testimony, the U.S. Holocaust Museum and Yad Vashem forget God and bear no witness to him at all. To accomplish that feat, they have to mangle the scripture that refers to him and/or put out of mind the master story that speaks of him. On display at both Yad Vashem and the U.S. Holocaust Museum are desecrated Torah scrolls, arks, and prayer shawls. But they are exhibited the way the British Museum shows artifacts from Greece and Rome—as antique remnants of long-dead cultures that worshipped long-dead gods. For the museums in Washington and Jerusalem, and for other such hallowed shrines of civil Judaism consecrated to the Holocaust cult, the story of the Exodus might as well be the tale of Jason's search for the golden fleece, and the Lord might as well be Zeus.

In ancient times, the cultic shrine was superintended by priests. Local shrines had local priests while national shrines, for example, the Temple in Jerusalem, had high priests. Without doubt, the Holocaust cult's High Priest is Elie Wiesel. His blessing is sought for every Holocaust museum and memorial, from the local *bamot* to the central *hechal* in Washington. Whether his name appears on a letterhead or whether he himself appears at a dedication, any effort to consecrate a site as a Holocaust memorial is almost unthinkable without at least his tacit approval. And like his predecessors in the Temple of old, Wiesel has found that being High Priest is not without its benefits. Lionized by Jews and non-Jews alike, he can command five-figure fees for his speaking engagements, to which he has been known to fly by private plane. He is a man whose honors have ranged from receiving the Nobel Peace Prize to throwing out the first ball at a World Series game. As if to underscore the apparent incongruity between his sorrowful-survivor public persona and his comfortable, prosperous private life, an article in *Moment* magazine asked puckishly, "Is Elie Wiesel Happy?"[56]

Of course, the office of High Priest has its limitations, too. The High Priest, almost by definition, can never question the value of the cult. Hence, Wiesel has never publicly questioned the wisdom of spending $167 million on the U.S. Holocaust Museum, although it could be argued that spending even half that much on scholarships to Jewish day schools would be a better way of reverencing the cult's great god, Jewish survival.[57] Nor has Wiesel ever publicly preached the cult's core gospel—"No silence ever again in the face of evil!"—to some of those who need to hear it most: Jews who stood by and said nothing as Palestinians during the *intifada* were beaten, tortured, and worse.[58] Counted among those Jewish bystanders were some of the cult's most ardent supporters, both inside Israel and out, for whom a word or two from their High Priest might have made a difference.

It simply may be too much to expect priests to confront their cult's rationale and practice. In ancient times, the priest was balanced by another religious figure, the prophet. In a sense, the prophet's role was remedial storytelling. By reminding Israel of its story, he reminded both priest and people that the object of veneration was neither the cult nor the community, but God—and God alone. Civil Judaism has its shrines, and it has its priests. But it has no prophets to remind it of a master story with a God beyond itself.

"You Troubler of Israel!"

In 853 B.C.E., Ahab reigned over the northern kingdom of Israel, and under him, the kingdom prospered. He maintained friendly relations with the southern kingdom of Judah as well as with the kingdom of Tyre. The only threat to his kingdom came from the rising Assyrian empire. A man of great political insight and skill, Ahab forged an alliance not only with the states friendly to him, but even with his enemy, Aram, to ward off the Assyrian host. The alliance met the Assyrians at the battle of Karkar and repelled them.[59] Ahab staved off the Assyrian threat to the kingdom of Israel for the next hundred and thirty years.

Yet the Bible mentions not one word about this historic accomplishment, nor does it praise Ahab as a wise and able king who ensured Israel's survival for more than a century.[60] Instead, the Bible, the Jewish People's sacred *Torah*, focuses on the story of Ahab's desire to obtain another man's vineyard:

Ahab said to Naboth, "Give me your vineyard, so that I many have it as a vegetable garden, since it is right next to my palace. I will give you a better vineyard in exchange; or, if you prefer, I will pay you the price in money." But Naboth replied, "The Lord forbid that I should give up to you what I have inherited from my fathers." Ahab went home dispirited and sullen. (I K21:2–4)

Ahab, great leader of Israel, rebuffed by a common Jew! What could be a greater insult? Here is a king, after all, who has done more to ensure Jewish survival than any leader since David. By rights, Ahab should be shown the highest degree of gratitude and respect by the Jewish People. Instead, a mere commoner from among that people rejects Ahab for the reason (in Ahab's eyes, the lousy reason) that that people's God and tradition prohibit him from complying with the king's wishes. Worse yet, especially to Ahab's non-Jewish wife, Jezebel, Naboth has the audacity to think that that God and Israelite tradition put him on an equal footing with the king, as if he, Naboth, belonged to a community ultimately answerable to another King. So Jezebel hatches a plot that eventually leads to Naboth's execution. As for Ahab, he sets off to take possession of the dead man's vineyard (Cf. IK21:11–16).

But although Naboth has been put to death, the story is not over. For God commands the prophet Elijah, another common Jew, to confront Ahab and to tell him of *his* impending demise due to the kind of leadership he has exhibited: "Because you have committed yourself to doing what is evil in the sight of the Lord, I [God] will bring disaster upon you . . . and make a clean sweep of you" (IK 21:20–21). As a kind of codicil to Ahab's fate, the biblical text adds a little further on:

Indeed, there never was anyone like Ahab, who committed himself to do what was displeasing to the Lord, at the instigation of his wife Jezebel. He acted abominably, straying after the fetishes just like the Amorites, whom the Lord had dispossessed before the Israelites. (I K 21:25–26)

The Bible attributes Ahab's downfall to his adoption (albeit at Jezebel's instigation!) of cultic observances foreign to the ways Israel had traditionally worshipped God; the act of killing Naboth on trumped-up charges to take his vineyard is but an expression of Ahab's forsaking both Israel's tradition and its God. The biblical term for Ahab's kind of illicit worship is *lelechet acharey hagilulim*— "following after idols"; the classical rabbinic term for it is *avodah zarah*—"alien service"; the sophisticated modern term for it is "civil Judaism."

For the Bible and much of the rest of Jewish tradition, Jews' ongoing physical existence is a necessary part of Jewish survival, but by no means a sufficient one. For such survival to be identifiably *Jewish*, from an historical as well as from a theological viewpoint, it must include the worship of God. That holy service is performed by enacting the commandments which are at the heart of God's covenant that made the Jews a people in the first place. Ignoring those practices and ignoring in whose service those practices ultimately are, the Jewish People ignores who it is. Without those practices, Jews may as well be Amorites, the prior inhabitants of Canaan mentioned in the Bible's condemnation of Ahab, those pagans whom God dispossessed because of their ungodly practices.

Such words cannot be glad tidings for the adherents of civil Judaism and the Holocaust cult. Especially now, almost a half-century after the Shoah, at a time when Jews in Russia and other former East bloc countries have a real opportunity to emigrate freely, and when Israel seems to be on the verge of true peace and security in the Middle East, the priests of the Holocaust cult seem to be whipping themselves into ever greater frenzies: a new, highly praised museum in Washington, a new, highly acclaimed movie in Hollywood, a slew of new, highly publicized exposés of Holocaust deniers.[61] Young may have explained the phenomenon best:

Without the traditional pillars of Torah, faith, and language to unify them, the majority of Jews in America have turned increasingly to the Holocaust as their vicariously shared memory. . . . When Israel came to be perceived as less a potential victim, it also became less a source of identification and pride among American Jews. As an identification with Israel waned during the late 1970s . . . the other half of secular American Jewish identity—Holocaust memory—assumed a greater proportion of Jewish time and resources.[62]

The redoubled efforts of the Holocaust cult's priests to preserve its central place in Jewish life represent a kind of fundamentalism. Fundamentalist movements manifest themselves by their conscious, organized opposition to the disruption of their (formerly) unchallenged world-view.[63] Hence, their reaction to challenge is not unlike Ahab's response when confronted by Elijah: "Is that you, you troubler of Israel?" Like Ahab, civil Judaism's leaders, when challenged, blame their critics for their communities' problems, reviling those critics as "self-hating Jews," "not community-minded," and "threats to Israel's security." Elijah's retort to Ahab still remains, some twenty-eight centuries later, the best rejoinder: "It is not I who have brought trouble on Israel, but you . . . by forsaking the commandments of the Lord and going after the *ba'alim*" (I K 18:17–18).

Unlike Ahab, civil Judaism's leaders are well-intentioned people. But like him, in their obsessive, even fanatical, preoccupation with survival *per se*, they have lost track of what counts as *Jewish* survival. Historically, at least, to identify as a Jew meant serving a particular God in a particular way as part of a particular community. But civil Judaism has discarded the God and disregarded the way, regarding only the community's survival as important. Civil Judaism and its Holocaust cult have become quite literally self-serving. And that may be the most dangerous worship of all—as the Holocaust cult's devotees should know better than anyone else, given the terrible powers unleashed by such idolatrous worship fifty years ago.

In Elijah's time, Jews were strongly tempted, like their king, to serve the *ba'alim*, the pagan gods whose worship was said to ensure fertility and thus the continued existence, the physical survival, of the people. But Elijah would not let the people and their leaders have it both ways. He would not let them devote their resources, *their lives*, to the *ba'alim* and then invoke God's name as mere etiquette, the very thing which, according to Woocher, civil Judaism characteristically does today:

In occasional speeches . . . God is invoked in a routinized, almost deistic, fashion—a deity who stands behind the world and Jewish tradition, but plays little or no active role in the working out of the contemporary destiny of either.[64]

Elijah refused to allow God to be invoked as a mere formality, as some religious nicety. He demanded that the people make a choice as to which deity, which power, brings life: "How long will you keep hopping between two opinions? If the Lord is God, follow him; and if Baal, follow him!" (I K 18:21).

Ahab made *his* choice. In the short to medium term, it worked. The Jews and their allies held the Assyrians at bay. Ultimately, however, the Assyrians prevailed—not merely because they overran the northern kingdom, nor simply because they dragged its inhabitants off to exile, but because while those deportees were in exile, they disappeared *as Jews*, becoming forevermore "the Ten Lost Tribes of Israel." Whatever security Ahab provided failed in the end to secure their continuing Jewish presence in the world.

When the southern kingdom of Judah fell to the Babylonians almost a century and a half later, its inhabitants were also sent into captivity. But unlike their northern neighbors, they did not disappear. For as their prophets, who went with them, constantly reminded them, the Power for their survival also went with them—the Power, that is, for their remaining Jews. Speaking on that Power's behalf, Isaiah proclaimed to all within hearing:

> Turn to Me and gain success
> All the ends of the earth!
> For I am God, and there is none else. . . .
> To me every knee shall bend,
> Every tongue vow loyalty.
> They shall say: "Only through the Lord
> Can I find victory and might. . . .
> It is through the Lord that all the offspring of Israel
> Have vindication and glory." (Is. 45:22–25)

In traditional Judaism, the first step toward repentance, toward changing one's ways, is turning back to God. For civil Judaism, there can be no step more important.

Notes

1. Primo Levi, *Survival in Auschwitz*, trans. Stuart Woolf (New York: Collier Books, 1993), pp. 65–66.

2. I do not mean "cult" in the popular sense of a secretive, relatively small group of the sort that followed David Koresh and Jim Jones. Instead, I mean it in the scholarly, academic sense of a system of religious worship. Thus, for instance, in speaking of "the Temple cult in Jerusalem," one would be referring to the animal sacrificial system observed there.

3. Cf. *Oxford English Dictionary*, 2d ed., s.v. "victim," and Joseph Amato, *Victims and Values: A History and Theory of Suffering*, foreword by Eugen Weber (New York: Greenwood Press, 1990), p. 99.

4. Originally, perhaps in an attempt to rejuvenate it, the Israeli rabbinate adopted the Tenth of Tevet, the fast day traditionally recalling the beginning of the Babylonians' siege of Jerusalem, as the day for remembering the Holocaust. See James E. Young, *The Texture of Memory: Holocaust Memorials and Meaning* (New Haven: Yale University Press, 1993), p. 267.

5. Tom Segev, *The Seventh Million: The Israelis and the Holocaust*, trans. Haim Watzman (New York: Hill and Wang, 1993), p. 434.

6. Robert Bellah, "Civil Religion in America," *Daedalus* 96 (Winter 1967):1–21.

7. NPR, "Fresh Air," 27 May 1993.

8. Charles S. Liebman and Eliezer Don-Yehiya, *Civil Religion in Israel: Traditional Judaism and Political Culture in the Jewish State* (Berkeley, Los Angeles, and London: University of California Press, 1983), pp. 1–5.

9. Jonathan S. Woocher, *Sacred Survival: The Civil Religion of American Jews* (Bloomington and Indianapolis: Indiana University Press, 1986), p. 77.

10. Ibid., pp. 67–68.

11. Ibid., p. 83; italics mine.

12. World Jewry, through the United Israel Appeal and other such philanthropies, contributed financially to the building of settlements in the West Bank—and thus also contributed morally to at least some of the violence perpetrated by the settlers.

13. Woocher, pp. 83, 182.

14. Robert Sam Anson, "Crazy in Cambodia," *Esquire*, August 1992, p. 134.

15. Steven T. Katz, *The Holocaust in Historical Context*, vol. 1: *The Holocaust and Mass Death before the Modern Age* (New York and Oxford: Oxford University Press, 1994).

16. Steven T. Katz, "History and the Holocaust," *William and Mary*, Summer 1984, 24–29.

17. Ibid., p. 25.

18. Ibid., p. 28; in the original text, Katz's words are italicized.

19. Katz, *The Holocaust in Historical Context*, p. 28.

20. The American Academy of Religion Annual Meeting in Washington, D.C., November 1993.

21. Cf. Katz, *The Holocaust in Historical Context*, p. 3.

22. Ibid., cf. pp. 28–31.

23. Phillip Lopate, "Resistance to the Holocaust," *Tikkun* 3, no. 4 (1989): 56.

24. Yosef Hayim Yerushalmi, *Zakhor: Jewish History and Jewish Memory* (Seattle and London: University of Washington Press, 1982), p. 10.

25. Katz states explicitly that his thesis about "the unique way in which Israel was chosen by Hitler for annihilation" in no way ought to be taken as some theological position, and especially not as "a secular or disguised form" of the traditional doctrine of God's having uniquely chosen Israel. See *The Holocaust in Historical Context*, p. 2, fn. 3.

26. That is, professional staff members of the UJA, Federations, etc., and the volunteer supporters of those organizations.

27. Woocher, p. 91; italics mine.

28. Ibid., p. 92.

29. Ibid., pp. 72–73.

30. Ibid., p. 72.

31. Ibid., cf. p. 74.

32. Young, p. 269. The Knesset placed the date for Yom Hashoah in the midst of two overlapping time spans. The first, the seven-week *sefirah*, marks the period of somber anticipation between the Jews' Passover deliverance from Egypt and their receiving Torah on *Shavuot* at Sinai. The second span encompasses the six-week timeframe during which the Warsaw Ghetto uprising occurred, a dark time that fits well with the traditionally solemn, even mournful, mood set by *sefirah*.

33. Ibid.

34. Ibid.

35. I witnessed this episode. Subsequent italicized anecdotal passages similarly reflect, unless otherwise noted, my own direct eyewitness (or earwitness) experience.

36. Given Herbert Friedman's sense of Jewish history as well as his own personal history—particularly his legendary ambivalence about being a rabbi—the notion of "mission" may have carried both military and religious connotations for him. In calling him "a chief rabbi of civil Judaism," I in no way mean to disparage him. Herbert Friedman is a great man who has accomplished great things for the Jewish People and the State of Israel—especially when compared to the largely ineffectual pulpit rabbis who were his contemporaries and the generally colorless communal bureaucrats who were his successors.

37. Some missions stop first at Auschwitz or Dachau before going on to Israel; in any case, the passage from Holocaust to Renewal remains intact.

38. Some missions may visit a development town, a revitalized poor neighborhood, and a *malben* home for the elderly in addition to, or instead, of an absorption center.

39. Woocher, pp. 149–150.

40. Ibid., cf. pp. 151–152.

41. Ibid., p. 133.

42. Young, p. 306.

43. Ibid., pp. ix–x. Looking at just the top three Holocaust memorial sites alone, we see that 1.8 million visited the U.S. Holocaust Memorial

Museum, over 1.3 million toured Yad Vashem, and more than 750,000 went to Auschwitz during 1993.

44. Amato, p. 47.

45. Remarks at the American Academy of Religion Annual Meeting in Washington, D.C., 22 November 1993.

46. Young, pp. 346–347.

47. Ibid., cf. p. 338.

48. Ibid., p. 337.

49. I witnessed this episode myself during a visit to the museum on, of all days, the thirtieth anniversary of President Kennedy's assassination, November 22, 1993.

50. Young, p. 344.

51. Remarks made at a session of the American Academy of Religion Annual Meeting, Washington, D.C., 22 November 1993.

52. Cf., e.g., David Wyman, *The Abandonment of the Jews* (New York: Pantheon Books, 1984), p. 295.

53. Young, p. 349.

54. Segev, p. 426.

55. See Chapter 3.

56. Yosef I. Abramowitz, "Is Elie Wiesel Happy?" *Moment*, February 1994, 32–37, 78.

57. For another interesting challenge to the wisdom of building yet one more Holocaust shrine, see Howard Husock's essay, "A Testament to The Diaspora," proposing a museum celebrating American Jewish life. *New York Newsday*, 19 september 1994.

58. Unpardonable acts such as these were well documented by a true worshipper at the altar of human rights, Amnesty International; see Chapter 6.

59. Whether the alliance defeated the Assyrians or merely fought them to a draw is a matter of scholarly dispute. Either way, however, the Assyrians withdrew.

60. The only way we know of Ahab's role in the battle of Karkar is through the monolith of the Assyrian king, Shalmaneser III, now in the British Museum. *Encyclopedia Judaica*, s.v. "Karkar," by Michael Avi-Yonah and Pin[c]has Artzi.

61. The film to which I refer is, of course, *Schindler's List*, and the kind of denier exposé I have in mind is Deborah Lipstadt's *Denying the Holocaust: The Growing Assault on Truth and Memory* (New York: The Free Press, 1993). Rabbi Marc Wilson first called this phenomenon to my attention.

62. Young, p. 348.

63. I am indebted to Professor Nancy Ammerman, an expert on the nature and history of fundamentalism(s), for helping me become clear about this point.

64. Woocher, p. 91.

Chapter 4

Is the Only Good God a Dead God?

Over the last few years, a certain "theological" text has been making the rounds:

> *"Shit Happens in Various World Religions"*
>
> TAOISM: *Shit happens.*
> CATHOLICISM: *If shit happens, you deserved it.*
> BUDDHISM: *If shit happens, it isn't really shit.*
> HINDUISM: *This shit has happened before.*
> JUDAISM: *Why does shit always happen to* us?

The last statement elicits a knowing nod from many Jews. To them, it wryly captures the nature of Jewish experience throughout history—a protracted story of suffering that climaxes with the Holocaust.

How, then, should Jews view their existence "after Auschwitz"? According to Richard Rubenstein's classic by that title, Jews, post-Holocaust, must come to see that they inhabit a world in which God is no longer alive. For those living in the shadow of Auschwitz, the caring, just God of Jewish tradition has died. Reigning instead as Lord of the world, says Rubenstein, is omnipotent Nothingness. Jews, like all other human beings, find themselves in a cold, impersonal universe. It is a realm in which there is nothing necessary, sacred, or "chosen" about Jewish existence. In such a world, talk about the redemption of the world is just that—talk.

When *After Auschwitz* was published in 1966, it caused quite a stir. Rubenstein became known as the leading Jewish exponent of the controversial "Death of God" theology. Here was a theology that denied the traditional Jewish beliefs in a just God, a chosen people, and a set of holy covenantal practices connecting the two. Earlier Jews would have taken such claims as apostasy; today, most Jews take them for granted. For these Jews, the logic of Rubenstein's argument is inescapable: After the attempted extermination of God's people, how can the Jewish People believe anymore in that God's existence?

God as Holocaust Survivor

Ironically, no matter how heretical Rubenstein's theological beliefs may appear, they nevertheless hold one key tenet in common with traditional Jewish thought: The fate of the Jews and the fate of the Jews' God are necessarily intertwined.

That axiom is certainly a basic theme resounding throughout the Exodus narrative. It provides the dramatic energy driving the plague cycle forward, goading any thoughtful reader sooner or later to ask: "Why *so many* plagues? If Israel's God is as mighty as the story would have us believe, then why go through this elaborate dumb show? Why not just bring Israel out of bondage and be done with it?" But that is the very question the narrative depicts God as answering before the seventh plague's onslaught:

By now I could have stretched forth my hand and stricken you [Pharaoh] and your people with pestilence, and you would have been effaced from the earth. Nevertheless, I have spared you for this purpose: in order to show you my power and *in order that my reputation be recounted throughout the world. (Ex. 9:15–16)

The master story of Israel's exodus from Egypt bears meaning far beyond the peoples of Israel and Egypt. It is a story meant to be for all the peoples of the world, such that as the Exodus master story unfolds, all the world hears who is its rightful lord. Neither Pharaoh nor even Moses can claim that title, for, in the end, no human can match God's life-sustaining power or merit the reputation ensuing from it. And on what does God's reputation as powerful, life-saving lord rest? On nothing more nor less than what happens to the Jewish People.

The notion that God's lot in the world is inextricably bound up with Israel's figures prominently in the story later on. When the people commit sacrilege by worshipping a golden calf, God goes into a blind rage, and in his fury, makes Moses an intriguing offer: "Let . . . my anger blaze forth against [the Israelites] . . . that I may destroy them, and make of you a great nation" (Ex. 32:10). God holds out to Moses the possibility of starting over "from scratch" by obliterating the current Israel in favor of a new one to be fathered by Moses himself—thereby making Moses a new Abraham in the bargain! Moses, however, ignores the offer and instead persuades God to relent. How? He asks God to consider the ruin he would bring to his reputation should he choose to ruin Israel:

Let not your anger, Lord, blaze forth against your people, whom you delivered from the land of Egypt with great power and with a mighty hand. Let not the Egyptians say, *"It was with evil intent that he delivered them, only to kill them off in the mountains and annihilate them from the face of the earth."* (Ex. 32:11–12)

But Moses also asks God to consider something else—the covenantal promises he has made:

Remember your servants, Abraham, Isaac, and Jacob, how you swore to them by your own self . . ." *I will make your offspring as numerous as the stars of heaven*, and I will give to your offspring this whole land . . . to possess forever." (Ex. 32:13)

Moses presses God to uphold his covenant with Israel's patriarchs, to whose offspring He has pledged abundant life. It as though Moses reminds God that if reputation stands or falls on any single thing, it is on the way one keeps—or breaks—one's promises. To *this* God, whose very name is first made known through a series of covenantal promises, no argument could prove more compelling: "So the Lord renounced the punishment he had planned to bring upon his people" (Ex. 32:14). For this God to keep his reputation intact, the Jewish People must be kept alive.[1]

But notice: it is *the life of the Jewish People* that God promises to preserve and *not the lives of individual Jewish persons*. Individual Jews may die, may in fact never live to see their lives redeemed or saved. After all, according to the Exodus narrative, generations of

Hebrews were born as slaves and later died as slaves.[2] What matters in terms of God's promise, and thus what matters for God's reputation, is that *the Jewish People survived* both Egyptian slavery and Egypt's attempts at genocide. The continued life of the people Israel points to a God alive to his commitments.

The Exodus tells us something else about God's promises to the Jews: no Jew can realize those promises alone. The wilderness, after all, holds a thousand different ways to die for those who try to strike out and make it on their own. Whatever portion of God's promise— of life's promise—individual Jews may attain comes only through continued participation in the corporate life of the Jewish People. Earlier, we saw how a community's rites and practices might be viewed as enactments of its master story's key aspects. Not for nothing, therefore, is Jewish prayer typically cast in the plural, its petitions, like its praises and thanksgivings, uttered in the language of "we," "us," and "our" rather than of "I," "me," and "my." No wonder, either, that Jewish tradition requires a *minyan*—a quorum of ten symbolizing the presence of the Jewish community—for the Torah service, when the covenant at Sinai is received once more, transforming a hodgepodge of individuals into "a kingdom of priests and a holy nation." And not surprisingly, in the benedictions of the *Amidah*, recited thrice each day, God's ultimate life-bearing promise to individual Jews—the promise of resurrection—is offered within the context of the enduring life of the entire people Israel, the pledge secured, it should be noted, by God's own good name:

Acknowledged are you, Adonai, our God and *God of our ancestors, God of Abraham, God of Isaac, and God of Jacob,* the great, mighty, powerful god . . . *who will bring a redeemer to their children's children, for the sake of his name,* out of love: King, Helper, and Shield. . . . *You revive the dead, so great are you to save.*[3]

By failing to see clearly that God's fortunes in the world are linked to those of his People, Rubenstein and other Holocaust-focused Jews have become blind to what counts as the most distinctive evidence of God's powerful presence on earth. Although the Nazis perpetrated the mass murder of millions of Jews, they ultimately failed to murder *the Jewish People*. While over one-third of the world's Jews were butchered, the empirical fact remains that Hitler's minions were unable to exterminate the world's remaining Jews, and that reality must count as heavily, if not more heavily, for talk of God's survival than of his death.

Looking for God in All the Wrong Places

The claim is not that the Exodus master story or any master story, including a Holocaust-based one, can or should shape our vision of life by showing us a one-to-one correspondence between each of its discrete components and the complex details of our lives. The claim is, however, that such a narrative trains us to spot certain motifs or patterns in our experience to help us better understand our existence. It is in this sense that Emil Fackenheim and Irving Greenberg have dubbed the Exodus an "orienting experience" through which we are to get our bearings for making sense of all the rest of life.[4]

Thus, reading our experience rightly means not misreading our master story. Fundamentalists, for example, tend to read such narratives in a way that correlates each and every item in the biblical text with some particular element of their current reality. But the models master stories offer us for making sense of our existence are more like the analog models of modern quantum physics than the scale models of toy train sets. Crucial for properly understanding the explanatory power of an analog model is comprehending the structural analogy it tries to draw between abstract phenomena not directly observable to us and other, more familiar features of our daily experience. The billiard ball model of gases, for instance, explains the interaction of colliding gas molecules—invisible to the naked eye—by comparing it to the motion of billiard balls striking one another on a pool table. So the Exodus narrative compares God saving Israel at the Sea— impossible to "see" in any straightforward sense—to a glorious rescue performed by a mighty warrior: "Sing to the Lord, for he has triumphed gloriously! Horse and driver he has hurled into the sea" (Ex. 15: 1, 21).

But notice how such analog models can be misinterpreted. Suppose that after we have presented the billiard ball model of gases, somebody pipes up, "This is all very nice, but tell me, which gas molecule is painted black and has an 8 stamped on it?" We would want to say that that person has misread the model, has misunderstood the model's meaning and import, has mistaken an analog model for a scale model. That should also be our response to two kinds of Jewish fundamentalists. The first kind, whose religious growth may have been stunted by some liberal Hebrew school, think they can dismiss God's existence by asking the question, "How can anybody believe in a big man high up in the sky reaching down to overturn Egyptian chariots with a 'strong hand and an outstretched arm' "?

The second kind of fundamentalist, whose intellectual growth may have been stymied in some Orthodox *yeshiva*, believe they can affirm God's existence by answering the question, "How high were the walls of water God piled up on the right and left of the fleeing Hebrews so that they could march through on dry ground?" Both kinds of fundamentalists misperceive the kind of model the Exodus story is and how such a model functions as an interpretative key for making sense of Jewish existence.

The incident at the Sea of Reeds, for instance, is just one more episode in a string of events whose purpose is to teach the Egyptians, the Hebrews, and all future audiences how and where to look for God at work in the world. Within this string of events are a series of occurrences typically referred to as "the Ten Plagues." But the narrative calls them by a different name—*signs*:

The Lord said to [Moses] . . ." You shall take some water from the Nile and . . . [it] will turn to blood. . . . Take with you this rod, with which you shall perform the *signs*." (Ex. 4:6, 9, 17)

I will set apart the region of Goshen, where my people dwell, so that no swarms of insects shall be there, that you may know that I, the Lord, am in the midst of the land. And I will make a distinction between my people and [Pharaoh's] people. Tomorrow this *sign* shall come to pass. (Ex. 8:18–19)

I have hardened [Pharaoh's] heart and the hearts of his courtiers, in order that I may display these My *signs* among them, and that you may recount in the hearing of your children and your children's children how I made a mockery of the Egyptians and how I displayed my *signs* among them—*in order that you may know that I am the Lord*. (Ex. 10:1–2)

As signs, these events point to something beyond themselves, but, as signs, they do not explain how they are to be read or understood, what they signify, or what significance they carry. Instead, the master story surrounding these "sign-events" provides the context for their correct interpretation. From within the interpretative framework supplied by the Exodus, Jew and non-Jew alike are to learn how to read this divine sign-language so that they may discern where to look—and, by implication, *where not to look*—for God active in the world.

Just consider another standard Rubensteinian, post-Holocaust challenge to any talk of God: "After Auschwitz, how can we speak any longer of a 'God of justice'? Babies bayonetted while their murderers died of old age, neither prosecuted nor punished, but at home, safe and warm in bed." Where, then, would an Exodus-based interpretative frame have us look to find the clearest, most distinctive signs of God's justice in such circumstances? Once again, the Exodus master story would direct our vision to the communal rather than individual level and to the long rather than short term. The Exodus narrative itself implicitly acknowledges the fact that evil individuals may escape punishment. The Pharaoh who initiated the Hebrews' oppression—including the drowning of the male Hebrew babies in an act of attempted genocide—died unrepentant and unpunished,[5] and only later did Egypt as a whole suffer the brunt of God's retribution. And, as with Egypt, so, too, with Germany: we can see God's justice if we view events from the right angle of vision. From such a standpoint, it matters that the German nation was defeated. From that perspective, it means something that the country that had sought to exterminate the Jews was itself virtually wiped off the map by the advancing Allied armies, as Germany ended the war not with a world-encompassing unified *Reich*, but with a *Vaterland* cut in two. In the last analysis, the post-Holocaust challenge to talk of God's justice, like the earlier one questioning talk of his presence, is not so much wrong as wrongly placed. Ignoring the Exodus master story, such challenges cannot help but fail to recognize the signs so characteristic of that narrative's leading character, whose justice and presence can still be discerned in the world.

And it is into the world—that is, into a *public, shared* world—that an Exodus interpretative framework directs us to find the signs of the living God among us. Hence, all the plagues, all the sign-events signifying who is truly lord of Egypt and of life, occur in fully public places—by the banks of the Nile, throughout the whole land of Egypt, at the Sea[6]—and in full public view—"before the eyes" (we repeatedly hear) of Pharaoh, his courtiers, the other Egyptians, and, of course, the Israelites.[7]

By contrast, many today look for signs of God in personal, private spheres. Given what might be called "the story of modernity," such a change should not astonish us. For the tale told by modernity is one of the progressive liberation of the individual from any and all social relationships that might tie or bind. In the words of R. W. B. Lewis, such a figure stands

emancipated from history, happily bereft of ancestry, untouched and undefiled by the usual inheritances of family and race; an individual standing alone, self-reliant and self-propelling, ready to confront whatever awaited him with the aid of his own unique and inherent resources.[8]

Is it any wonder that the novel is *the* literary creation of the modern age? With its focus on the individual's inner, psychic life as the realm in which all real, meaningful drama occurs, the novel recounts its stories of individual liberation on a stage far smaller and very different from the one on which the Exodus plays out its saga of a people's release from bondage.

It is not only "radical" or liberal Jewish thinkers such as Rubenstein who have been captivated by modernity's siren song. Other Jews, who see themselves as "traditionalists," have also been distracted by its alluring call, have also lost sight of the Exodus, and have thus also gone looking for God in all the wrong places. James Kugel has written a book, *On Being a Jew*, whose title page inscription describing it as a "Brief Presentation of Jewish Practice and Belief, being written as a dialogue in defense of tradition."[9] intentionally alludes to the poet Judah Halevi's medieval tract, *The Kuzari*, originally entitled *The Book of Argument and Proof in Defense of a Despised Faith*. In Halevi's work, a rabbi discusses the truth of Judaism with a non-Jewish monarch known as the Kuzari, the King of the Khazars. Thus, Kugel, too, fashions a dialogue between a believing Jew, the Sephardic banker Albert Abbadi, and a nonbeliever—in this case, the secularized American Jewish graduate student, Judd Lewis.

To direct Judd to God's presence, Albert points to the biblical image of the *mishkan*, the wilderness "Tent of Meeting" where Moses and the people could find the divine presence "residing." Albert explains to Judd that although the universe itself cannot contain God's majesty, and although God surely might have chosen some more awe-inspiring natural site from which to reveal his presence, he nevertheless had the people construct the relatively small space enclosed by the *mishkan* so that he might fill it —and thereby their lives as well. Continues Albert,

And this is the most basic principle of our way, to open up such a space in our lives and in our hearts. . . . [Jewish observance] is also a structure . . . that keeps open the heart in the same fashion. . . . So long as the *inside of you* remains unbreached, you might be standing at the entrance of the holiest part of that *mishkan*, yet you would *still be quite blind to God's presence*, because there would be *no place inside you in which to receive the impression*.[10] (italics added)

Kugel's image of the heart as an inner *mishkan* in which to encounter God's presence is both brilliant and moving. Nevertheless, with its emphasis on the inner life of the individual as *the* decisive locus for coming in contact with the divine, Kugel's argument takes us in the exact opposite direction followed by Halevi eight centuries ago. At the outset of Halevi's dialogue, a philosopher, a Christian, and a Muslim are summoned to see if they can interpret the Kuzari's recurring troubling dream. In it, the king is told that his "way of thinking is pleasing to God," but not his "way of acting."[11] Significantly, the king doesn't even flirt with the idea of interviewing any Jews, because, like virtually everybody else in the (medieval) world, he perceives them to be "of low station, few in number, and generally despised."[12] However, when those summoned by the king repeatedly cite as support for their respective positions the biblical history and tradition of the Jews, the monarch's opinion changes and he finds himself "compelled to ask the Jews. . . for I see that they constitute in themselves the evidence for the divine law on earth."[13] Thus, the king summons a rabbi, who opens his testimony with a capsule summary of the Exodus master story linking the Jewish People's presence on earth with God's: "I believe in the God of Abraham, Isaac, and Israel, who led the children of Israel out of Egypt with signs and miracles, who fed them in the desert and gave them the land." [14]

Even so, why should the Kuzari be impressed? After all, God's rescue of Israel from Egypt was a sign, a miracle, performed long ago. "What significant miracle," the king might ask, "has Israel's God performed lately?" Witness then, O King of the Khazars, the miracle, the sign, right before your eyes: the very presence of this rabbi in your midst! The continued preservation of that rabbi and his people down to the king's own time is a miraculous sign, especially when, as the king himself had noted only a little while ago, the Jews have been so low in station, numbers, and esteem. The Jews' survival, despite their having been battered and brutalized throughout history, provides the world with powerful testimony about the Jews' powerful God, King of the World.

As for the King of the Khazars, he finds such testimony truly compelling, for he eventually converts to Judaism, that is, to the observance of the acts constitutive of traditional Jewish practice. In other words, the king does *not* convert to the acceptance of some abstract universal truth of reason about "the nature of the Divine" discovered through inward reflection. Indeed, his dream had already assured him that his way of *thinking* pleased God. Instead, he had been informed again and again that what he needed was *a way of acting* likewise God-pleasing. Hence, the rabbi directs the king's attention "outward" toward a people distinguished throughout history by its performance of certain practices, namely, the *mitzvot* or commandments, through whose observance that people publicly and corporately enacts God's will on earth. Consequently, by adopting the Jews' distinctive way of life, the king and the rest of the Khazars become part of the body politic of the Jewish People, God's most distinctive *incarnation* in the world.

No one is claiming that Jews can have no personal religious life, as if their corporate experience were all that mattered. What is being claimed, however, is that Jews' shared, public experience is primary, and that whatever private, inner experience Jews may have is dependent on it. As Gershom Scholem, the dean of Kabbalah scholars, pointed out long ago, even Jewish mystics pursued their esoteric studies and practices communally while being notably reticent to speak or write about their own individual mystical experiences.[15]

But what happens if we lose sight of where to encounter God most distinctively? What happens if we turn our attention to an individual, private world over the short run rather than to the corporate, public one over the long term?

When Bad Things Happen to Good Gods

On New York's Upper West Side, near Harlem, a rabbinical student was mugged and stabbed. During his recuperation in the hospital, he shared a room with a Roman Catholic man, who was recovering from a terrible car wreck. One day, the man turned to him and said, "I know you're not a Catholic, but you are a divinity student, and there's been one question which has been troubling me all the time I've been lying here in this bed: Why did God let me live? I should have been killed in that car wreck! It's the stuff tragedy is made of—a father leaving behind a young wife and small children! But I didn't die; I'm not even going to be maimed! So my question is just this: Why did God let me live?!"

The rabbinical student thought a minute, paused, and then replied, "Gee, I don't know. I haven't had that course yet."

But apparently Rabbi Harold Kushner has had that course; at least, that's what he suggests in his 1980s runaway best-seller, *When Bad Things Happen to Good People*. For Kushner, the focus of that course was his child's death of a rare disease. Reflecting on that individual tragedy led Kushner to conclude that he had "seen the wrong people get sick . . . be hurt . . . die young." As a result of his own experience, Kushner felt compelled to "rethink everything he had been taught about God and God's ways," and he knew he had to write a book "to help other people who might one day find themselves in a similar predicament."[16]

What insight does Kushner draw from his son's death that might comfort others? "God . . . did not send the illness and could not prevent it."[17] Kushner counsels that some bad things happen to good individuals "for no reason, [because] there is randomness in the universe." Individual suffering brought on by such randomness cannot possibly reflect any kind of divine choice or decision—else how could we call it "random"? According to Kushner, we need to understand that "randomness is another name for chaos . . . and chaos is evil . . . because by causing tragedies at random, it prevents people from believing in God's goodness." Having asked, "Could it be that God does not cause the bad things that happens to us?" Kushner answers emphatically, " '*Yes*,' misfortunes do not come from God at all."[18]

One reads Kushner's conclusion, and one wonders how his message could possibly comfort anybody: "Look out! There's random evil loose in the world *that even God cannot control!*" Perhaps the explanation lies that in our secular, modern age, people find consolation—and confirmation—in the view that even if there is a God, he is no less vulnerable, ultimately no less impotent, than they. Or, to put it another way, misery loves miserable company.

But even if we can explain Kushner's popular appeal psychologically, we dare not embrace his position theologically. It snatches away the last theological morsel many post-Holocaust Jews have allowed their anorexic religious faith: monotheism. What Kushner has held out instead is a universe in which there are two powers at work—the god of goodness and the force of random evil. That kind of move is certainly tempting; conjuring up two (or more) powers to account for good and evil in the world is certainly easier than pegging everything ultimately on just one. But before we make that move and call such stuff "Jewish" or even "biblical," we might do well to recall what Robert Frost said about blank verse: It's like playing tennis without a net. And if you play tennis without a net, is the game you're playing really recognizable *as tennis* any longer?

Why did Rabbi Kushner's son die? Why do specific individuals suffer specific ills? Jews don't know; they haven't had that course yet. Instead, Jews have only been schooled to follow the Exodus narrative so that they might learn to follow the kind of divine pathmarks of Jewish history that can keep them on course with God as they make the long trek toward our promised destination. If, like Kushner, they lose sight of those signposts pointing God's way, they may also well lose track of the truth about their lives.

It is just such errancy that characterizes Kushner's reading of the Book of Job, which he enlists as biblical support for his theory of evil on the loose. Kushner thinks the book asks (and answers) the question, "Why do bad things happen to good people?" But that is not the book's question. To that question, we get an answer early on: Job has lost his property, his children, and his health due to a bet between God and Satan as to whether Job, under the weight of his suffering, will curse the Lord. Accordingly, the bet itself raises the book's real question: How should good people remain true to the God they proclaim God of the world when the world, *their* world, is full of suffering?

Given how Kushner misses the centrality of that question, it seems inevitable—and highly revealing—that he should also overlook the book's most famous passage: "The Lord has given, and the Lord has taken away. Blessed be the name of the Lord" (Job 1:21). What do Job's words mean? In particular, what does it mean to "bless the name of the Lord?" And in the face of unmerited suffering, what might "blessing the Lord's name" mean for our speaking the truth about God—and about ourselves?

We have come across the importance of God's "name" before. In the Exodus where Israel is brought out alive while Egypt is overwhelmed by all manner of death-dealing evil, God's name is synonymous with his reputation *as God*. He, not Pharaoh or any other pretender god, *is* the Lord in whose hand is held human life—and death. As for the word translated in English as "blessed," it comes from a Hebrew root meaning "knee" and connotes the act of kneeling, of reverently acknowledging. Consequently, when Job utters those famous words, in light of—and not in spite of—everything that has happened to him, he is acknowledging God as the Lord of everything. Later, Job reaffirms his undivided commitment to that one Lord when he responds to his wife's urging that he curse God: "Should we accept only good from God and not accept evil?" Significantly, in making this affirmation as well as the earlier one, Job has done nothing more nor less than affirm the truth, for as the biblical text goes on to observe quite pointedly, "In all this, Job said nothing sinful."[19]

The rabbis of the Talmud wove Job's truth-telling into the fabric of Jewish practice. Because those rabbis, unlike Kushner, were monotheists, they taught that we are obliged to acknowledge God as the ultimate source of the bad as well as the good that befalls us. Using Job 1:21 as a cornerstone, the sages fashioned a distinctive Jewish observance pertaining to death and mourning. Upon hearing of the death of a close relative or loved one, a Jew is required to rend his or her garment at the lapel, symbolizing the wish to tear one's heart out in anguish. Then, at that most painful, seemingly godforsaken moment, a Jew recites the confessional, *tzidduk hadin,* whose passages express what for a Jew is the truth of what has taken place:

Acknowledged are You, Adonai, our God, the world's king, the true judge, . . . who kills and makes alive. . . . The Lord has given, the Lord has taken away. Acknowledged be the Lord's name. . . .

as Lord of *both* good *and* evil. Audiences sometimes ask Kushner how he can hold his theological views and still function as a traditional rabbi; he has been known glibly to reply that when the need arises, he simply trades his theologian's hat for his rabbinic one. But if that is his response, such that his theology does not inform his practice (or vice versa!), then one can only harbor deep suspicions that not only his theology is flawed, but also the pastoral care he offers as a rabbi. In the face of death and suffering, we all want to say to others—and have others say to us—something that is psychologically helpful and supportive. But Jewish tradition teaches that we can only take comfort in what is true —that no matter how "meaningful" something may be, if it is false, it ultimately cannot, *will not,* console us but will leave us more bereft than before.

By contrast, in acknowledging God as the ultimate source of even the most horrendous suffering, Job and Jews maintain their integrity by wholeheartedly persisting in speaking the truth. Strikingly, Job only speaks falsely when he presumes (like his "friends") to explain why he suffers, making assertions about God's motives and disposition for which he lacks sufficient evidence or warrant:

> *In His anger* He tears and persecutes me;
> He gnashes His teeth at me;
> *My foe* stabs me with His eyes. . . .
> He rushed at me *like a warrior.* . . . (Job 16:9,14)

In the end, such unwarranted assertions trigger God's well-known rebuke to Job out of the whirlwind:

> Who is this who darkens counsel,
> *Speaking without knowledge?*
> Gird your loins like a man;
> *I will ask and you will inform me.*
> Where were you when I laid the earth's foundations?
> *Speak if you have understanding.* (Job 38: 2–4)

Confronted by the truth of God's rejoinder, Job again faces up to the truth about himself—and us—as he confesses to the Lord:

> I know that You can do everything,
> That nothing you propose is impossible for You.
> *Who is this who obscures counsel without knowledge?*
> *Indeed, I spoke without understanding*
> *Of things beyond me, which I did not know. . . .*
> Therefore, I recant and relent,
> *Being but dust and ashes.* (Job 42: 2–3, 6)

Earlier, Job was surely right in asserting that he did not deserve the suffering he experienced: The book's prologue tells us as much! But, as the prologue and the rest of the book make clear, Job was definitely wrong in assuming that he could truly explain the grounds for his suffering, for he was never in position to be privy to God's wager with Satan or otherwise know about God's rationale. Consequently, in presuming that he could be in position to speak truly about God's motives, Job was in essence presuming to be God and not man. It is exactly for this false presumption, for such presumptuousness, that God rebukes Job from the whirlwind and for which Job then repents, acknowledging the true limits of his—and all human—existence.

The Exodus, like Job, reminds us that in speaking of God, even if we can ultimately ascribe to him some general level of responsibility for everything that happens to us, we cannot impute to him either specific motive or corresponding blame for each and every woe we encounter. Hence, while we must say that God is ultimately, at some level, responsible even for the Holocaust,[20] we dare not say that God himself directly caused the Holocaust or that the Holocaust came as divine retribution for some transgression committed by the Jewish People. The Exodus narrative never suggests that Egypt's oppression of Israel is the result of God's punishment of Israel's sin. On the contrary, says the narrative, Israel's suffering comes from Egypt's sin. From the Exodus master story's perspective, it is possible for the Jewish People to be victimized through no fault of its own—or its God's.

But some Jews, like insurance adjusters gone berserk, have been obsessed with placing fault with the Holocaust's victims. Some so-called "religious" commentators have tried to rationalize what happened to the victims by arguing that since Germany was Reform Judaism's birthplace, the Holocaust originated there as divine retribution. (Meanwhile, some secular Zionist figures have alleged that German Jews "deserved" what happened to them because they allegedly failed to confront the reality of what was going on around them as the Nazis rose to power.) However, neither the Exodus nor our position as human beings warrants our giving some detailed explanation why, for instance, Eastern European Jewry, famed for its piety, nevertheless perished in the Holocaust.[21] From the standpoint we do occupy—one framed by a particular story and the traditional practices that have grown out of it—there is only one fully truthful answer we can give as to why during the Holocaust such bad things happened to such good, God-revering people: *We do not know.* In giving such an answer, we are not trying to spare God's honor. Nor, for that matter, are we trying to spare God our anger or our pain. If God *is* God, he ought to be able to take both our anger and our pain. No, we are only trying to say the truth, especially in those circumstances where we must not say anything else at all, lest we speak falsely, victimizing the victims once more and in the process, adding yet more evil to the world.[22]

And yet, while confessing such ignorance in one area, we are not thereby committing ourselves to a thoroughgoing agnosticism in all areas. I know of a rabbi who believes that after the Holocaust, we cannot say that God is either good or bad—only that God just *is.* But why should anyone worship or serve a deity like that? If such a deity's mere power, detached from any moral consideration, is the only reason we can cite for giving it our reverence, gratitude, and praise, then what is the difference between vowing fealty to that kind of god and pledging loyalty to some Mafia don—or some Pharaoh in Egypt?

After the Holocaust, many Jews, like the aforementioned rabbi, act as if no other Jews—indeed, no other human beings—have ever suffered so great a catastrophe. Such an attitude reflects, of course, a typically modern viewpoint, a particularly modern story, which would have us believe that all prior human history affords us no usable past, only the refuse of the past, such that the events of our generation are without parallel in human experience. But the rabbis who lived at the end of the first century may be a generation of Jews with quite a bit to say to us. For theirs was a generation that witnessed the destruction of the Second Temple and the slaughter of a million Jews in its defense; theirs was a generation that repeated Job's confession while rending garments for loved ones slain in the rebellion; and theirs was a generation that, without flinching at either its suffering or the truth, decreed that God be acknowledged at the start of each morning's prayer as "Fashioner of light, Creator of darkness, Maker of peace, *Creator of everything.*"[23] In the midst of all the death around them, the sages of that generation of Jews looked up, post-catastrophe, and saw the Jewish People still breathing, albeit barely, and they said something they still say to us three times a day through the worship service they composed as substitute for the fallen Temple's service:

We gratefully acknowledge that you are Adonai, our God, and the God of our ancestors, throughout all time. *You are the rock of our lives, the shield of our triumph from generation to generation. We thank you . . . for your miracles that are daily with us . . .* evening, morning, and noon. . . . For all these things, let your name be acknowledged and exalted, our King, continually forever. . . . Acknowledged are you, Adonai, 'the Good' is Your name, and thus, *to You it is fitting to render praise.*

But very bad things can happen even to so good a God if we talk with complete disregard for the Exodus master story through which we learn to talk about that God most clearly and distinctly. Notice, for instance, what happens when Kushner attempts to speak about God apart from that core story's framework:

How seriously would we take a person who said, "I have faith in Adolf Hitler, or in John Dillinger. I can't explain why they did the things they did, but I can't believe they would have done it without a good reason." Yet people try to justify the deaths and tragedies God inflicts on innocent victims with almost these same words.[24]

If we take the Exodus as foundational for making whatever claims we would justifiably make about God, there is no credible way to compare God—the God who brought Jews "out of the land of Egypt, out of the house of bondage"—with Adolf Hitler or John Dillinger any more than we might reasonably compare Harold Kushner with Jimmy Swaggart. Kushner's analogy sounds plausible only if we ignore the particular master story that depicts God as not only having a distinctive character but also as *being* one.

Admittedly, views such as Kushner's appear attractive, precisely because by consistently disregarding what we do know of this character called "God," they give us greater leeway to say all kinds of things about him, whether true or not, and thus, make it a good deal simpler for us to fit the shattered pieces of our lives together: a sphere of evil, a sphere of good, and an easy-to-follow explanation of the relationship between the two. Kushner's words may appear especially compelling, because they are drawn not from some learned tome on theology, but from his own first-hand experience. Who among us would venture to challenge, let alone criticize, the religious views of someone who has experienced the tragedy born of a child's death? Nevertheless, a Christian philosopher, Nicholas Wolterstorff, has done just that—after losing his own son in a freak mountain-climbing accident:

Seeing God as the agent of death is one way of fitting together into a rational pattern God, ourselves, and death. There are other ways. One of these has been explored in a book by Rabbi Kushner: God too is pained by death, more even than you and I are; but there is nothing much he can do about it.

I cannot fit it all together by saying, "He did it," but neither can I do so by saying, "There was nothing he could do about it." I cannot fit it together at all. I can only, with Job, endure.[25]

At times, like Job, like Wolterstorff, like the children of Israel making their way through the wilderness, we, too, must endure.[26]

Enlisting in God's Service

For those life stories shaped by the Exodus master story, endurance means more than mere survival. Against the backdrop of the Exodus, the endurance of the Jewish People through history is perseverance in telling the world a truth crucial not only to its own survival, but to its own deliverance as well: there is only one true Lord with whom the world can dependably join ranks to save it from every Pharaonic attempt to enslave it—whether Ramses II's in ancient times or Hitler's in our own. Only by enlisting with God can the world, like the Jews, ultimately arrive at the place where it might at last settle into a life of promise.

Notions of "joining ranks" and "enlisting" are quite appropriate for the kind of life Jews are called to live and the kind of people Jews are called to be. In the Exodus narrative, the Israelites are repeatedly referred to as God's "ranks" or "troops":

You shall observe the [Feast of] Unleavened Bread, for on this very day I brought your *ranks* out of the land of Egypt. (Ex. 12:17)

I will lay My hand upon Egypt and deliver My *troops*, My people the Israelites. (Ex. 7:4)

At the end of the four hundred and thirtieth year, to the very day, all the *troops* of the Lord departed from the land of Egypt. (Ex. 12:41)[27]

For all who read history through Exodus-framed lenses, Jews are God's chosen, hand-picked troops, recruited to be in his service as a kind of expeditionary force. Those who set out with him on this long march through the wilderness will find the going hard, and those whom they encounter on the way will typically treat them as lowly outcasts—despised, discounted, and, at times, seemingly doomed to die. Although the call to give up, surrender, and go over to the other side will most often come from external foes, on occasion it will issue even from those supposedly within the Lord's own camp.

At the beginning of the Palestinian intifada, an Atlanta synagogue sponsored an educational program designed to acquaint the local Jewish community with various political, ethical, and theological issues surrounding the uprising. A panel of speakers, spanning a broad spectrum of viewpoints, headed the program; further underscoring the event's significance was the fact that for the first time in the community's history, Reform, Conservative, and Orthodox rabbis shared the same pulpit.

Eventually, the opportunity to address the crowd (numbering over 1,600) came to the community's leading Orthodox rabbi. Over the course of thirty years, he almost single-handedly had forged a strong Orthodox communal presence and had come to be viewed by many as the voice of Jewish tradition in Atlanta. He had been preceded by a speaker who had tried to remind the audience of something apparently forgotten by Israeli authorities. Those authorities had been trying to crush the intifada by indiscriminately firing at Palestinian men, women, and children as well as by literally trying to beat the Palestinians into submission, aiming, in the words of then Defense Minister (later Prime Minister) Yitzhak Rabin, "to break their bones." This speaker concluded his remarks by urging the audience to remember that in the words of practically every story-based blessing that Jews utter in acknowledging their Lord, he is not only Eloheynu, "our God," but also Melech Ha'olam, "King of the World," and hence, the Palestinians' God as well, Palestinians who, like Jews, are created in his image. At that, the champion of Orthodoxy got up and declared, "There may be times to pray to God, but now's the time to pass the ammunition!" The crowd broke out into thunderous applause.

By responding to that rabbi's call, those assembled had abandoned their God to serve two other gods—brute force and raw power, idolatrous Nazi gods if ever there were ones. Their "voice of tradition" had in fact issued a call for mutiny and desertion from the cause.

Others, however, are still willing to remain under God's command. They remember the initial victory won in Egypt long ago, and they know that to achieve the promised final triumph over the forces arrayed against their Lord—pretenders to his throne as King, usurpers of his name as God—those who have signed on with him must be able, above all, to endure *to the end*. To be a Jew is to be able to persist on a mission, to persevere for the duration—forty years, four hundred years, or even forty times four hundred. Many, perhaps most, Jews who dedicate themselves to God's cause in the world will fall before full victory is achieved. And because their story's ending is not yet resolved, because their promised destination is not yet even in sight, who can say? Perhaps Jews are not on a noble quest, but only on a fool's errand. But at least the choice is clear: To be a dedicated Jew is either to be among the brave of history or to be the butt of history. And what is God's stake in all of this? He can be no true Commander without troops, no true King without subjects, no true God without us. Thus, he must take care to ensure that those who have staked their lives on his sacred reputation survive.

Those Jews who have staked their lives on him, those who signed on at Sinai, know their assignment: to rally the whole world to his service. To discharge its duty faithfully, the Jewish People, like the rest of the world's peoples in time to come, must keep following its Commander's lead, its marching orders for the campaign ahead.

Notes

1. Thus, the idea of Israel's suffering as punishment for sin is subordinated to the larger notion of God's name or reputation. That dynamic is also evident elsewhere in the Hebrew Bible. For example, God announces in Ezekiel 36:16ff. that he will end Israel's exile in Babylonia—initially caused by Israel's practices, which defiled God's holy name—not due to any particular merit on Israel's behalf, "but for my holy name, which you have caused to be profaned among the nations," who wrongly see Israel's misfortune as a sign of God's weakness. In the end, God's maintaining his name governs whatever good or ill befalls Israel.

2. Cf., e.g., Ex. 12:40–41.

3. Or, as the rabbinic sages put it in the Mishnah, that early compendium of Judaism's basic principles and precedents, "*All* Israel has a portion in the world-to-come." (Sanhedrin 10:1)

4. See Emil Fackenheim, *God's Presence in History* (New York: New York University Press, 1970), and Irving Greenberg, "Judaism and History: Historical Events and Religious Change," in *Perspectives in Jewish Learning*, vol. 1, eds. Stanley Kazan and Nathaniel Stampfer (Chicago: Spertus College Press, 1977).

5. See Ex. 2:23: "And it happened that after a long time, the king of Egypt died, and the Israelites cried out under their bondage . . ."

6. Even though the district of Goshen is spared some of the plagues, that in itself is but another *public* manifestation of God's power and presence.

7. See such texts as Ex. 4:30, 7:20, and 11:3.

8. R. W. B. Lewis, *The American Adam* (Chicago: University of Chicago Press, 1955), p. 5.

9. James Kugel, *On Being a Jew* (San Francisco: HarperCollins, 1990).

10. Ibid., pp. 36, 37.

11. Judah Halevi, *The Kuzari*, Hartwig Hirschfield, trans. (New York, Shocken, 1964), p. 35.

12. Ibid., p. 40.

13. Ibid., p. 44.

14. Ibid.

15. Gershom Scholem, *Major Trends in Jewish Mysticism* (New York: Schocken Books, 1946), pp. 15–22.

16. Harold Kushner, *When Bad Things Happen to Good People* (New York: Shocken, 1981), pp. 1, 7, 4.

17. Ibid., 2nd edition, pp. xiv–xv.

18. Ibid., pp. 46, 53, 30, 44.

19. Job 2:10.

20. After all, one might argue, had God not given human beings genuine freedom, neither Hitler nor the Nazis would have been able to abuse that freedom in such horrific ways.

21. Or why American Jewry, notoriously unobservant, came through the Holocaust unscathed.

22. See Terrence Tilley's masterful book, *The Evils of Theodicy* (Washington, D.C: Georgetown University Press, 1991).

23. This is part of the *Yotzer* benediction; cf. Isaiah 45:7, which is its scriptural underpinning: "I fashion light and create darkness, I make peace and create *evil*—I the Lord do *all* these things."

24. Kushner, p. 19.

25. Nicholas Wolterstorff, *Lament for a Son* (Grand Rapids, MI: William B. Eerdmans Publishing Company, 1987), p. 67.

26. Cf. the next chapter for the difference between this sense of "endurance" and Emil Fackenheim's.

27. Cf. also Ex. 6:26,12:51, and 13:8: "Now the Israelites went up armed out of the land of Egypt." (NJPS)

Chapter 5

A New Sinai, a New Torah, and the 614th Commandment

Over a quarter century ago, Emil Fackenheim projected a Holocaust-framed vision of Jewish survival that was an eerie reworking of the traditional, Exodus-based rationale for the Jewish People's existence. Citing Elie Wiesel's comparison of the Holocaust to Sinai in terms of "revelatory significance," Fackenheim wrote that post-Auschwitz, "we [Jews] must endure because we are *commanded* to endure."[1] Traditionally, Jews believed that 613 commandments were given as Torah at Mount Sinai.[2] But Fackenheim heard from the "Commanding Voice of Auschwitz," the new Sinai, a new Torah teaching a new, 614th commandment: "Jews are forbidden to hand Hitler a posthumous victory."[3]

Ironically, Fackenheim and his new *mitzvah* for modern Jews—"Survive to spite the *goyim*"—prove a point made three centuries ago by the world's first modern Jew, Baruch (a.k.a Benedict) Spinoza: "That [the Jews] have been preserved in great measure by Gentile hatred, experience demonstrates."[4] More ironic still, Spinoza used that very point to anchor his argument, not for how the Jewish People might survive, but for how it might be made to disappear. He noted how the kings of Portugal and Spain had treated their Jews in different ways—with very different outcomes. The king of Portugal, after having compelled the Jews in his country to become Christians, still discriminated against them. As a result, although converted, they continued to live apart and maintain a separate identity. By contrast, the king of Spain, after having forced the Jews in his country to convert, saw to it that they

were admitted to all the native privileges of Spaniards and deemed worthy of filling all honorable offices. [Thus,] it came to pass that they straight-[a]way became so intermingled with the Spaniards as to leave of themselves no relic of remembrance.[5]

From Spinoza's perspective, Hitler's great mistake was trying to make the Jews disappear by murdering them: he could have had the same result by killing them instead with kindness. Three hundred years later, Spinoza's advice to societies on how to remove Jews from their midst has proved essentially correct. How else to explain the timing—or the urgency—of Fackenheim's new *mitzvah* for contemporary Jewry? The open society of the United States has produced 1.3 million adults and progeny of Jewish descent who currently follow another religion—about the same number of Jewish children (i.e., about the same proportion of the Jewish future) the Nazis' managed to kill off.[6]

In that respect, the life story of Baruch Spinoza, the first modern Jew, should serve as a cautionary tale to those who would try to appeal to other modern Jews along Fackenheim's lines. Spinoza lived in the relatively open society of Amsterdam. There, he rejected the traditional Jewish tenet of divine authorship of the Bible, maintaining that the Bible's only real value lies in providing the undiscerning masses moral norms that the more enlightened can derive by reason alone. More significant, though, was how Spinoza lived his life after being excommunicated from the Jewish community for his heretical views. He did not become a Christian but simply lived as an alienated, unaffiliated, non-practicing Jew—in other words, as that most modern of personages, a "human being." He lived, that is, just like most American Jews today.

For the Spinozas of our day, Fackenheim's new Torah of "survival as spite" can hardly be compelling. Now that the cold war seems to have ended with peace apparently breaking out in the Middle East, the injunction to survive stands in need of more, not less, justification. No wonder some of the current "survivalist" leadership of the American Jewish community look so much like old cold warriors.[7] With their #1 bogeyman gone, their raison d'être seems likewise to have evaporated and, with it, their ideological conception of the Jewish People as downtrodden and beleaguered.

Can it be any surprise that the American Jewish Committee found itself forced to produce a booklet and a whole study course devoted to the question "Why Be Jewish?"[8] That question, perhaps more than any other, constitutes the most basic challenge to Fackenheim's 614th commandment to "Just Be Jewish!"—an imperative as devoid of any real content or rationale as the "Just Do It!" of a sports shoe ad. So much, then, for Fackenheim's new commandment. But what about the traditional *mitzvot*? What rationale might there be for their observance?

Observing the Commandments Through Observing the Story

Post-Spinoza, two rationales for observing the commandments will *not* work. The first is any naked appeal to "God's will." Spinoza himself characterized that kind of move as an attempt "to fly to the refuge of ignorance."[9] As he rightly saw, that explanation explains nothing unless we learn more about who this deity is. What if the one we worship turns out to be Ba'al or Moloch—or David Koresh? If our sole concern is survival, following the commands of that kind of god might well prove our undoing. To learn the identity of any god, including that God whom Jews have traditionally claimed to serve, we must come to know a deity's unique character by making out his/ her/its characteristic pattern of activity displayed over time or (to say the same thing) through a story in which each one's distinctive character cumulatively unfolds. And a story-context is exactly what the Exodus narrative provides us concerning the Lord's character. We follow God's direction, not because his *will* bids us do it, but because *he* bids us do it—*he*, the one who established his character by keeping a promise to redeem his people from Egypt and who can therefore be trusted to keep true to that character by preserving that people in the future.

If an appeal to "God's will" without any further reference to his hallmark character traits will not in itself serve as ground for following the commandments, then neither will dividing them into two types, the "moral" versus the "ritual." As Spinoza showed, such a distinction ultimately undermines the commandments' religious context as well as their observance. For if any "reasonable person" anywhere can deduce the so-called "moral commandments," who needs the Bible or, for that matter, the rest of Jewish tradition? As for the remaining "ritual" commandments, moderns can, following Spinoza's lead, easily deem them vestiges of a primitive law code and then chuck them without hesitation or regret.[10]

But such a division of the commandments between "moral" ones on the one hand and "ritual" ones on the other can nowhere be found in the Exodus narrative or, for that matter, anywhere else in the Bible.[11] After all, the oft-repeated biblical rationale for Israel's observing the *mitzvot* is neither "You shall be moral, for I, the Lord your God, am moral," nor "You shall be ritual-obsessed, because I, the Lord your God, am ritual-obsessed." Instead, Israel hears only one, very different rationale for keeping the commandments: "You shall be holy, for I, the Lord your God, am holy."[12]

Hence, the Jewish People's following God's commandments depends on its ability to follow (in both senses!) a story that reveals the character of that God as well as the requisite character of that God's people. As illustrations I propose to examine two Jewish practices, one long-standing and largely uncontroversial (i.e., Jewish courts' preservation of their integrity), the other of relatively recent origin and fraught with controversy (namely, Jewish women's inclusion in the *minyan*).[13] Using these two apparently disconnected practices as examples, I hope to make clear how the Exodus master story can (i) generate commandments, (ii) broaden their scope, and (iii) even correct their observance, if need be.

i: Generating the Commandments—Barring Bribes in Jewish Courts

To refer to a story as the ground—that is, as the source and justification—for the value we place on judicial integrity must sound extremely odd to most moderns.[14] After all, what could appear more self-evident to any decent, thoughtful human being than that it is always and everywhere wrong for a judge to accept a gift from a litigant? And yet, for the majority of human beings who have walked this earth from ancient times to our own, such a practice has not been considered blameworthy but entirely legitimate. One dissenting voice, though, issued from the Book of Deuteronomy. From the Deuteronomic writers' perspective, judges who regularly pocketed presents from litigants were not to be seen as engaging in some neutral practice called "judicial gift-taking": instead, they were to be viewed as *guilty of accepting bribes*. We can only understand these writers' unique outlook if we see it within the context of the

Exodus master story which depicts the character of God, of his people Israel, and of the relationship between them.

In the 1960s, the anthropologist Marcel Mauss showed that in many cultures, reciprocal gift-giving has been the social engine responsible for generating much of the interchange among people, affecting everything from dinner party invitations to legal contracts.[15] Although the word "gift" suggests something given freely, "with no strings attached," we learn from earliest childhood that often just the opposite is true. We draw up a list of other children to invite to our birthday party. Our mother looks at the list and tells us that we need to add Richard's name to it. We protest that we don't like Richard, but our mother replies that Richard invited us to his party. When we say we didn't ask to be invited to his party, Mother says (getting more annoyed all the time), "It doesn't matter—this is just what nice people do!" And so we come to learn that "gifts" may place obligations on us to respond to their givers in kind. We also learn that a failure to reciprocate may be more than just improper. As Mother tried to teach us, the failure to reciprocate may also be unwise, entailing consequences that may be literally uninviting.

In fact, where the principle of reciprocity is in play, much more is frequently at stake than guest lists. In societies where the principle of reciprocity is common, it typically finds its way into the law courts, where gifts are presented to judges *as a matter of course*. A person comes to court and hands the judge a gift that the judge later reciprocates by handing down a verdict in that person's favor.[16] Such judicial reciprocity is considered neither unseemly nor out of place.[17] On the contrary, what is considered illegitimate is either side's failure to reciprocate—as a sixteenth-century B.C.E. official report from Nuzi (in what is now Iraq) makes clear:

Thus H. the wife of Z.: "I gave one sheep to P as *tatu* [the gift of a petitioner to a superior], saying, 'Concerning my fields, attend to my lawsuit with K.' But he did not attend to my lawsuit, and when I spoke [to him] concerning my sheep, he struck me and kept my sheep."[18]

It is easy, of course, to dismiss this kind of practice and perspective as peculiar to societies culturally remote from own. But before we do that, we should stop and reflect on the power our society routinely gives to political action committees, known as PACs, by virtue of their "gifts" to politicians' campaign chests. As Lyndon Johnson reputedly once said about a candidate who had been given a hefty, perfectly legal "donation" for his re-election bid, "He may be a sumbitch, but at least he's our sumbitch. When you buy him, he stays bought!"

That "wisdom," so common from ancient times to modern, even finds expression in certain places in the Bible. The Book of Proverbs, written as savvy advice to young men interested in getting ahead in the world, warmly endorses the use of *shochad*—a word often translated as "bribe" but whose root meaning is "gift":

He who offers *shochad* finds it works like a charm; he prospers in all he undertakes. (Prov. 17:8)

A gift in secret placates an angry man; *shochad* slipped under the cloak pacifies great wrath. (Prov. 21:14)

With reciprocal gift-giving so generally accepted, how—*on what grounds*—did the Deuteronomic writers come to oppose it?

Part of the answer lies in the different story base the Deuteronomic writers used as the foundation for their distinctive outlook. Pagan deities typically had stories framing their birth, growth, and even death,[19] and those stories tended to include an episode recounting the world's creation. Often, the gods and the world were generated out of the same primordial "goop"—the only difference being that the gods at creation received more "goop" than did the rest of creation, and consequently, more power, too. But at bottom, the gods and the world shared a common nature and thus an inherent natural link.

Not so the God of whom the Exodus master story speaks. As we hear of Pharaoh and the other Egyptians being by struck by plague after plague, we may, as we remarked in the last chapter, start wondering why God doesn't simply bring Israel out of Egypt and get it over with. As we saw, the narrative gives God's answer right before the plague of hail—"in order to show you my power, and in order that my reputation resound throughout the world" (Cf. Ex. 9:14–16). Or as the biblical scholar Brevard Childs has put it, "The major theme of the plague story [is] the revelation by God of his nature to Pharaoh, to the Egyptians, and to all men."[20] For "nature" should be substituted "character," because it is character, after all, that a narrative reveals. Thus, the creation story of Genesis 1 depicts God's character as unlike all others, for unlike the pagan deities, this Deity comes with no tale of his birth or "personal life."[21] Instead, the Genesis 1 story makes it absolutely clear that while God created the world and is concerned about the world, God is radically different from the world.

The Torah characterizes such radical differentness as *kadosh*, "holy," and the paradigm of holiness is the Lord.[22] God is *kadosh* precisely because he is fundamentally different from everything else in the world—including those whom the world worships as gods. That holiness, that otherness, extends in turn to the people Israel through its being set apart from other peoples by its entering into a fundamentally different relationship with God, namely, the covenant at Sinai:

Now, therefore, if you will faithfully obey my voice and observe my covenant, you shall be my treasured possession among all peoples. Indeed, all the earth is mine, but you shall be to me a kingdom of priests and a holy nation. (Ex. 19:5–6)

What makes Israel so essentially different from other peoples is its performance of the distinctive practices, that is, the *mitzvot* or commandments, that constitute its covenant with God. In short, Israel has the character it has—different, holy, *kadosh*—because God has the character he has. By performing the *mitzvot*, God's commandments, Israel makes manifest God's holy character to the world.

The story-based holy character shared by God, his people, and their covenant illuminates certain *mitzvot* whose rationale would otherwise remain obscure, doomed either to be "defended" by some talismanic appeal to "God's will" or dispatched to the realm of "ritual" or "morals." Deuteronomy 14:21, which ends with the commandment "You shall not boil a kid in its mother's milk," has suffered just this sort of (mis)treatment through the ages.[23] A few commentators nonetheless noticed the words immediately preceding the prohibition on seething a baby goat in its mother's milk: "For you are a holy people to the Lord your God." In the twelfth century, Maimonides guessed what twentieth-century archaeologists and biblical scholars confirmed: Various Canaanite cults regularly practiced fertility rites by making a kind of "cream-of-baby-goat gumbo" that participants then drank in order to coerce the gods into making their flocks, fields, and women fertile.[24] Such rites of sympathetic magic "worked" on the story-formed assumption that the gods shared and were subject to the same created natural order that humans inhabited. By ingesting two powerfully symbolic elements of life—a newborn and (its) mother's milk—as a now death-laden potion, the fertility rite's participants could "reverse the power flow" between the gods and themselves to compel the divine beings to submit to the will of human beings.[25]

No practice could have been more unbecoming Israel or its God, given Israel's story-dependent conception of itself and its God. If Israel's God was the Holy Other, it was because he was so wholly other, the divinity who was quite literally "not of this world." As a result, no natural "levers" or "buttons" were available to his worshippers to force him to do their bidding. If an Israelite were to practice sympathetic magic by quaffing down a helping of baby-goat gumbo, what would that act attest? That neither God, nor Israel, nor the covenant between them was all that different—all that *kadosh*—from Israel's pagan neighbors.

Against this backdrop, what comes next in Deuteronomy 14:22ff. makes perfect sense. The passage speaks of the Israelite's obligation to tithe, and once more, only a few commentators, medieval and modern, have rightly understood why these verses follow immediately after the prohibition of a Canaanite fertility rite. An Israelite, faithful to the holiness of his or her God, people, and covenant does not practice a fertility rite at the agricultural year's outset to compel the deity to grant a bountiful yield. Instead, at the agricultural year's end (i.e., after the harvest) and whether the year's yield has been bountiful or not, the faithful Israelite brings a tithe as an act of gratitude. The community of Israel observes these commandments not primarily because they are expressions of God's will to be obeyed, but because they are manifestations of God's character to be embodied in Israel's ongoing story.

This storied understanding of the connection among God, Israel, and the commandments also makes clear the rationale for Deuteronomy's opposition to judges' accepting gifts from litigants. In Deut. 16:16–17, we once more find Israel commanded to gratefully acknowledge God on each of the pilgrimage festivals following the various harvests.[26] Then, unexpectedly, "out of the blue," comes the commandment outlawing judicial bribe-taking:

Judges and officers you shall appoint for your tribes in all the settlements that the Lord your God is giving you, and they shall judge the people with just judgments. You shall not pervert judgment; you shall show no partiality; you shall not take *shochad* [i.e., a gift meant to influence, obligate, or *bind* a judge, viz., a bribe], for *shochad* blinds the eyes of the wise and undermines the cause of those in the right. Justice, justice you shall pursue, that you may live and inherit the land the Lord is giving you. (Deut. 16:18–20)

Most commentators have seen this passage condemning bribery as breaking off the discussion of various "ritually oriented" commandments regarding tithes and other festival observances and moving on to a new set of commandments having a "moral focus."

The passage, however, is no break with what has come before, but a continuation of it—linked to it by the common theme of God's holiness and the corresponding holiness required of those who would be in his service. Human judges in Israel were seen as stand-ins for the Divine Judge; King Yehoshafat's charge to his newly appointed judges (in IIChronicles 19:6–7) makes explicit that relationship: "Look to what you are doing, for you do not judge on behalf of man but on behalf of the Lord . . . [with whom] there is no . . . partiality nor taking of *shochad*." Like the Israelite farmer, the Israelite judge is part of "a kingdom of priests" in the service of a holy God, and he knows full well that the character of his actions reflects on the character of his Lord. Consequently, his Lord, beyond all coercion or manipulation in the agricultural realm, is equally beyond all such illegitimate efforts to influence, sway, or bribe him in the judicial realm. In the last analysis, the Israelite judge who would take *shochad*, like the Israelite farmer who would practice a fertility rite, would by that very act disavow the holiness—that is, the different-ness, the specialness—not only of his God, but also of his people and its covenant.

In sum, there is a common thread of justification that runs from the commandment that prohibits boiling a kid in its mother's milk through the one that prescribes tithes to the one that proscribes judges' taking bribes. That thread follows a storyline that cumula-tively unfolds the character of the narrative's central character—God. Significantly, much of Deuteronomy is cast as Moses' telling Israel's story to the people as he approaches death and they ap-proach the Promised Land. In Deut. 4:32–40, through a short-story version of a longer narrative that begins with the Creation and cli-maxes with the Exodus, Moses reminds Israel how it came to be—and why:

For what great nation is there that has a god so close at hand as is the Lord our god whenever we call upon him? Or what great nation has laws and rules as perfect as all this Teaching [Hebrew: *Torah*] that I set before you this day? . . . You have but to inquire about bygone ages . . . ever since God created humankind on earth, from one end of heaven to the other: has anything as grand as this ever happened, or has its like ever been known? Has any people heard the voice of a god speaking out of a fire, as you have, and survived? Or has any god ventured to go and take for himself one nation from the midst of another by prodigious acts, by signs and portents, by war,

by a mighty hand and an outstretched arm and awesome power, as the Lord
your God did for you in Egypt before your very eyes? . . . And because he
loved your ancestors, he chose their descendants after them; he himself, in
his great might, led you out of Egypt, to drive from your path nations greater
and more populous than you, to take you into their land and assign it to you
as a heritage. . . . Observe his laws and commandments . . . that it may go
well with you and your children after you. (Deut. 4:7–8, 32–34, 37–38, 40)

In the end, keeping God's commandment is much more than merely
following some rule or precept. More basically, it is following a
story—the Exodus from Egypt.

Admittedly, the idea that any justifiable ethic must be grounded
in some story-formed ethos may sound odd. We are accustomed to
thinking that any "reasonable person" knows what's right and wrong
apart from any story. Reflect, then, on this story:

> In a course on legal ethics at a noted California law school,
> the professor (now a distinguished federal judge) posed a
> hypothetical question to the soon-to-be-graduated law students in
> the class. "Suppose," he said, "you were at the end of a long trial
> on which your client had already spent hundreds of thousands,
> perhaps even millions of dollars, and a 'bag man' representing the
> trial judge approached you, letting it be known that if your client
> were to make $10,000 available, the judge would issue a favorable
> verdict. Your client, of course, could decline to pay, but then . . .
> who knows how the verdict might come out? The bag man closes
> by advising you to sell the proposal to your client as just another
> legal fee or court cost."
>
> The professor then added that the history of corrupt American
> judges shows that it is extremely difficult to catch, prosecute, or
> convict one of them, because they are so very practiced at what
> they do. The professor concluded by asking the students what
> they would advise their clients to do.
>
> The answer given by each and every student? "I'd tell my
> client to pay the bribe."

The professor's reaction was revealing. All he could do was to
keep sputtering, "You can't do that—it's just plain wrong!" To modern ethicists who follow the lead of Immanuel Kant, the professor's
reiterated assertion counts as the essence of a moral claim. Lacking
any larger context of explanation or justification, narrative or other-

wise, it is an imperative with "no ifs, ands, or buts": "You just ought not to do something, because you just ought not to do it!" But to some of us, the professor's utterance sounds like something else entirely, namely, the invocation of a taboo. For what is a taboo, but the bald declaration that "in our tribe, that's just not done!"[27]

In the end, my claim is not merely that the Jewish people's practices, whether enjoined or forbidden, have a story-context. More basically, it's that *any* community's practices have *got to have* a story base—or else remain simply unjustifiable.[28]

ii: Broadening the Commandments' Scope—Freeing Female Slaves

It was to Israel's story that the Deuteronomic writers hearkened when they expanded the range of Israel's practices. Rather than issue sheer fiats, the Deuteronomists followed out the story's implications and thereby expanded its application. Thus, in Deuteronomy, Moses doesn't merely recite Israel's story—he interprets it, drawing out its significance for the life of the people, now and in the future. Exodus 21, part of what scholars call "the Book of the Covenant,"[29] reflects Israelite practices initiated near the time of the people's conquest and settlement of Canaan. Hardly surprising for a people with strong memories of its own enslavement, the Book of the Covenant begins with slavery restrictions: "When you acquire a Hebrew slave, he shall serve six years; in the seventh year, he shall go free, without payment" (Ex. 21:2). At the very least, the Exodus repudiated lifelong servitude,[30] and the Book of the Covenant displays that insight by strictly limiting the number of years one Israelite could be in servitude to another. Moreover, because an Israelite typically became enslaved because he was unable to pay his debts, the Book of the Covenant specifies that an Israelite slave goes free after six years even if he is still unable to pay off his debt. The commanded practice, then, provides the way for Israel to live out the implications of the Exodus story in its own continuing story.

Four or five centuries later, Deuteronomy, written as a reform document, significantly revises the earlier laws governing the release of slaves:

If a fellow Hebrew, man or woman, is sold to you, he shall serve you six years, and in the seventh, you shall set him free. When you set him free, do not let him go empty-handed: Furnish him generously out of the flock, threshing floor, and vat, with which the Lord your God blessed you. (Deut. 15:12–14)

No longer is it sufficient for a master/creditor merely to forego his outstanding debts upon freeing his slave in the seventh year. Now, he must provide generously for the newly freed slave out of his own possessions. The rationale? The very next verse, Deut. 15:15, supplies the answer: "Remember that you were slaves in the land of Egypt, and the Lord your God redeemed you; therefore I enjoin upon you this commandment today." When those Israelites freed from Egyptian servitude departed, they did not leave empty-handed, but, as the narrative reminds us, "the Lord disposed the Egyptians favorably toward the people" so that they left Egypt with much silver and gold.[31] From its Exodus-informed vantage point, the Deuteronomic reform regards those Israelites to be freed in its own day as having never truly been slaves in the first place—only "hired hands" owed their back wages.[32] By attending to the particulars of the Exodus story more closely, the Deuteronomic writers came to see the broader scope of the commandment more clearly.

But compensating the freed slave was not the only reform the Deuteronomic writers made when they broadened the scope of the earlier practice: "If a fellow Hebrew, man *or woman*, is sold to you, he [or she] shall serve you six years, and in the seventh, you shall set him [or her] free." In the Book of the Covenant, Israelite women are not included among those to be set free at the end of six years. How to account for the change?

One thing will certainly not account for it—the (all-too-predictable) contemporary appeal to "women's rights." Not only does such language not exist in biblical (or, for that matter, rabbinic) Hebrew, neither do the assumptions about the relationship between individuals and communities that underlie any claim to such rights. For moderns, communities are simply collections of individuals who, theoretically having existed as individuals before there were any communities, possess certain inherent, inalienable rights that every community must respect. But if the child psychologists are right, even as (and *especially as*) infants we do not exist naturally as solitary, socially disconnected beings. At this point, up pops a political theorist to tell us that we have got it all wrong: "Talk about 'individuals' with their 'natural rights' in some 'state of nature' preceding civil society is not to be taken as an historical fact. It is a theoretical construct that grounds the value we place on individual liberty and equality." But what would our theorist say to a Christian traditionalist who grounds

Church teaching about original sin—and hence, the "value" of Jesus' atoning life, death, and resurrection—in a "theoretical construct" about a garden inhabited by the first man, the first woman, and a talking snake? Quite likely, the theorist would dismiss it as "mere myth." Then why not dismiss a story about a state of nature and a social contract on the same grounds? One thing, after all, is factually certain: No one has ever come into this world totally detached from other human beings anymore than some Adam has been born into the world without a belly button. Ultimately, talk about free-standing individuals and their inherent rights is, in Jeremy Bentham's memorable phrase, "nonsense upon stilts,"[33] and to the extent that no one has ever been able to produce such a right for public inspection, belief in them is, in Alasdair MacIntyre's apt terminology, "a superstition."[34]

For the story the Torah tells, individuals do not confer an identity on a community, but the other way around. At Sinai, the birthing of a new community gives birth to a specific identity for a group of individuals who prior to that are nothing more determinate than what the Torah calls "a mixed multitude" (Ex. 12:38). That new community comes into existence, not because some individuals choose to limit their natural rights in favor of acquiring some civil rights, but because that hodge-podge of recently freed Hebrew slaves and their Egyptian hangers-on who saw the writing on the wall (more precisely, the blood on the doorposts) en masse encounter God and agree to share a covenant of common obligations. At the heart of the Exodus master story, as opposed to the fiction told by moderns, is not an array of rights, but a set of duties, not a random collection of individuals, but a covenant-bound community embarked on a common quest.

To ask again: How to account for Deuteronomy's extension of the duty to free Hebrew slaves to include Hebrew women, too? To answer again: by its extension of the detailed implications of the Exodus narrative. As the story detail that the Israelites had not gone out of Egypt empty-handed eventually led to the practice of lavishing provisions on newly freed Hebrew slaves, the story item that Israelite women were liberated from Egypt alongside Israelite men likewise led to broadening the scope of the seventh year's release to include female Hebrew slaves as well as their male counterparts.

If the Exodus narrative truly is the Jewish master story, then by rights it can and should provide the guide for making sense of Jewish practice. Without the Exodus master story providing the context for those practices' origin and rationale, they lose the context for their meaning and cannot help appearing arbitrary. As such, they might as well be the fickle dictates of some capricious Greek deity—one whose character emanates from a decidedly non-biblical narrative. True, some people point to a practice's seeming arbitrariness, its apparent senselessness, as proof of its "God-givenness." But eight hundred years ago, Maimonides crafted a stinging riposte to such persons:

It is as if . . . man were more perfect than his Maker; for man speaks and acts in a manner that leads to some intended end, whereas the deity does not act thus, but commands us to do things that are not useful to us and forbids us to do things that are not harmful to us. But He is far exalted above this; the contrary is the case—the whole purpose consisting in what is useful for us, as we have [elsewhere] explained on the basis of [*the story-shaped Deuteronomic*] dictum: "For our good always, that He might preserve us alive, as it is at this day."[35]

In Hebrew, the word *Torah* means "teaching," and it stems from a root that means "direction."[36] In that sense, the *mitzvot* are God's directions to the Jewish People for enacting the Exodus master story. If there is any overall instruction or command coming out of the Exodus master story, it is that we Jews are to *become the story*. Jews are not simply enjoined to study Torah, but to be Torah. Without the Torah's practices, the Exodus master story remains just a story. Put another way,[37] stories without practices are empty, and practices without stories are blind—hence the emptiness of much of liberal Judaism with its lack of any real "Thou shalts" or "Thou shalt nots" and hence the myopia of much of Orthodox Judaism with its inability to see beyond the individual rulings laid down by the *Kitzur Shulchan Aruch*.

iii: Correcting the Commandments' Observance— Dealing Uprightly with Gentile Judicial Authorities, Counting Women in the *Minyan*

No one is claiming that each and every *mitzvah*, each and every obligatory Jewish practice, must ultimately be traceable for its source or justification back to the Exodus narrative any more than we would claim that America's maximum legal speed limit of 65 mph must ultimately derive from the American master story surrounding the Revolutionary War. We would claim, however, that at the very least, *a community's practices must not contradict a com-*

munity's master story. It is a master story that can and should serve as the corrective lens through which we ought see more clearly the communal practices in which we are engaged. In that sense, it is a master story's vision that can and should lead to a distorted practice's revision.

The practice and abolition of slavery in America is a case in point. As Gary Wills has shown,[38] Americans in Abraham Lincoln's time tried to hold fast to two contradictory inclinations. On the one hand, they revered the Declaration of Independence—and the "freedom story" it grew out of. On the other hand, many of them also embraced slaveholding. Lincoln felt these two dispositions could not coexist in one mind. Once the contradiction was pointed out, one or the other simply had to be given up. To that end, Lincoln himself distinguished between

the Declaration [of Independence] as the statement of a permanent ideal and the Constitution as an early and provisional embodiment of that ideal [in so far as the Constitution countenanced slavery], to be tested against it, kept in motion toward it.[39]

Although America's "Torah," the Constitution, recognized the traditional practice of American slavery as legitimate, Lincoln implicitly appealed to the Declaration and America's founding story to uproot that practice when he began the Gettysburg Address by saying, "Four score and seven years ago our fathers brought forth on this continent a new nation, conceived in Liberty, and dedicated to the proposition that all men are created equal." The theme of equality, of equal liberty, might be said to be Lincoln's *midrash*, that is, according to the literal meaning of the term, what Lincoln "drew out" of the American master story. Once drawn out, that theme became so compelling to Americans that the Constitution, America's core body of *halacha*, was subsequently amended to ban slavery and to provide for equal protection under law.[40] Lincoln was right: Americans could not hold the vision of equal liberty and at the same time hold on to the practice of slavery. One or the other had to be let go.

And so it is for Jews, their story, and their practices. When practices contradict the story, one or the other must simply be let go. Earlier, we saw how the Jewish practices barring judicial bribe-taking and freeing female slaves emerged from the Jewish master story. Now, we need to examine how some of the Jewish practices surrounding judges and women later ran contrary to the story—and how they might be put back on track with the storyline again.

At one level, the seeds of Deuteronomy's teaching against judges taking bribes struck deep roots among the talmudic and medieval rabbis, who themselves regularly functioned as judges. The rabbis were always eager to build a protective "fence around the Torah" so that its commandments might not be trampled, even inadvertently.[41] Consequently, to protect the integrity of Jewish courts, they expanded the concept of *shochad* to include any sort of favor or largess whatsoever.[42] A corrupt rabbinic judge is almost impossible to find in any classical talmudic or medieval text.[43]

But as committed as the rabbis were to maintaining the integrity of Jewish courts, they were to just that degree oblivious to Jews' corrupting the judicial character of non-Jewish legal systems. A former justice of Israel's Supreme Court summed up the matter best by saying that the "bribing of non-Jewish rulers, officials, and judges was regarded as legitimate at all times."[44] We might be tempted to try to justify such behavior by invoking the famous rabbinic maxim that "saving a life takes precedence over everything."[45] Try—but not succeed. Many of the reported incidents of bribery have nothing at all to do with preserving life but with preserving cash, for example, by offering a "gift" to a Gentile official in return for a lower tax rate.[46]

Strikingly, such practiced corruption runs afoul of three separate *halachic* principles: (1) the prohibition of taking advantage of someone's "blind-spot," (such as the avariciousness of a non-Jewish official who might be easily tempted by a bribe);[47] (2) the obligation to establish just courts, incumbent on Jews and non-Jews alike as one of the so-called Noachide Laws;[48] and (3) the affirmation that *dina d'malchuta dina*, that except in very limited cases, "the law of the land is the law"—and especially so in tax matters where tax evasion is tantamount to theft.[49] Though the rabbis normally went to great lengths to reconcile apparent contradictions in Jewish law, remarkably, they did not even make the attempt, did not even feel the need, to square the practice of corrupting non-Jewish officials with any of these potential *halachic* barriers to it. So intellectually agile at creating legal fictions or at otherwise reinterpreting other practices they found theologically or ethically problematic, the rabbis in this area remained silent. Here, not only did they not attempt to justify the practice—they didn't even bother to comment on it.

Once again, we might be tempted to spring to the rabbis' defense, explaining their silence as simply "hard-headed," "clear-eyed" acceptance of "the facts of life" based on the Jewish community's sorry experience with Gentile rulers through the centuries. But "the facts" are never just "out there" for the taking. They always come framed within a story-context—and especially when the facts put into evidence are implicitly (or explicitly) prefaced by the words, "History shows that. . . ." If the rabbis truly did accept the goings-on before them as just the "facts of life," then they also accepted, at least in this case, a story different from the Exodus as the backdrop against which to make their judicial decisions and display their judicial character.

Sadly, the rabbis, for whom an Exodus vision shaped practice in Jewish courts, became blind to that vision as it applied to Jews' practices toward non-Jewish officials. The contradiction between the world-embracing story the rabbis espoused and the practices they countenanced vis-à-vis the wider, non-Jewish world weakened the credibility of their claim to serve the God of the world as members of that people who are to make manifest his character to the world. To hold on to both that formative story and those deformed practices is to hold on to a contradiction. Either the story or the practices must be given up. Giving up the practices means letting go of a narrated interpretation of human life better suited to another people. But to give up the story means giving up what it means to be a Jew.

What it means to be a Jew and how that is bound up with the Exodus master story is precisely what's at issue in the story-contradicting practice of *not* counting women as part of a *minyan*. The *minyan*, the quorum of ten symbolizing the presence of the Jewish community, signifies another presence as well. Consider those parts of the service that require a *minyan* for their performance: the summons of *barchu*, the congregational reading of the Torah, and the recitation of any *kaddish* or *kedusha*. What these different service parts share in common is their communal proclamation of God's presence to the world—*barchu* through its general invitation to come worship God, the Torah reading through its corporate recitation of God's historic deeds, and each *kaddish* or *kedusha* through its public declaration of God's holiness. Thus, the practice of the *minyan* articulates the deeply-held, age-old, Exodus-forged Jewish conviction that it is in the presence of the community of Israel that God's presence in the world is most distinctively—and distinctly—made known to the world.

As the practice of the *minyan* stands, however, part of that last statement stands in need of correction: It should instead read "in the presence of the community of te Israel's *males*. . . ." Some may argue, citing both Scripture and Talmud, that the practice of constituting the *minyan* solely from Jewish men is supported by a tradition going back to the Israelite spies who brought back bad reports to Moses about the Promised Land. As that "congregation" was constituted by ten Jewish men, so, too, every Jewish congregation must consist of at least ten Jewish men.[50] But such an argument is as muddleheaded as the Roman Catholic Church's (allegedly narrative-based) practice of calling only males to be priests since Jesus called only males to be his disciples. It's also true, however, that Jesus called only Jews to be his disciples, and yet the Church has never said that only Jews could be priests![51] It is one thing to take a master story seriously, it is quite another to take it woodenly—and it is the former rather than the latter that those who would faithfully enact a community's core story are called on to do.

Still, there is a more substantial piece of story-based support to bolster the claim of those who would maintain that only Jewish men should constitute the *minyan*, that traditional symbol of the Jewish community. Thus, someone might contend: "If the community of Israel, the Jewish People, was brought into existence by its entry into a covenant at Sinai, then look at *the gender* of those to whom the covenant was offered. First, in preparation for receiving the covenant, Moses, following God's instruction, issued the warning, 'Be ready for the third day: do not go near *a woman*' (Ex. 19:15). Second, when the terms of the covenant were finally disclosed, notice to whom by implication they were addressed: 'You shall not covet your neighbor's house: you shall not covet your neighbor's *wife . . .*' *(Ex. 20:14). If this is not clear narrative*—and *halachic*—evidence that only Jewish males are to be the basis of the *minyan*, then what is?!"

We are, it seems, in Lincoln's position prior to the Civil War. There was a foundational document, the U.S. Constitution, which implicitly recognized slavery as a legitimate American practice. Moreover, the Constitution launched something called "the United States of America" in the first place, replacing with a federal republic the loose association of states created by the Articles of Confederation. We recall what Lincoln did. He did not say, well, the Constitution doesn't really mean what it seems to mean when it talks about slavery, so what we need to do is to get the Supreme Court or some slick lawyer to come up with a nifty new interpretation to that effect. Instead, Lincoln appealed to a higher source than the Constitution— or rather, to a deeper, more basic source: the American master story of the Declaration and the War of Independence. He believed that one of the distinctive themes of that story, equal liberty for all, was powerful enough in most Americans' minds to overcome the traditional practice of slavery and the prejudice(s) that went with it and so extend liberty to all who lived within America's borders.

Including Jewish women in a *minyan* faces a similar problem—and requires a similar solution. The foundational document of the Jewish People—the Sinai covenant and the Torah practices it enjoins—implicitly bars Jewish women from being counted as equal members of this covenant-formed community. What, if anything, could justify setting aside the traditional practice? What, if anything, could justify setting aside—or rather, *extending*—the traditional practice so as to include women as full partners in the *minyan*?

Exactly the same thing that justified extending the traditional practice of freeing slaves in the seventh year to include Israelite women as well as Israelite men: "Remember that you were slaves in the land of Egypt, and the Lord your God redeemed you; therefore I enjoin upon you this commandment today" (Deut. 15:15). Jewish women as well as Jewish men were redeemed by God from Egyptian bondage. Through the redemption of the Israelite slaves, men *and women*, God redeemed his own reputation: "Egypt shall know that I am the Lord when I stretch out my hand over Egypt and bring out the Israelites from their midst" (Ex. 7:5). From the fourth plague on, Egypt suffers the plagues' full brunt while Israel (in Goshen) remains unscathed as God's saving presence in Israel's midst becomes increasingly evident. Thus, God, through Moses, warns Pharaoh:

I will set apart the region of Goshen, where my people dwell, so that no swarms of insects shall be there, that you may know that I the Lord am in the midst of the land. And I will make a distinction between my people and your people. Tomorrow this sign shall come to pass. (Ex. 8:18–19)

By making a distinction between the Israelites and the rest of the population, God distinctively makes known his presence to both Egyptian and Israelite. Ultimately, Israel protected, Israel delivered, Israel alive is the unmistakable sign of God's distinctive, holy, active presence in the world.

In fact, that is just what Israel proclaims after having been saved alive by God at the Sea of Reeds: "Who is like you, O Lord, among the gods? Who is like you, majestic in holiness, awesome in splendor, working wonders?" (Ex. 15:11). And notice: as *all* Israel has been redeemed from Egyptian slavery, *all* Israel joins in proclaiming God's redeeming presence to the world:

Miriam the prophetess, Aaron's *sister* took a timbrel in her hand, and *all the women* went out after her in dance with timbrels. And *Miriam* sang to them: "Sing to the Lord, for he has triumphed gloriously; horse and driver he has hurled into the sea!" (Ex. 15:20–21)

What, then, is it that the *minyan* finally signifies? Not merely the presence of the Jewish community, but God's own presence, too. Indeed, as the Exodus master story tells it—and as the *minyan* re-tells it every day—it is through the surviving presence of the community of the Jewish People in the world that God's own presence is most clearly made known to the world. As Jewish women were counted among those God rescued in the Exodus from Egypt in an-cient days, so, too, in our day they ought to be counted in the *minyan* among those who can rightfully proclaim God's saving pres-ence to the world.

The Story's Outcome and Keeping in Line with Its Storyline

Bringing Jewish women fully into the Exodus narrative's storyline also has important consequences for bringing another group into full participation in the community of the Jewish People: non-Jews. The apostle Paul was right. Being part of a community based on God's covenant with Abraham depended on being born into it; consequently, Gentiles would always be "the outs." But Paul missed the significance of the Sinai covenant for those not born Jewish. In a very real sense, those who were first offered that covenant in the wilderness were not members of the Jewish community either, be-cause there was no Jewish community, no Jewish People, until they entered it. At Sinai, a new community was born precisely because its would-be members (God included!) were willing to undertake a set of mutually-binding obligations spelled out by common prac-tices. Because of Sinai, belonging to the Jewish people was no longer simply or primarily a matter of biology but of theology, that is, of sharing the same conviction-laden, practice-filled, and God-partnered way of life called Torah.

That the early (i.e., first and second-century) rabbis surely held this view is indicated by the story-based liturgical choices and formu-lations they made. They changed *Shavuot*, variously known as "The Feast of Weeks" or "The Feast of First Fruits," from a purely agricul-tural festival into a celebration of *matan Torah*, the giving of the Torah covenant at Sinai. Significantly, among their choices of spe-cial biblical readings for that day was the Book of Ruth, the quintessential conversion story of a non-Jew's coming to share the Jewish way of life: "For wherever you go, I will go; wherever you lodge, I will lodge; your people shall be my people, and your God my God. Where you die, I will die, and there I will be buried" (Ruth 1:16–17). The rabbis' choice of Ruth becomes even more telling—and their conviction that the Sinai covenant could transform *any* human life even more emphatic—when we notice that Ruth was a Moabite, of whom Deuteronomy says,

No . . . Moabite shall be admitted into the congregation of the Lord; none of their descendants, even in the tenth generation, shall ever be admitted into the congregation of the Lord. . . . You shall never concern yourself with their welfare or benefit as long as you live. (Deut. 23:4,7)

No matter, say the rabbis; even a Moabite can become one of us, "the congregation of the Lord." Once again, the seemingly clear-cut rule, what lawyers call "black letter law," becomes revised in light of the broader master story's vision.

Following that storied vision's lead, the rabbis taught that coming into the service of God means entering into the covenant God offered at Sinai. The rabbis asked an insightful question about the ordering of the biblical passages that make up the *Shema*: Why does the passage that begins "Hear, O Israel, the Lord is our God, the Lord Alone" (Deut. 6:4–9) precede the passage that begins "If you will heed My commandments"? (Deut. 11:13–21) The answer the rabbis give must not be overlooked: "In order that one should first accept on himself the yoke of the Kingdom of Heaven and afterward accept on himself the yoke of the commandments."[52] For the rabbis, *becoming a subject of God, King of the World, entailed becoming subject to his commandments.*

In the *Alenu*, the prayer near the close of every service, the horizons of that conviction take on world-encompassing proportions. Though the exact origins of the prayer are obscure,[53] its plain meaning is not. After reaffirming the unique destiny God has allotted the Jewish People, namely, to acknowledge him as the "King of kings of kings," those Jews chanting the prayer then declare:

We therefore hope in you, Lord our God, soon to see your splendor . . . perfecting the world through the Kingdom of the Almighty. . . . Then will all the inhabitants of the earth recognize and know that to you every knee must bend, every tongue pledge loyalty. . . . May they all then give honor to the glory of your name, and *may they all accept the yoke of your kingdom,* and may you rule over them soon and for all time.

Liberal Jews read those words about accepting the yoke of God's kingdom and feel that they have already been fulfilled through the spread of "monotheism" since Christians and Muslims now also acknowledge God as "King of the World." But liberal Jews fail to appreciate those words' traditional implication. For to truly accept this particular, storied God as King is to accept the commandments, those covenantal practices that form the basis for being—and here Yiddish may express it best—a *landsman* of his realm.

Recall the last chapter's discussion of Judah Halevi's *Kuzari*. As we saw, the stimulus for the dramatic dialogue that unfolds in the story is the recurring dream of the King of the Khazars in which he is told that although his way of thinking is pleasing to God, his way of acting is not. That nocturnal message nicely sums up *the* religious issue of the medieval world in which Halevi lived. Unlike the ancient, pagan world, Jews were not arguing with other traditions about whether there was only one God or many gods; Jews, Christians, and Muslims all agreed that there was only one true God. What they profoundly disagreed about, however, was the proper way to serve that God. In that context, the *Kuzari* is not merely a "defense of a despised faith." As evidenced by the king's eventual acceptance of Judaism, it is, more fundamentally, a conversion tract. For Halevi whose fictional convert-king inhabits a realm at the far edges of the known world, as well as for the early rabbis who sought and made converts all over the world from Rome to Babylonia, the God of Sinai and the Sinai covenant itself were not merely to be "available" to non-Jews: both that God and that covenant were meant for them.[54] Or, as Solomon Schechter succinctly stated the matter at the turn of the century, "Judaism means to convert the world."[55] The rabbis, Halevi, and Schechter knew that in any true dialogue about religion, what's at stake is convincing someone of the validity not of a point, but of a way of life.

What distances Jews such as Halevi, the rabbis, and even Schechter from contemporary liberal Jews is that the former were not the products—or the victims—of a mushy pluralism that, because it considers all religions equally true (and, thus, equally false), judges them only according to how "meaningful" they may be to their adherents. For Jews like Halevi, Judaism is to be embraced as a way of life because it holds out a truthful way of life, that is, it is true to the reality of human life in this world, a world whose true king is God—*the Jews'* God. Jews like Halevi believed that Christianity and Islam were truer than Ba'al worship, but they also believed that truer still was Judaism, with its story-bound characteristic practices that mirror the story-framed character of God. Maimonides, as usual, may have said it best. Like Halevi an inhabitant of a medieval world dominated by Christians and Muslims rather than by Jews, he, too, nevertheless believed in history's eventual unfolding when all humankind will come to acknowledge the truth of the Torah and its covenantal practices:

And all these things that have transpired [including the ascendancy of the religions connected] with Jesus the Nazarene and this Ishmaelite who came after him [i.e., Muhammad] are nothing but a means of preparing the way for the King Messiah and of *perfecting all the world to serve the Lord as one*. . . .

How? The world has already been filled with words about the Messiah and words about the Torah and words about the commandments, and these things have spread even to the farthest isles and even to the most unenlightened peoples, who debate about these matters and about the Torah's commandments. These [i.e., Christians] say, "These commandments *were* true but have already become invalid at this time. . . ." And these [i.e., Muslims] say, "These matters are hidden and not according to [the commandments'] plain meaning. . . ."

But when the true King Messiah arises . . . these [Christians and Muslims] will immediately repent and know that *their forefathers inherited falsehood and that their prophets and forefathers erred.*[56]

Views like that, which implicitly claim that religious tradition is more about truth than about "meaning," are, of course, anathema to the adherents of the dominant faith of the late-twentieth-century West: liberalism. Liberals are liberal about everything, after all, except their own orthodoxies.

But if liberal Jews, from their direction, have missed what is truly ecumenical (a word whose root means "world-encompassing") about the Jewish People's being founded on a covenant of shared practices, Orthodox Jews have also missed it from theirs.

In the midst of a large, prosperous American city with a similarly large, rather prosperous Jewish community, there is small Orthodox synagogue, a one-room affair so tiny it could easily be called a "shtiebl." The room has few windows and their venetian blinds are always lowered. One day, someone went to raise the blinds to let in some light. The synagogue's rabbi, an octogenarian originally from the Ukraine, immediately hurried over and told the person to leave the blinds down: "I don't want the goyim to see what we're doing in here."

*At about the same time, another Orthodox rabbi from a much
larger synagogue was asked about his willingness to assist with a
conversion. He proudly responded that in his more than thirty
years in the pulpit, he had not performed a single one.*

The word *orthodox* means "regular belief," but those two rabbis'
beliefs would have seemed anything but regular to their rabbinic
forebears. In the first few centuries of the Common Era, Jews prosely-
tized left and right. According to Salo Baron, one of the most eminent Jewish historians of this century, the world's Jewish population
exploded to such an extent that "every tenth Roman was a Jew . . .
[and] every fifth . . . inhabitant of the eastern Mediterranean was a
Jew."[57] What led to this large-scale conversion of non-Jews to Judaism? Baron writes,

The very stability of the Jewish way of life, as the rabbis realized, even the
spectacle of a large community eating and abstaining from the same foods,
often impressed sensitive pagans. Disturbed by the anarchical diversity of
modes of living and worship, many of the latter found escape in the inner
security of the Jews' strictly regulated behavior. The inhabitants of the ever-
growing metropolitan centers, in particular, . . . more readily succumbed to
the Jewish example as their uprootedness from ancestral soils had rendered
meaningless their old shrines and territorially bound forms of worship.[58]

The practices themselves, not some abstracted theology of "the oneness of God," attracted non-Jews to Judaism. For nearly three centuries, Jews continued to convert great numbers of non-Jews to Judaism.
That practice ended, however, when the Roman emperor Constan-
tine converted to Christianity in 311, paving the way for a series of
edicts that gave Christians a monopoly on the "conversion market"
while barring Jews on pain of death.

How grotesque that those two Orthodox rabbis opposed conversion on the basis of a tradition inaugurated not by Jews, but by
Christians. For the old rabbi of the *shtiebl*, his Jewish way of life was
to be shuttered away from the world rather than displayed to it as a
potentially compelling alternative. As for the Orthodox rabbi who
bragged that he had never converted anybody to the Sinai covenant,
he might as well have boasted of his opposition to the advent of the
Kingdom of God. For that *is* the intended future outcome of the
Exodus master story. It is the hope given voice in the last line of the
Alenu near the close of every service: "The Lord shall be King over
all the earth; on that day, he shall be the one and only Lord, with his

name the only one."[59] In the last analysis, the Exodus becomes a master story not merely for the Jewish People, but for all people. As for Torah, it becomes instruction in a set of practices that spell out not only what it means to be Jewish, but what it means to be human. Thus understood, Jewish survival, as narrated by the Exodus and as practiced through Torah, becomes a kind of performance art showing the world what it truly, fully, means to live.

"By Their Fruits Shall Ye Know Them"

If one of the hallmarks of a story worth adopting is its ability to germinate a whole field of communal practices, then compare the bounty of practices with deep roots in the Exodus master story with the paltry few gleaned from the Holocaust's thin soil of "Jewish survival." At this chapter's beginning, we saw that thinness evident in Fackenheim's desiccated doctrine of "survival as spite"—a *"mitzvah"* weak on justification and in the hands of a Spinoza, dangerous in potential implication. Now, before this chapter ends, we need to examine the other great commanded practice springing up from the Holocaust: "Remember the past so that it does not happen again."

And yet, remembering, studying, even understanding an event is no guarantee that it can or will be prevented from recurring. From the earliest days of civilized human habitation on this planet, we have had countless examples of wars that were fought for the acquisition of territory, and such wars have been researched, analyzed, and retold by generations of historians and scholars. Nevertheless, such wars continue to be fought today—as in Bosnia, for instance. Indeed, if anyone seems to have remembered "the lesson of the Holocaust," it seems to be the Bosnian Serbs, who have learned all too well that if you attempt genocide, the rest of the world will likely just stand by and dither.

Oddly enough, even at the most elementary level of its own goal of ensuring Jewish survival, of simply making sure the number of Jews in the world holds steady or increases, a Holocaust-based civil Judaism has sprouted a stunted practice. Though there have been calls for higher Jewish birth rates, when is the last time such high priests of the Holocaust cult as Elie Wiesel have called for conversion as a means of replenishing the Jewish People's ranks? As for the American Jewish survivalists who are the "leadership" of the UJA, AIPAC, and Israel Bonds, why should we treat their cries of alarm any differently from those of American Gentile survivalists who, taking to the woods with stores of food and ammunition, warn of an always-approaching political Armageddon? The *machers* of the American Jewish community, for all their vaunted political and economic power, don't even possess the power to keep Jews—particularly young Jews—wanting to remain Jews, as reflected by the high intermarriage and even higher nonaffiliation rates.[60] In the end, the Holocaust-as-Jewish-master-story can nourish neither the body of the Jewish People nor its soul.

If our stories, our identities, and our lives are tied, then our choice is not between living out some story or living out no story, anymore than we have a choice between having some identity or no identity. It is only a matter of *which* story and *which* identity we are finally going to be living out. The Exodus' pride of place may well have been taken by the emaciated account of Jewish existence provided by the Holocaust. But the Holocaust story can produce only the puniest of Jewish identities. As such, that Holocaust-bound narrative may spell death not only for the Exodus master story, but for the proper self-understanding, *the very character*, of the People about whom that story would tell.

Notes

1. Emil L. Fackenheim, *God's Presence in History: Jewish Affirmations and Philosophical Reflections* (New York: Harper Torchbooks, 1972), pp. 84, 95; these essays originally constituted the 1968 Charles Deems Lectures given at New York University.

2. Makkot 23b.

3. Fackenheim, p. 84.

4. Benedict de Spinoza, *A Theologico-Political Treatise and a Political Treatise*, trans. and with an introduction by R. H. M. Elwes (New York: Dover Publications, Inc., 1951), p. 55.

5. Ibid., pp. 55–56.

6. Barbara Skolnick Hoenig et al., *Jewish Environmental Scan: Toward the Year 2000* (New York: Council of Jewish Federations, 1992), p.3. Worse yet, the CJF 1990 Population Survey predicts that by the year 2000, the rate of intermarriage will climb to 70% of all Jewish marriages—with only 5 to 10% of the offspring of those marriages being raised as Jews. Cf. pp. 26–27.

7. During the first ten months following the historic handshake between Yitzhak Rabin and Yasser Arafat on the White House lawn, the Conference of Presidents of Major American Jewish Organizations, American Jewry's leading "umbrella organization," faxed out not one news release to hail Israel for the risks that it had undertaken in search of peace

with the Palestinians. Moreover, the Conference, which from time to time takes out full-page ads in the *New York Times* to sponsor various positions, has in that time run no such ads to support Prime Minister Rabin's moves. *Jewish World News*, August 1994, p. 27. See also the page 1 article in the 14 September 1994 *Wall Street Journal*; its headline reads "Burden of Peace, American Jews Grapple With an Identity Crisis," and its close asks, "Without trouble, what is there left to talk about?"

8. Barry W. Holtz and Steven Bayme, "Why Be Jewish?" (New York: The American Jewish Committee, 1993). (Significantly, the December 1992 issue of *Moment* magazine took the same question as its focus.) In addition to producing the aforementioned booklet and study course, the AJC ran an advertising campaign in the *New York Times* on the theme "What Being Jewish Means to Me"; the ads featured such luminaries as Elie Wiesel, Senator Joseph Lieberman of Connecticut, and the writer, Ann Roiphe. Revealingly, as the title of the ad campaign suggests, such ads could answer the question of "Why Be Jewish?" only by giving various individuals' personal preferences, as though identifying as a Jew were on a par with liking chocolate ice cream.

9. Benedict de Spinoza, *Ethic* in *Spinoza Selections*, ed. and with an introduction by John Wild (New York: Charles Scribner's Sons, 1958), p. 139.

10. See Spinoza, *A Theologico-Political Treatise*, Chapter V, "Of the Ceremonial Law." Significantly, though this move of ignoring one class of commandment has typically been made by liberal Jews, Orthodox Jews have made it also, but in reverse, by focusing on the 'ritual' *mitzvot* while tending to jettison the moral ones.

11. Nor does that division appear in rabbinic literature. To be sure, the rabbis talk about those commandments that exist between God and a human being versus those between one human being and another. But in and of itself, that division is not synonymous with "the moral" versus "the ritualistic"—especially since the rabbis lacked even the very language to make such a distinction. And besides, even the distinction the rabbis *did* make is not clear-cut: Do the commandments enjoining sexual abstinence between husband and wife during menstruation fall into the category of practices that obtain between God and a human being? Or the category of practices between one human being and another? Or both?

12. Cf., e.g., Lev. 19:2.

13. At the outset, let me say that I am aware of the highly charged and highly divisive nature of counting women in the *minyan*. I know of no synagogue where the inclusion of women in the *minyan* has been accomplished without causing considerable pain and anger to those who opposed it, people who have often been genuinely sincere in their conviction. Sadly, however, sincerity and depth of feeling are no more guarantors of the validity of a religious conviction than they were for the once devoutly held conviction that the earth was the center of the universe.

14. For a longer, more detailed version of my argument here, see my article, "The Story of the Moral: Gifts or Bribes in Deuteronomy?" in *Interpretation* 38 (January 1984) : 15–25.

15. Marcel Mauss, *The Gift* (New York: W.W. Norton and Co., Inc., 1967), pp. 31–45. Consider, for instance, the standard contract form. Whether

in its classical Roman formulation—"*Do ut des*" ("I give that you may give")—or in its contemporary expression as an exchange of considerations, the principle of reciprocity is clearly in evidence.

16. Or, alternatively, the judge delivers *first*, giving the decision a litigant desires with the implicit understanding that later the litigant will give the judge something he or she finds equally desirable. Or again, in societies without any professional or permanent judiciary, a gift may serve as a kind of "access payment"; we give the judge a gift, and, in return, he or she gives attention to our case.

17. Even when the system works decidedly in favor of the wealthy and the powerful, who can always provide bigger gifts; the judge is just giving them what is due them.

18. J. J. Finkelstein, "The Middle Assyrian Sulmanu Texts, " JAOS 72:78–79 (1952).

19. Cf., e.g., Yehezkiel Kaufmann, *The Religion of Israel: From Its Beginnings to the Babylonian Exile*, trans. and abrdg. Moshe Greenberg (New York: Shocken Books, 1972), and Nahum Sarna, *Understanding Genesis: The Biblical Heritage of Israel* (New York: Shocken Books, 1970).

20. *The Book of Exodus: A Critical Theological Commentary* (Philadelphia: The Westminster Press, 1974), p. 150.

21. Significantly, most biblical critics agree that the first chapter of Genesis was perhaps one of the last pieces of the Pentateuch to be composed, and, hence, the portrayal of God and his character in that chapter is the result of the cumulative depiction of the Lord recounted by other biblical texts.

22. For the root meaning of *kadosh* as "different," "separate," or "set apart," see *A Hebrew and English Lexicon of the Old Testament*, s.v., *ad loc*, and Sifra on Lev. 19:2.

23. For instance, the first-century philosopher, Philo of Alexandria, and the medieval biblical commentator, Abraham Ibn Ezra, both took the prohibition as a bar to cruelty toward animals. By contrast, the 1885 Pittsburgh Platform of Reform Judaism categorized it as "mere ritual," which could consequently be discarded.

24. Maimonides *Guide for the Perplexed* 3.48; on the basis of a Ugaritic text discovered at Ras Shamra in 1928, biblical scholars such as H. L. Ginsberg, Theodore H. Gaster, and Hans Kosmala made their own determinations which, in essence, agreed with Maimonides. For a full citation of the sources, see my *Interpretation* article cited in note 11.

Since the article was first published, an important monograph, " 'A Kid in Milk'?: New Photographs of *KTU* 1.23, Line 14" by Robert Ratner and Bruce Zuckerman, appeared in the *Hebrew Union College Annual*, no. 57 (1986), pp. 15–60. In their article, the writers claim that the cuneiform characters of the Ugaritic text are not as clear as earlier scholars had thought them to be and that, consequently, the relationship between that text and Deut. 14:21 is not as clear-cut either. Even so, the authors (to their credit) conclude that "the evidence does not allow us totally to exclude the possibility that *KTU* 1.23, line 14 associates a kid and milk, nor does it allow us to prove beyond all doubt that the passage has no relevance to the famous biblical text" (p. 52).

25. Ancient magic has been called "sacred technology." It might be

helpful, therefore, to think of the dynamics of a fertility rite of sympathetic magic in ways similar to those we employ when we think about the chain reaction accompanying nuclear fission. By dismantling or splitting certain natural bonds, we release an enormous amount of energy, which, if we act at precisely the right time in precisely the right way, we can harness to our will.

26. The celebration of *Shavuot*, for example, followed the barley harvest.

27. Cf. Alasdair MacIntyre, "Can Medicine Dispense with a Theological Perspective of Human Nature?" (Mimeographed), pp. 5–6, and T. Englehardt, ed., *The Foundations of Ethics and Its Relation to Science*, vol 3.

28. For an elaboration of this point, see my *Theology and Narrative: A Critical Introduction*, rev. ed. (Philadelphia: Trinity Press International, 1991), Chapter VI.

29. On the basis of Ex. 24:3; cf. Childs, pp. 440–496.

30. Or in the case of the Egyptians, afterlife-long servitude as well.

31. Ex. 11:3; cf., also, Ex. 11:2 and 12:35–36.

32. Or as Deuteronomy 15:18 puts it when it "consoles" the former "master," "When you set him free, do not feel aggrieved, for in the six years, he has given you double the service of a hired man."

33. Jeremy Bentham, *The Works of Jeremy Bentham*, ed. John Bowring, vol. 2: "Anarchical Fallacies" (Edinburgh: W. Tait, 1843–59), p. 501.

34. Cf. MacIntyre's *After Virtue*, 2nd ed. (Notre Dame, In.: University of Notre Dame Press, 1984), p. 70.

35. Maimonides, *Guide for the Perplexed* III, 31.

36. Significantly, the term for Jewish law, *halacha*, comes from a root meaning "to walk" and by extension, is a "way of walking."

37. And with apologies to Kant!

38. Gary Wills, *Lincoln at Gettysburg: The Words that Remade America* (New York: Simon and Schuster, 1992).

39. Ibid., p. 101.

40. In the Thirteenth and Fourteenth Amendments.

41. Cf. Yevamot 21a on Lev. 18:30.

42. The Talmud reports many episodes of rabbis disqualifying themselves from hearing cases where there might have been even the slightest appearance of partiality or favoritism, as in the case of Samuel, a third-century Babylonian sage:

He was crossing [a river] on a plank when a man came up and gave him his hand. [Samuel] asked him, "What is your business here?" The other responded, "I have a lawsuit." [Samuel] replied, "I am disqualified from judging your case." (Ketubot 105b)

The rabbis similarly took with utmost seriousness the notion that, for better or worse, their own judicial character attested to the story-based character of the ultimate judge—God. As Maimonides put it, a rabbi called on to be a judge "should know Whom he judges, before Whom he judges, and Who will exact judgment from him in the future should he deviate from the true course." (Mishneh Torah, Hilchot Sanhedrin 23:8).

43. Indeed, the only example I can find appears in a remark by the

sixteenth-century traveler *cum* commentator, Rabbi Ovadiah of Bertinoro. Commenting on Bechorot 4:6, he complains of a greedy rabbinic judge, who, in his opinion, overcharged for the writing and granting of a *get*, a Jewish bill of divorce. And lest someone suggest that the sources are silent on the subject of rabbinic corruption as part of a "cover-up," it should be noted that the sources contain no such cover-ups in other areas where we might expect to find them as, for example, in the case of Elisha ben Abuya, a talmudic sage who committed apostasy.

44. *Encyclopedia Judaica*, s.v. "Bribery," by Haim Hermann Cohn. For examples of what Cohn means, together with the complete lack of self-consciousness with which Jews engaged in the bribing of non-Jews, see the following Talmudic sources: Shabbat 116a-b; Yevamot 63b; Avodah Zarah 71a. Cohn himself reports that in medieval bills of debt between Jews, one finds, alongside the amount actually owed the creditor by the debtor, an additional amount to cover the creditor's expenses in having to bribe a non-Jewish official to pursue the party in arrears.

45. Cf., e.g., the discussion in Yoma 85a-b.

46. Cf., e.g., Avodah Zarah 71a.

47. See Pesachim 22b and Maimonides, Mishneh Torah, Hilchot Sanhedrin 23:2; the rabbinic principle is derived from Lev. 19:14: "You shall not place a stumbling-block before the blind." The rabbis were forced to give this rather farfetched interpretation of the verse in order to find some basis for proscribing bribe-*giving*. The Bible itself only outlaws bribe-*taking*!

48. See Sanhedrin 56a and note also Maimonides' nuanced inference in the Mishneh Torah, Hilchot M'lachim 8:10, that Jews may not therefore undermine Gentile courts.

49. Cf. Nedarim 28a; Gittin 10b; Baba Kamma 113a; Baba Batra 54b, 55a.

50. See Num. 14:27 and the rabbinic interpretation of it in Megillah 23b and Sanhedrin 74b.

51. Another version of this argument is that since Jesus was a man, only men can be priests. It, too, however collapses in the face of the fact that while Jesus was a Jew, no one would claim that only Jews can be priests. Clearly, those opposed to the ordination of women as priests may have additional reasons for their position. If so, those reasons need to be put forward explicitly.

52. Berachot 2:2.

53. Some scholars say it originates from the time prior to the destruction of the Second Temple, while others attribute it to the third-century Babylonian sage, Rav. Cf., e.g., A.Z. Idelson, *Jewish Liturgy and Its Development* (New York: Schocken, 1960), pp. 116 and 316, and Joseph Heinemann, *HaTefilla B'Tkufat HaTanna'im V'HaAmora'im* [Prayer in the Period of the Tanna'im and the Amora'im] (Jerusalem: Magnes Press, 1966), pp. 173ff.

54. Some have taken the so-called Noachide Laws incumbent on non-Jews as establishing a "two-track" system for living righteously, with Jews being bound by the full complement of commandments in the Torah. But both the Talmud (Avodah Zarah 64b) and Maimonides (Mishneh Torah, Hilchot M'lachim 8:10) reflect perspectives that view the Noachide commandments as the minimal requirements needed for a non-Jew to be treated

as a *ger-toshav*, i.e., as a resident-alien whose presence is to be tolerated by the larger, normative culture around them. Moreover, in the Jerusalem Talmud (Avodah Zarah 2:1), the Noachide Laws are viewed as a preparatory step on the way of non-Jews' universally coming to accept the whole of Torah as binding on them. Thus, in a recent article, "The Jewish Legal Model," *Harvard Law Review* 106 (February 1993), Suzanne Last Stone has aptly written:

> Although nothing more is promised by the messianic idea than the restoration of the full practice of Torah, Torah law is designed to bring about nothing less than collective spiritual, intellectual, and social perfection. Maimonides's messianic doctrine, in turn, is a philosophic elaboration of themes already evident in the earlier midrashic discussion of the messianic days. The messianic age is not the end of days, but a redemptive phase of history. Messianic redemption is a public, communal event. There will be a reign of peace in which evil . . . disappears, so *that humanity will be able to devote itself to the study and fulfillment of the law. Thus, the transformation of human nature and society that will occur in the messianic age is the result of the more perfect fulfillment and understanding of the Torah's laws that the age itself makes possible.*" (p. 881; italics mine)

55. Solomon Schechter, *Aspects of Rabbinic Theology: Major Concepts of the Talmud* (New York: Schocken, 1961), p. 77.

56. Hilchot M'lachim 11:4; italics added.

57. Salo Baron. *A Social and Religious History of the Jews*, vol. 1: *To the Beginning of the Christian Era*, 2nd ed. (New York: Columbia University Press, 1952), p. 171.

58. Ibid., p. 174.

59. Taken from Zechariah 14:9.

60. See Skolnick Hoenig, p. 46; only 40% of Jewish households affilate at any given time with a synagogue, which in all likelihood is the one Jewish organization that Jews given to affiliation would join in the first place.

Chapter 6

The Household of Israel: Is Anybody Home Besides Anne Frank and Eleazar ben Ya'ir?

> *Everyone agrees that the Holocaust teaches what awaits a nation in exile that has no state power of its own; had Israel been established before the Nazis came to power, the murder of the Jews could not have been possible. Everyone agrees that the Holocaust led to the establishment of the state and that its survivors were at the center of the struggle for independence.*
>
> Yitzhak Arad, Director of Yad Vashem[1]

The Holocaust as master story holds out only two choices for Jewish identity: victim or hero. Seen through the lens of the Holocaust, the Jewish past is an epic of suffering that culminated in the murder of 6,000,000 men, women, and children. From that perspective, the Jewish People's future will look exactly like its past unless Jews heroically and unrelentingly resist the world's undying anti-Semitism.

Many, perhaps most, contemporary Jews in America and Israel have accepted this Holocaust-framed vision of Jewish history. But the images it provides Jews, particularly the self-images, are malformed. They mutilate Jews' self-understanding and mangle the truer depiction of Jewish existence rendered by the Exodus.

The Jew as Victim

*Two Jews are about to be shot by a firing squad. The commander
of the squad asks them if they have any last words. One of the
Jews shrieks, "We're innocent!" The other Jew turns to him and
says, "Shh! Don't make trouble!"*

Soon after the Holocaust, Israelis contemptuously began using
the Hebrew word *sabon*, "soap," to refer to the Nazis' victims. Although the fat of murdered Jews may not actually have been turned
into soap, the utter disdain native-born Israelis expressed toward the
death camps' victims was real enough.[2] Tales about European Jews
going to the gas chambers like so many "sheep to the slaughter"
reinforced *sabras'* general scorn for Jewish life in the Diaspora,
where, they believed, Jews had been harassed, hounded, and humili-
ated for close to two millennia—without so much as offering a peep
of protest.

American Jews, though understandably not as thoroughgoingly
Zionist as their Israeli counterparts, nevertheless agreed implicitly
with the Zionist assessment of Diaspora life. Well before the full
horror of the Holocaust became public knowledge, an upsurge in
American anti-Semitism gave American Jews good reason to feel
uneasy. They knew of the Ku Klux Klan's resurgence in the twen-
ties, of Father Coughlin's vitriolic radio broadcasts in the thirties,
and of Jewish refugees in the early forties being turned away despite unfilled immigration quotas. At war's end when the concentration camps and their pathetic survivors were liberated for all the
world to see, American Jews' sense of self-esteem could hardly have
fallen lower as their sense of apprehension rose ever higher. By
1945, the Roper pollsters were warning "that anti-Semitism has
spread all over the nation and is particularly virulent in urban
areas."[3] The centuries-old image of the Jew as defenseless prey had
stalked the Household of Israel even to the shores of America, that
land lauded by one of its Jewish immigrants, Irving Berlin, as
"crowned . . . with brotherhood, from sea to shining sea."

Hence, after the Holocaust most Jews had little trouble swallow-
ing a story that portrayed all prior Jewish history as a grim saga of
powerlessness and passivity. The Jew's unchanging role in that epic
of suffering? At worst, a contemptible weakling, at best, a pathetic
nebisch. Throughout the late forties and fifties, the Nazis' victims

evoked more revulsion than sympathy from Jews in Israel and the United States. The sole exception may have been Anne Frank, whose diary when published in 1947, transfigured her into "the symbol of the persecuted Jewish child."[4]

Nevertheless, the depiction of all Jewish history as one long episode of victimization is profoundly false. Although Jews certainly have suffered many savage episodes of persecution—for a people over three and one-half millennia old, it would truly be astounding *not* to find such episodes—a chronicle focusing on such experiences alone fails to yield the whole story. As David Biale has shown in his useful survey, *Power and Powerlessness in Jewish History: The Jewish Tradition and the Myth of Passivity*,[5] Jews throughout their history have often been a power to be reckoned with. In 117, after Alexandria's non-Jews tried to strip its Jewish population of their rights, the city's Jews staged a riot so severe that Roman troops had to be summoned to restore order. Medieval Jews, far from being helpless "wanderers," were permitted like knights (and unlike commoners) to carry weapons—which they used with considerable skill to defend themselves during the First and Second Crusades. In 1648, Jews did not stand by to wait passively for Bogdan Chmielnicki and his Cossacks to descend on them; instead, they converted their synagogues into forts and passed communal ordinances requiring "every householder [to] have as many guns as the number of men." In sum, the Holocaust-inspired narration of Jewish history portraying Jews as docile doormats is simply incorrect.

It is also deeply anti-Semitic. Its assessment of Jews essentially agrees with the worst that the enemies of the Jewish People have historically said about us: that we have been spineless, that we have been cowards, that we have been less than human. The Holocaust master story's characterization of our ancestors is at its core character assassination.

The 1961 trial of Adolf Eichmann in Jerusalem represented an attempt to retract such slander where the Holocaust's victims and survivors were concerned. The prosecution's chief aim was essentially an educational one. It sought, through survivors' testimony, to induce younger Israelis to identify with the victims, and by the trial's conclusion, that goal had been achieved. Many Israelis had not ever heard the horrific stories the witnesses told, and the survivors' testimony set in motion a process of identification with the victims and their suffering. One Israeli, Haim Guri, for whom the survivors had initially aroused intense shame, wrote toward trial's end:

We must ask absolution from untold numbers whom we have judged in our hearts, we who lived outside that realm [of the Holocaust]. We often judged them without having asked ourselves what right we had to do that.[6]

By 1992, a reversal in Israelis' attitudes toward the victims had become so complete that a survey of teachers' college students reported almost 80% of them agreeing with the statement, "We are all Holocaust survivors."[7]

All?

Whoever has listened to survivors tell their stories cannot help being moved. Who among us can truly fathom what they endured? How many of us could endure it ourselves? Can we even endure listening to their accounts? Perhaps the most basic comfort we can give survivors comes from our willingness to listen to their stories of what happened, no matter how painful (or repetitious) those narratives may be. But while listening empathetically to victims' stories is one thing, letting victims' stories define our reality morally and politically is something else again.

In one concentration camp, a sadistic Nazi guard hitched up an elderly rabbi to a cart and made the rabbi pull him around the camp, whipping him all the while. Finally having had enough "fun," the guard told the rabbi to get back to work. One of the inmates came up to the rabbi and asked, "Wasn't it horrible for you to have to pull that cart?" The rabbi replied, "It would have been more horrible for me to be driving it."[8]

In the camps, there were only two choices: to be a victim—or a victimizer. But the larger world outside the camps, *our* world, has many more choices and much more complexity. Therapists try to impress just such truths on abuse victims. They try to get these people to see that they have more options than being either the abused or the abuser. In the wider world outside the abuse situation, that is simply a too-narrow choice fraught with moral and psychological danger. Victims' continued inability or unwillingness to see a wider range of alternatives is a sign of pathology.[9]

You would never know that by looking at the number of squatters staking claims to victimhood on the contemporary American moral and political landscape. Partially fueled by (excesses in) the civil rights', women's, and recovery movements, a whole cottage industry of victimhood sprang up in the United States in the late 1970s and

1980s. It was as though by claiming to be victims who had suffered moral wrongdoing, some people believed they were immune from moral wrongdoing themselves—and from any moral criticism. Being a victim thus offered not only a privileged position from which to define the good, but, more important, to be equated with the good. Claimed victimhood consequently carried with it significant moral and political leverage over those cast in the role of victimizers.[10]

Best of all, virtually anybody could claim to be a victim. One of the recovery movement's leading figures, John Bradshaw, has contended that "approximately 96 percent of the families in this country are dysfunctional to one degree or another."[11] Claiming victim status has become so popular, in fact, that even some recent Jewish theology has jumped on the bandwagon. David Blumenthal, holder of an endowed chair of Jewish Studies at Emory University, has written a book entitled *Facing the Abusing God: A Theology of Protest.*[12] One can only wonder: Does God need to go through a 12-step program? Or do we?

Blumenthal has not been the only Jew to mine the vein of victimhood for its potential moral and political riches. In the mid-1980s, the World Jewish Congress adamantly opposed the construction of a Carmelite convent at Auschwitz. One WJC official against building the site was Gerhard Riegner, the man who had provided President Roosevelt with the first authoritative information about the Nazis pursuing a policy of genocide toward Europe's Jews. When Riegner was asked about the reason for the WJC's opposition to the convent, he replied that as a part of the Jews' national memory, Auschwitz should not be appropriated by anyone else. Besides, he said, it was also an important political asset.[13]

When it came to exploiting Jews' victimization, Menachem Begin, Israel's first Holocaust-survivor prime minister, had no peer. Other Israeli prime ministers and governments before Begin had put the Holocaust to political uses. The first place they typically took visiting dignitaries was Yad Vashem. Begin went further, though, never missing an opportunity to "remind" foreign officials (and anybody else within earshot) that the Jewish People had been victimized by other peoples throughout history. Thus draped in the invincible moral aura of victimhood, Begin would go on to assert that no nation could ever therefore legitimately level any moral criticism at either the State of Israel or the Jewish People. A few weeks after Israel's incursion into Lebanon in 1982, Begin told the Knesset, "No one, anywhere in the world, can preach morality to our people."[14]

But Begin's view undercuts the very thing that gives a victim's testimony its moral power, namely, its universal application—even to, and perhaps most especially to, the one giving the testimony. Begin and other would-be Holocaust exploiters cannot have it both ways. They cannot use the memory of the Holocaust as both a moral sword and shield—a sword of moral criticism with which to prick the consciences of others and a shield to deflect the sting of that selfsame criticism from their own consciences. That kind of tactic ultimately defiles all invocations of the Holocaust's memory, perverting them from moral acts into acts of cheap moralizing.

The result of such moralizing, of the invocation of the Holocaust as a talisman to ward off every moral challenge to the Jewish People and the Jewish state, is that many people (including Jews) will simply stop listening to what victims rightly have to say. To be sure, the intended audience will dutifully nod and outwardly respond with the appropriate mea culpas (or *al cheyts*). Inwardly, however, they will put their minds—and hearts—on autopilot and attend to other things. In many ways, what will increasingly happen to Jews when they speak about the Holocaust is what already happens to African-Americans when they speak about slavery and racism: "Nice people" listen *but do not hear*. Can it be any wonder that Jews and blacks seem to be competing so fiercely over which of them should win the gold medal in the "Victim Olympics"? Hence, the grotesque spectacle of a black scholar trying to make a case that blacks rather than Jews should take first prize in the history of suffering:

It is a simplistic notion of slavery which makes it easy for people to compare their holocaust to our holocaust. They don't understand that going to the ovens knowing who you are, is damn well better than walking around for 100 years not knowing who you are. . . . Our holocaust in America is worse than the holocaust in Europe.[15]

The competition between Jews and blacks for the title of "Greatest Victim in the World" will likely grow only more intense. Even now, blacks are following close on Jews' heels by trying to build a museum memorializing slavery and racism in Washington, D.C., lest Jews have a moral monopoly on that plum political market with their Holocaust museum on the Mall. Of course, as the marketplace of victims becomes increasingly crowded with more and more competitors, Jews and blacks will have to hawk their wares more stridently to make themselves heard above the din.

Perhaps worst of all, though, a "Gresham's Law of Victimization" will likely take effect: Bogus victims will drive out real ones.

Bradshaw considers even Hitler a victim. "Hitler," he has said, is "a cruel caricature of what can happen . . . if we do not stop . . . family rules that kill the souls of human beings."[16] And yet, if everybody counts as a victim, then nobody really counts, because the lines between victims and victimizers will become hopelessly blurred.[17]

In contrast to a Holocaust-inspired story that disparages victims or contemporary politics that deifies them, how does the Exodus master story ask us to view those who have undergone hideous suffering?

In the first place, it would have us realize that one can become a victim through no fault of one's own. At the story's outset, the Egyptians victimize the Hebrews for no other reason than that there are so many of them. Pharaoh tells his people (1:9), "Look, the Israelite people are much too numerous for us." So Israel's oppression begins, but even as the people are oppressed, they continue to flourish, so much so that "the Egyptians came to dread the Israelites" (1:12). What could be the cause of Israel's affliction? Might it be their migration from the promised land to a land ruled by Gentiles? Or perhaps their failure to arm themselves properly? No, according to this story, they are victimized as a consequence of God's promise of fertility to Abraham and his descendants. In other words, God's blessing has become Israel's curse. According to this story, at least, those who would be God's subjects will always be vulnerable in a world that stands in opposition to God's rule. From the point of view of the Exodus, Jews may become victims without having necessarily done anything wrong at all.

If the Exodus' opening verses show us that people may become victims through no fault of their own, a passage near its end demonstrates that victims bear no special immunity from behaving in morally faulty ways. The Israelites have just been rescued by God at the Sea. So how do these recently redeemed victims of oppression express their gratitude?

Then Moses caused Israel to set out from the Sea of Reeds. They went on into the wilderness of Shur; they traveled three days in the wilderness and found no water. They came to Marah, but they could not drink the water of Marah because it was bitter. . . . *And the people grumbled against Moses.* . . .

Setting out from Elim, the whole Israelite community came to the wilderness of Sin . . . on the fifteenth day of the second month after their departure from the land of Egypt. . . . *The whole Israelite community grumbled against Moses and Aaron . . ."If only we had died by the hand of the Lord in the land of Egypt, when we sat by the fleshpots, when we ate our fill of bread!* For you have brought us out into this wilderness to starve this whole congregation to death." (Ex. 15:22–25; 16:1–3)

Part of the Exodus narrative's compelling power stems from its ability to tell us the truth about ourselves, most especially when we would prefer not to hear it. In our time, the jarring truth it would have the Jewish People hear is this: Even victims can still sin.

Even those who would reject the Exodus in favor of more modern wisdom, such as that which comes from psychotherapy, must acknowledge that truth. After all, who is more likely to grow up to be a child abuser than the child of an abuser? We Jews have certainly shown over the last several years just how much we have learned from our historical abusers. In January 1987, an Israeli-government panel, the Landau Commission, reported that over the previous two decades, Israel's secret service, the *Shin Bet*, had routinely tortured Palestinians during interrogation. The commission nevertheless gave the *Shin Bet* permission to continue the practice according to certain unspecified "guidelines for limited psychological and physical pressure," that is, through the continued use of torture and intimidation. As for the *Shin Bet* officials involved, the commission recommended that they be let off because those officials—and here the commission used words with a chilling familiarity—"were just carrying out orders."[18]

Nor is that the only example of us Jews passing on to others the same abuse that we have suffered. Near the close of 1992, Israel expelled without trial several hundred Palestinian "troublemakers." Because these Palestinians were essentially stateless people who held no passports, they were welcome by no country. Their situation, in short, resembled that of countless generations of Jews through the ages. Exposed and vulnerable, the expelled Palestinians eventually ended up in a no-man's land between Israel and Lebanon. When Prime Minister Rabin was asked to defend the summary mass expulsions, he replied that Israel was simply following the 1945 procedures laid down by Britain, or, as he referred to it, "the mother of all democracies." This was the same Britain, of course, that in 1945 was deporting Jewish refugees from Palestine who had nowhere else to go.[19]

However, Jews have recently committed an even greater abuse. And it is an abuse we ourselves have experienced, perhaps, in fact, the worst abuse ever experienced—namely, others' silence while we suffered. Elie Wiesel has made a virtual career of reminding people how silence made the Holocaust possible. But during the *intifada*, when Israel was routinely using its army with disproportionate, of-

ten lethal, force against Palestinian civilians while regularly round-
ing up scores of Palestinians for detention camps, where was Wiesel's
voice to be heard? Arthur Hertzberg, editor of the classic text, *The
Zionist Idea*, asked that very question in an open letter to Wiesel:

In the memory of the Holocaust we have been reminded by you that silence
is a sin. You have spoken out against indifference and injustice. Why are
you making a special exception of Israel? Do you think our silence will help
Israel? The [sacred] texts that [Jews] study and restudy teach the contrary. . . . To be silent gives free reign to the armed zealots of ages past, and
of this day.[20]

If there is nothing inherently wrong about having been a victim,
there is nothing intrinsically right about it either. As the Exodus
master story and the recent story of the Jewish People both make
clear, victims are in the end neither subhuman nor superhuman, but
merely human. As they are not necessarily to be reproached for what
has happened to them, neither are they are necessarily beyond re-
proach because of it.

The Jew as Hero

*"We were the very first that revolted from [the Romans], and
we are the last that fight against them; and I cannot but esteem it as a favor that God [has] granted us, that it is still in
our power to die bravely and in a state of freedom. . . . Let our
wives die before they are abused, and our children before they
have tasted of slavery; and after we have slain them, let us
bestow that glorious benefit upon one another mutually, and
preserve ourselves in freedom, as an excellent funereal monument for us. . . . Let us spare nothing but our provisions; for
they will be a testimonial when we are dead, that we were not
subdued for want of necessaries, but that, according to our
original resolution, we have preferred death over slavery. . . .
Certainly our hands are still at liberty, and have a sword in
them; let them, then, be subservient to us in our glorious design; let us die before we become slaves under our enemies, and
let us go out of the world, together with our children and our
wives, in a state of freedom."*

Eleazar ben Ya'ir, commander of the Jewish rebels on Masada[21]

If the Jew-as-victim represents one fictitious character emanating from the Holocaust story, then the Jew-as-hero represents the other. In spite of—or because of—the general disdain Israelis originally felt for the victims, attempts soon arose to refurbish the Jewish People's image. Memory of the Nazis' victims soon became linked with the memory of those who resisted the Nazis. As we've seen before,[22] the date for commemorating the Holocaust was at first pegged to the date of the Warsaw Ghetto Uprising. In the end, the official name for the observance became "Holocaust, Rebellion, and Heroism Memorial Day." The full official name of Yad Vashem reflects a similar linkage: "The Memorial Authority for the Holocaust and Heroism." A tale of heroic Jewish resistance began to be spun. As Tom Segev writes with reference to Yad Vashem,

The Jewish attempts to resist the Nazis are described in detail, and the visitor gets the impression that the Jews fought a war with the Nazis. In the Israeli culture of memory Holocaust and heroism stand side-by-side, as if they were equal in force and in historical importance, complementary halves of a single entity.[23]

Along similar lines, an early *kibbutz*, Yad Mordecai, displays a statue of its namesake, Mordecai Anielewicz, the Warsaw Ghetto Rebellion's leader. The statue, a reworking of Michelangelo's *David*, stands clothed in battle dress and holds a grenade. Engraved nearby is a quotation from one of Anielewicz's last letters to an aide: "The last desire of my life has been fulfilled. Jewish self-defense is a fact. I am content, happy that I was among the first Jewish fighters in the ghetto."[24]

In the fifties and sixties, the theme of heroic resistance leading to a martyr's death reached its zenith on the wilderness plateau of Masada. After the fall of Jerusalem in 70, Jewish zealots led by Eleazar ben Ya'ir held out on Masada against the Tenth Roman Legion for three years before taking their own lives. Almost two thousand years later, newly inducted Israeli soldiers started scaling the plateau to receive their first rifles and vow, "Masada shall not fall again."

But if not, why take the vow at Masada in the first place? That is, why not take such a vow at a place of *successful* resistance, at a spot where resistance resulted in life rather than in death? More fundamentally, if for almost two millennia, generations of Jews did not even allude to the Masada story, why does our generation so enthusiastically invoke it? Just what kind of story is it?

> *Once, 960 men, women, and children left the society in which they lived, because they felt it was corrupt—and corrupting. They moved* en masse *to a wilderness to be left alone to lead the kind of life they desired.*
>
> *After a time, some representatives of the society they had left came out to their wilderness home. They greeted these outsiders with violent resistance. In the end, however, all the men, women, and children gave up their lives rather than give up their way of life.*

What story is here recounted? Most Jews today would instantly answer "Masada." But why not answer "Jonestown"? Maybe the answer is "Both." Significantly, the Masada story comes to us by way of the first-century Jewish historian, Josephus, who relates the incident in his work, *The Jewish Wars*. Written in the form of a Roman chronicle for a Roman audience, it attempted to put the Jews' rebellion in a somewhat more favorable light.[25] What better way to lend some nobility to the Jewish rebels on Masada than by ending their story the same way that noble Romans (such as Seneca) ended theirs, by way of suicide?

Two thousand years later, the storyline of that essentially non-Jewish narrative apparently has mass appeal to Josephus' descendants, both in Israel and the United States. In the early sixties, for example, American Jews made a best-seller of Leon Uris's *Mila 18*, an historical novel about the (doomed) Warsaw Ghetto Revolt; later, they helped make a ratings success of a mini-series about Masada starring Peter O'Toole. Meanwhile in Israel, despite such impressive triumphs as the 1967 Six-Day War, the 1976 rescue of Jewish hostages at Entebbe, and the 1982 bombing of the Iraqi nuclear reactor, the specter of a Masada-like "heroic" death continued to haunt the Jewish imagination. Soon the "Masada Syndrome" was joined by two others. The "Samson Syndrome" conjured the image of an Israel severely weakened, but still strong enough to bring down its adversaries with it in a nuclear holocaust, a holocaust initiated this time by Jews. For its part, the "Bar Kochba Syndrome" recalled the rebel whose band made its last stand against the Romans in 135 at Betar in the Judean hills; modern Israel, if necessary, would also fight to the last in and for the Land of Israel.[26] Every powerful story told by post-Holocaust Jews seemingly ended in the death of the Jewish People. An inextricable bond somehow started to develop between Jewish heroism and death. But historically, a narration of heroic, self-sacrificial martyrdom was understood by Jews to be somebody else's master story: Christians'.

In 135, in the aftermath of Bar Kochba's defeat at Betar and around the same time Christians had been gaining a reputation for their willingness to let themselves be martyred like their master, the rabbis were taking steps to severely limit martyrdom as an option for Jews:

They took a vote and concluded in the upper room of the house of Nitza in Lod that regarding all the transgressions prohibited in the Torah, if they [i.e., the Romans] said to a man [i.e., a Jew], "Transgress and do not let yourself be killed," let him transgress and let him not be killed. . . . (San. 74a)

The biblical prooftext on which the rabbis' based their ruling was Leviticus 18:5, where God commands the observance of such laws and rules "through the performance of which [a person] shall live." Therefore, inferred the rabbis, God gave the commandments so that Jews might live by them—not die because of them. Though this general rule subsequently became greatly qualified, the basic principle nevertheless remained intact. Maimonides underscores that principle by noting that a Jew who suffers death rather than commit a permissible transgression "is himself to blame for his death."[27] Which is exactly as it should be. If the Jewish People is God's embodied presence on earth, then both God and his People have a stake in preferring life over death.

Something is therefore odd about Jews of all people adopting a storyline, be it Jesus' or Jonestown's, that equates heroism with death. Every bit as problematic is letting Masada set the benchmark by which to gauge resistance, for it begs the most important question: What specifically counts as heroic *Jewish* resistance?

Is suicide, for instance, an example of such resistance? Those who take Masada as their model might well answer "Yes."[28] But the answer from Jewish tradition and from, for example, the traditional Jews of Poland is emphatically "No!" Although for several months following *Kristallnacht*, suicides accounted for more than half the deaths among Germany's highly assimilated Jewish population, the number of suicides in the Warsaw Ghetto by contrast was "trifling."[29] Traditional Jews understood a crucial difference between the martyr and the suicide: True martyrs do not lay hands on themselves.[30]

Moreover, by too readily embracing the story of Masada or the Warsaw Ghetto (as though these were Jewish versions of the legend of the Alamo or of the Spartans at Thermopylae), we too easily are led to make resistance synonymous with a resort to violence. But powerful, nonviolent evidence of Jewish resistance during the Holocaust came from those Jews who struggled to cling to their story, the Exodus, in defiance of the Nazi story. In the words of one commentator, "Unquestionably, the recounting of the story of the Exodus strengthened [Jews'] belief that the Jewish people—if not particular individual Jews—would outlive Hitler as they had outlived Pharaoh."[31] Somehow, Jews managed to observe Passover in the concentration camps by eating *matzah*, by refraining from *chametz* (leaven), and even by holding seder meals. When circumstances made it impossible to observe such practices, some Jews still tried to keep even their nonobservance faithful. Thus, the rabbis of Bergen-Belsen composed a prayer for those compelled to eat leaven; strikingly, they modeled it on the prayer traditionally recited before the obligatory eating of *matzah*:

Our Father in heaven, it is known and revealed before Thee that it is our will to do Thy will and observe the festival of Passover through the eating of *matzah* and by not violating the prohibition of [c]*hametz*. For this our hearts are grieved—that our enslavement prevents us and we are in danger of our lives. Behold, then, we are prepared and ready to fulfill Thy commandment of "Thou shalt live by them and not die by them." . . . Therefore it is our prayer unto Thee that Thou keep us alive and preserve us and redeem us speedily so that we may observe Thy statutes and do Thy will and serve Thee with a perfect heart. Amen.[32]

Those Jews' lives attested to what they believed was true—and false—in life. In this, they were practicing the witness commanded of Jews in Leviticus 22:32: "You shall not profane My holy name, that I may be sanctified in the midst of the people Israel—I the Lord who sanctify you." Jewish tradition calls such witness "*kiddush ha-Shem*," literally, "sanctification of the Name," and those who give such witness are called *k'doshim*, "sanctified" or "holy" ones. As we have seen before, the name or reputation of the holy God depends on what happens in the life of those who would be his holy People. In the Middle Ages, the word *k'doshim* became synonymous with those Jews who could testify to the truth of life only by giving up their lives. But once again that medieval figure, Maimonides, provides a much needed corrective, especially for those of us who, misled by the distorting vision of the Holocaust, stand in need of such correction. As Maimonides reminds us, being one of God's *k'doshim*, one of those whose very life declares the sanctity of God's name, has more to do with living one's life than with losing it. Hence, Maimonides closes his discussion of *kiddush haShem* not with talk about how the faithful Jew should die, but about how such a Jew should live:

Pleasant in interaction with fellow-creatures . . . dependable in business dealings . . . engaged in Torah study . . . behold, such a one sanctifies God's name, and of such a one, it is written in Scripture [Is. 49:3], "You are my servant, Israel, in whom I will be glorified."[33]

Truly Jewish resistance is not about showing that Jews can die as heroically as non-Jews nor, for that matter, that Jews can kill non-Jews as well as non-Jews can kill Jews or even one another. Instead, the testimony of genuine Jewish resistance stands against the falsehood of the world. The English word *martyr* comes from the Greek translation of the Hebrew *eyd*, meaning "witness." Through what one does with one's life, one witnesses to the truth of life. The witness of real Jewish resistance testifies that in the midst of a world that is godless, Jews can still be godly, that in the midst of a world that would declare God non-existent, there is yet a people whose very life still declares him *God*.

It is that way of life the Exodus story speaks of, and it is within the context of that story that Jews are to learn what counts not only as resistance but also as heroism. Who is the hero of the story? On one level, it is Moses; on another, it is God. What makes them heroes? Certainly not their eloquence or communications skills. As Moses repeatedly stammers out, "I am slow of speech and slow of tongue,"[34] and that impediment becomes God's own as time and again he chooses to use Moses as his mouthpiece. Nor are Moses and the Lord "natural leaders" who have a knack either for getting along with people or for getting people to do what they want. If anything, both God and Moses seem to have a fairly short fuse and they often seem ready to abandon Israel rather than to lead it.

But lead it they do, and therein lies the Exodus-based quality that makes them heroes: faithfulness. The word that typically expresses that term is *chesed*, and it appears over two hundred times in Scripture. *Chesed*, faithfulness, is exactly the quality, the core virtue, needed by the heroes of a story that is the narrated keeping of a promise:

Go forth from your native land and from your father's house to the land that I will show you. I will make of you a great nation, and I will bless you; I will make your name great, and you shall be a blessing. I will bless those who bless you and curse him who curses you; and all the families of the earth shall bless themselves by you. (Gen. 12:1–3)

While stories such as the ones surrounding Masada may celebrate "going out in a blaze of glory," the narration of the Exodus from Egypt gives glory instead to those who remain faithful, steadfast, devoted. For that is the persistence needed by a people who must outlast an oppressive sojourn in Egypt before it can set out for its promised place, which, like it, will be known throughout history as "Israel." In between Egypt and that Land is a forty-year trudge through a wilderness—hardly an enticing prospect for those who would be eternal victims or instant heroes.

The Household of Israel, A Home to Outsiders with a Covenant-in-Residence

If the Holocaust-inspired identities of victim and hero are so shallow, how could they have taken hold so deeply in contemporary Jews' consciousness? For the last two hundred years, another story has been hard at work undermining the Exodus' moorings as the foundational narrative for Jewish self-understanding. That story was one only the Enlightenment could tell, and its central character, as we have seen earlier, was not a community, but the individual.[35] That Enlightenment story was—indeed, *is*—so powerful that to this day it still profoundly affects the way that Jews hear their own story of the Exodus. When American Jews read of Passover's being *zman cheyruteynu*, "the festival of our freedom," the Exodus becomes for them a kind of precursor to Jeffersonian democracy, with its central value of individual liberty. When Israeli Jews read of the Exodus from Egypt, their attention skips to the journey's destination, the Zionist homeland where the right to national self-determination can be exercised. Both of these Enlightenment-guided understandings are not so much misreadings as attenuated readings of the Exodus narrative. For the Exodus to be the kind of freedom story American Jews take it to be, it would have to end at the crossing of the Sea. There, finally, the Israelites are free from the oppressive hand of an Egyptian George III. For the Exodus to be the kind of national liberation yarn modern Zionists would spin, the story, *the journey*, needs to be much shorter, taking the direct route along the coast from Egypt to Canaan, avoiding the wilderness altogether.

What the American and Israeli readings of the Exodus share
with the Enlightenment account of human history is a virtual disregard of the significance of community, particularly if community
means anything more than a collection of autonomous individuals.
For the Enlightenment, community, family, and tradition are little
more than background scenery in the drama of an individual human
life. That is the deeper reason why an Enlightenment-grounded narration of the Holocaust continually throws up for Jewish identity
images of individuals—the pathetic victim, the lone hero—apart
from any broader communal context. Similarly, when American
and Israeli Jews view the Exodus narrative through an Enlightenment framework, a huge blind spot results. Whether they tell the
story so that it ends at the Sea or instead skips right to the invasion of
Canaan, each of their readings has a glaring omission: The stop at
Sinai where a community comes into being and the individuals of a
heretofore undifferentiated mass gain an identity. What happens to
a "Jewish" community or polity when it loses sight of that story-
piece? And what can restoring that piece do for the fragmented Jewish identity of our time?

i: Restoring the Judeo-American Reading of the Exodus[36]

Most American Jews use the word "community" the way most
American politicians use the word "friend"—with ease and emptiness. The crux of what makes community (i.e., common goals pursued by common means) is largely absent from American Jewish
life. One sign of its absence is the frantic way American Jews look for
it. They join synagogues, they form *chavurot*, they affiliate with
various Jewish organizations to find it. And yet, true community
remains elusive.

Vibrant, lively community eludes many American Jews because
even as they look for it, they carry with them the infection that kills
community in contemporary American life: a culture of consumer-
ism based on individual preference. Despite their vaunted theological differences, American Orthodox, Conservative, Reconstructionist, and Reform Jews all practice the same kind of Judaism—
Consumer Judaism. For the only thing their synagogues *require for
membership* is the payment of monetary dues. Such synagogues are
like religious 7-11s. When American Jews get a craving for something sweet and gooey—a bar or bat mitzvah, a wedding, a baby-

naming—they drop in, plunk down their money, savor their choice, and then drive away, until the craving overcomes them again. The "members" of such synagogues are essentially nothing more than consumers exercising their individual preferences in the market-place. As for the congregational board of directors, they basically operate as a management team keeping tabs on market share and income. And the rabbi? He or she takes the role of counter help whose job it is to keep the individual customers satisfied so they keep coming back to this particular franchise outlet rather than to that other religious Stop 'N Shop down the street.

From what the statistics tell us, business has not been good.[37] Most American Jews do not belong to any synagogue at all, those who do belong generally do not attend services regularly, and those who do attend typically sit next to people whose concerns and commitments they do not know, whose lives they therefore cannot possibly know. Consequently, many American Jews encounter in the synagogue the same two social demons that bedevil them outside it: anonymity and alienation. No one knows them, and no one cares that no one knows them. Calling such a collection of random individuals a "community," even a "congregation," is the height of *chutzpah*. The only things such individuals generally share in common are their names on a mailing list.

Because they hold little or nothing in common but their individual preferences and tastes, American Jews inevitably wind up chasing will-o'-the wisps. They seek synagogues that are "warm." But what counts as "warmth"? And who determines what counts as warmth? Or they look for congregations that make them feel "like family." But to which "family" are we referring? The Waltons? Or the Mansons? And just what does being a "family congregation" mean? Does it mean that no single, divorced, or widowed Jews are welcome? (Unfortunately, too often, that is exactly what it means.) Or does it mean that if I go bankrupt or my health insurance runs out, the congregation will be that place where, in Robert Frost's words, "when you go there, they have to take you in"? When so much depends on such ill-defined individual feelings, preferences, and tastes, it can hardly be surprising that American Jews have so little success in finding what they are looking for. No wonder, either, that so many young American Jews remain unfazed by their parents' appeals and admonitions not to intermarry. If at the heart of American Judaism is nothing more than mere preference, why deny the heart its preference?

Fortunately, Moses did not come down from the mountain and

say to the people, "I have met the Lord, and I really like him. He's so warm, and welcoming, and, well, just *nice*." Significantly, it's that Sinai episode of the Exodus that the Judeo-American telling of the story omits, in fact, never even gets to. As we've seen, the Judeo-American version reaches its climax at the crossing of the Sea. That version relates the story as though God's command to Pharaoh were simply "Let my people go!" But according to the honest-to-God Exodus story, God's repeated directive to Pharaoh is significantly different: "Let my people go *that they may serve me!*" (Ex. 10:3) Contrary to a Judeo-American reading, the Exodus' goal was not merely to set the people free from Pharaoh's service. It was to make them free for God's service. Entering into God's service meant entering into a covenant of mutually binding commitments. It was by virtue of entry into that covenant that the community of the Jewish People came into being. A covenant of commitments transformed a mongrel mob into a community with a distinctive identity and destiny. To transform American synagogues from collections of random individuals into cohesive communities, what kind of covenantal commitments need to be undertaken?

One answer, of course, would be all the commandments in the Torah. But in our consumer society, where even Orthodox synagogues are minimalist synagogues in so far as they require only monetary dues for membership, our answer needs to focus on those shared practices that are *indispensable* for the possibility of Jews sharing *community* with one another.

Somewhere along the way, even the most Jewishly illiterate of us have heard in one form or another the saying, "The world stands on three things: on *Torah*, on *Avodah*, and on *Gemilut Chasadim*."[38] In other words, the world of any recognizably Jewish community depends on three core practices: study, worship or prayer, and acts of covenantal faithfulness. These are the three core practices Jews must keep alive to keep their story-based community alive. Study lets Jews know their story and its implications, prayer (*tefilla* in Hebrew) enables Jews to ask God for the strength to act on that story, and covenantal faithfulness—*chesed* for short—makes it possible for Jews to act the story out. In a sense, these three practices give an Exodus-led people their headings. *Torah* directs Jews "inward" so that they can internalize who and what they are to be. *Tefilla* directs Jews "upward" to seek Heaven's help so that they can become such people. *Chesed* directs Jews "outward" into the world to show how such a people, how such a community, can make a difference to the world.

Belonging to such a covenant-based community would mean observing this triad of practices and the commitments they express. It would mean spending a specific amount of time each week in communal Torah study and a specific amount of time each year attending worship services, particularly those that include the reading of the Torah. Most important, belonging to a community with a covenant at its core would mean keeping faith with that community and its covenant by supporting it not only financially, but through the performance of *ma'asim tovim*, "good deeds" such as visiting the sick, comforting the mourner, feeding the hungry, and sheltering the homeless. Members of a covenant-based community could of course take on additional *mitzvot*, but without shared commitments to at least *torah*, *tefilla*, and *chesed*, it's impossible to see how there could be any *Jewish* community at all.

Someone might object: "With the operative words in American society, 'autonomy' and 'choice,' how can we possibly make requirements for synagogue membership?" We already do. Every synagogue requires the payment of yearly monetary dues—which is why they are called *dues*. In fact, the keeping of those monetary commitments is virtually the only covenantal practice, the only *mitzvah*, observed by most American Jews. As important as that *mitzvah*—known as *tzedakah* - may be, it is insufficient to nourish any Jewish community or any Jewish soul beyond a mere subsistence level. Besides, what is the message it sends young Jews? Being Jewish, being part of the Jewish community, depends on money and virtually nothing else. What message could be more repulsive, especially to the young?

Jews seem to have forgotten that money, like survival, is not an end in itself, but only a means to an end. From the standpoint of the Exodus as well as of later Jewish tradition, wealth, survival, and, as we have seen, even freedom itself all gain importance only when they are put into the service of God. Communities are only rightly called Jewish when their resources are of such service. Losing sight of that goal and mistaking means, such as money, for ends, we will likely continue to lose young Jews' allegiance, because we will never even address, let alone answer, their most basic question, "Survival to what purpose?" Unless we become clear about what ought to be the goals, the point, of Jewish communal life, an assemblage of *machers* at a big-givers' dinner will continue to pass for Jewish "community" while what passes for Jewish "life" will continue to be ostentatious parties right out of *Good-bye Columbus*.

Perhaps no practice better illustrates just how deformed Jewish communal life has become than the observance of bar and bat mitzvah. Bar/bat mitzvah is a Jewish puberty rite. Like most such rites of passage, it is ideally a communal celebration of a young person's entry into adulthood by becoming skilled in a practice necessary for the community's continuation. For some human communities, it is hunting, for others, it is procreation. What "survival skill," then, does the puberty rite of bar or bat mitzvah celebrate? Traditionally understood, it celebrates a child's being called up to the Torah for the first time. On that occasion, the community rejoices that another Jew has demonstrated that he or she can *handle Torah*,[39] a skill whose regular practice the community cannot live without.

Except that most American Jewish "communities" do live without it. So what can they possibly celebrate except the celebration, each blowout trying to outdo the one preceding it? When Jewish children complain that they don't learn much worth knowing in Hebrew school, no one should doubt them. Given the skills contemporary Jewish communities rely on and the practices they hold dear, Hebrew schools should revise their curricula to emphasize fundraising and party-throwing.

Jews must realize that a school, any school, only works when it exists within the context of a community whose commitments and practices it passes on so that that community will live on. Most synagogue Hebrew schools (and even, I suspect, many Jewish day schools) fail, because they exist apart from any true community. They certainly do not exist within the context of a community living in the framework of a covenant. But if a synagogue were to covenant around the communal practices of *torah*, *tefilla*, and *chesed*, the focal points of its educational program would become clear. Each year, children's skill in these practices could be deepened; each year, such depth could be tested and demonstrated; and each year, the storyline of that community—and the Jewish People—could be extended toward the future.

Somebody, no doubt, is wondering, "What kind of Judaism would this be—Conservative, Reform, Orthodox, Reconstructionist?" It could be any of them if synagogues affiliated with these movements were willing to reorganize around a shared covenant. What would make such a synagogue distinctive would not be its affiliation but its formation, not its denomination, but its organization. What to name what I've proposed? Perhaps "Covenantal Judaism" would be best. At least as compared with the other current descriptors of Judaism (e.g.,

Orthodox, Conservative, etc.), ours comes from an actual Hebrew word, one as old the Hebrew Bible itself—*brit*. Still, "Covenantal Judaism" does sounds a little odd, if only because it sounds so redundant. How, after all, could there be any kind of historically recognizable Judaism—or any sort of genuinely Jewish community—that did not have a covenant at its heart?[40]

Are synagogues the only possible venues for building covenant communities? No. *Chavurot*, for instance, could easily organize around covenants of shared practices. However, not all Jewish organizations would find the exodus from an American model of membership to a Jewish one so smooth. Jewish federations have long prided themselves on being the "secular" arm of the Jewish community. They have not meant by that, of course, that they have no religious commitments. *Tzedakah* is a Jewish religious commitment if ever there was one, and many federation professionals and volunteers are religious, even observant Jews. But issues about God, Torah, and the People chosen to be God's-People-through-Torah typically have no place on federation agendas. As the word "secular" implies, federations have historically wanted a separation between *shul* and state. But when your communal master story is the Exodus, such separation is not only impossible, but also undesirable. According to that story, if God is not part of the community, there is no community. From the perspective of that narrative, if God's covenant with the community does not provide the framework for addressing communal issues, *that* should be an issue.

The American master story and its Judeo-American rendition of the Exodus may exalt the individual, but if the traditional Exodus narrative is your story, the very last thing you aspire to be is a lone individual. For who would want to be Pharaoh, the one person in the story who repeatedly and disastrously insists on demonstrating his individual autonomy? Everyone knows, except him, that his attempted assertion of individual will is an illusion, in reality only compulsive willfulness leading to ruin. And anyway, as we've said before, on a long desert trek, the worst thing you can do is strike out on your own: there are a thousand different ways to die in the wilderness. To keep any hope at all of reaching your place of promise, you need to stay close to others, to an Other, and to the relationship that binds all of you together. To be able even to know that, let alone to be able to do it, American Jews must restore the narration of the Jewish community's covenantal birth at Sinai to its rightful place in their recounting of the Exodus master story.

ii: Restoring the Judeo-Israeli Version of the
        Exodus Story

In its own way the standard Israeli reading of the Exodus master
story is as defective as the Judeo-American rendition. The Judeo-
Israeli version also misses the story's climax: Sinai. Many Israelis
mistakenly assume the climax is the Israelites' entry into the Land.
And yet, the story-shaped world fashioned by the Exodus portrays a
people "on the way" but not yet home. Note where the Jews' paradigmatic Torah (i.e., the Five Books of Moses) ends: with the people
preparing to enter the Land, but having not yet entered. The Jews of
the fifth century B.C.E. who decided that the Torah should end with
Deuteronomy (and not with the Book of Joshua where the Land's
settlement actually begins) had themselves only recently returned
to the Land from exile in Babylonia. Starkly put, they knew that
even in the Land, a Jew could still be in Exile.[41]

For what constituted the Land's promise was not some special
quality of the land itself (the way pagan nature-worshippers would
have it), but the kind of communal life practiced in it. Such a life is
not the result of the people's acting autonomously through some feat
of self-determination. Instead, according to the Exodus narrative, it
is the outcome of the people and God acting together at Sinai. Given
the Exodus' sequence of events, Sinai is the necessary precondition
for this particular people's living in this particular land. Following
the logic of the storyline, Israel's settlement of the Land presupposes
its agreement to a host of practices outlined at Sinai. If at Sinai, God
becomes Israel's king and Israel his subjects, then in the Land no one
should be subject to any laws but his. In other words, the Land of
Israel, inhabited by the People Israel, faithful subjects of the King of
Israel, can legitimately be home to no other polity than the Kingdom of Heaven on earth. Consequently, breaches of the Sinai covenant can—and do!—result in the removal of the people of Israel
from the Land and the (human) kings of Israel from the throne.
Conversely, restoration of those covenantal breaches results in restoration of all to their promised places.

Any Jewish state that fails to recognize the central role of the
covenant for its politics is illegitimate as a *Jewish* state. Whatever
political theory or rationale it might espouse likely springs from
somebody else's story. Such a story is easy to identify in the case of
the ancient Jewish monarchs against whom the prophets railed. The
old Canaanite myths of Ba'al, Anath, and gods other than the Lord

too often claimed the allegiance of the kings (and queens) of Israel and Judah.

We moderns, though, have been seduced by a different story. Stemming in part from the Enlightenment and in part from the Holocaust, it tempts us to worship that most dangerous of modern gods— ourselves. In the form of modern political Zionism, it would have us believe that the fate of the Jewish People is in the hands of the Jewish People alone, a people whose task in history is to do nothing more than survive.

Zionism essentially claims that the Jewish People rightfully ought to have its own state in the Land of Israel as the fundamental remedy to the problem of Jewish life in the Diaspora. On this much, virtually all Zionists agree. They disagree, however, about the specific nature of the problem the Diaspora poses for Jewish life and, hence, about the remedy itself. The two most dominant forms of Zionism, Herzlian and Revisionist, reflect just such disagreement. They also reflect the difficulties in store for a Jewish state that has forgotten the Jewish People's Exodus master story.

For Theodor Herzl and Herzlian Zionism, the overriding problem for Diaspora Jews is their fundamental, irremediable differentness from the non-Jews around them. As a Viennese correspondent covering the Dreyfus trial in Paris, Herzl became convinced that in France, Jews would ultimately never be considered Frenchmen, as in his native Austria, they would never be deemed true Austrians. In all places, he concluded, Jews were forever doomed to lead an abnormal existence. The remedy, therefore, would be the creation of a place where Jews might live a normal existence as a people like any other, that is, as a people with its own nation-state.

As many have pointed out, Herzl's position is paradoxical at best and self-defeating at worst: for Jews to be a people like any other, they must stop being Jews. Herzl's Zionism in this respect reflects his own fairly thin Jewish identity. At the time he reported on the Dreyfus case, he himself was a rather highly assimilated Jew, who had invested a significant amount of time in trying to convert young Jews to socialism. More revealing still, Herzl at one point was prepared to accept Uganda as the site for his proposed Jewish homeland.

Though Herzl's work was absolutely crucial for realizing the Zionist dream of a Jewish state, his hope that that state's establishment would make Jewish existence normal has gone unrealized. If anything, the years since the Holocaust and the establishment of the State of Israel have been among the most "abnormal" in Jewish history. After having been off the front pages of history for almost 2,000 years, Israel and the Jewish People are featured almost daily in newspapers and newscasts. If the State of Israel shows anything about the Jewish People, it is that, for better or worse, we are not like other peoples—nor likely ever to be. For Jews, therefore, only one question truly matters: "*How* should we be different?"

Ze'ev Jabotinsky's Zionism answers that question no better than Herzl's. For the Revisionists, the problem confronting Jews in the Diaspora is the unrelenting, not infrequently murderous anti-Semitism of Gentiles. A Jewish state thus becomes a safe haven and citadel from which a strong, united Jewry can defend itself. But just as the establishment of a Jewish state has not made Jewish existence any more normal, it has also not made Jewish existence any safer, particularly for those Jews who live in the Jewish state. Indeed, Israel is the one place in the world where a Jew faces greatest odds of being killed simply because he or she is a Jew.

But Revisionist Zionism has far deeper, far more disturbing flaws than that. To think that the State of Israel alone can save Jews in peril is dangerous fantasy. Why should anyone suppose that the State of Israel by itself could have defeated the Nazi forces when the combined forces of the United States, Britain, and the Soviet Union barely managed to do it? Moreover, even if there had been a State of Israel during the Holocaust, how effective could it have been in rescuing Europe's Jews? David Wyman estimates that by the time hard evidence of the Nazi genocide first reached the West in mid-1942, two million Jews had already been murdered, with the killing continuing full-bore and with the Nazis in control of most of Europe. Wyman surmises that even if there had been concerted action by the Allies to save Jewish lives, at most, they (and presumably a State of Israel had it existed) would have been able to save several hundred thousand lives, a by no means insignificant number, but certainly nowhere near six million.[42] Furthermore, even with a Jewish state established, the rescue of Jews in peril still significantly depends on the aid and goodwill of non-Jews. For instance, before Israel could serve as a haven for Jews from Ethiopia and the Soviet Union, the United States had to act to pry open those two countries' doors so that Jews could leave in the first place.

Nor will it suffice to attribute such U.S. action to the "political clout" of American Jews, who have learned post-Holocaust, so the standard "argument" runs, that they must be vocal in speaking out. In 1985, when President Reagan was about to visit a German military cemetery in Bitburg in which SS men were buried, American

Jews protested vigorously. One of them, Elie Wiesel, happened to be going to the White House to receive a medal. Television carried the event live. When it came time for him to speak, Wiesel looked at the President and before a national audience implored him not to visit the cemetery: "That place, Mr. President, is not your place. Your place is with the victims of the SS." Reagan went anyway. He wanted to keep good relations with the Germans—as though the Germans might somehow turn instead to the Russians for good relations. Despite their having had far more access to America's President and despite America's having had far less at stake, Wiesel and the American Jewish community proved to be just as ineffective as those American Jews fifty years ago who pleaded with the Allies to bomb Auschwitz, only to be told that it was not in the overall interest of the war effort. In the balance of power, even with a strong American Jewish community and a stronger Jewish state, the Jewish People still ultimately lacks the power to be the sole determiner of its own fate. Much of that power still remains in large part where it always has, namely, in the hands of non-Jews—and of God.

For a secular, Revisionist, Holocaust-dependent Zionism, no message could be worse. Worse yet, however, is the underlying assumption of such a Zionism, because it implicitly grants the worst thing the enemies of Zionism have ever said about it, namely, that it is racist.[43] What is the underlying assumption about non-Jews reflected by Revisionist Zionism? Just this: You can't trust *any of them*—not the ones who fought with the Allies against the Nazis, not the ones who sheltered Jews from the Nazis, not even the ones not yet born. At long last, it seems, a form of the toxic, age-old teaching of the Church has taken hold of Jewish hearts. As the Church once condemned for eternity a whole people on the charge of deicide, Jews now condemn for all time a whole people on the charge of genocide. Strikingly, the Torah points to eventual reconciliation even with those Nazis of ancient times, the Egyptians, who were the first to employ genocide and slave labor as means to exterminate the Jewish People: "You shall not abhor an Egyptian, for you were a stranger in his land" (Deut. 23:8).

In light of the Exodus master story, the significance of the stranger takes on a special meaning, especially the stranger living in the midst of a Jewish state: "You shall not wrong a stranger or oppress him, because you were strangers in the land of Egypt."[44] Again and again in the Torah, God unconditionally enjoins those who would be faithful members of the community he redeemed to show care for those who are outsiders with respect to that community. For a Jewish state, insider politics must make room for outsiders—particularly for those outsiders living there closest to us, those strangers from whom we have tragically become most estranged: Palestinians. Even in our homeland, we must make accommodations for such outsiders in a way that lets them reside among us. The last chapter discussed Emil Fackenheim's 614th commandment meant to prevent Jews from giving Hitler a posthumous victory through intermarriage and assimilation. But there are other ways to let the Nazis triumph. One way is for Jews, history's outsiders par excellence, to forget the Exodus story and adopt the Nazis' master story in its place. The Nazi story says that the outsider, the alien, the stranger are threats to the well-being of the body politic, bacteria and vermin that must be extirpated without mercy. If Jews succumb to the Nazis' story by implicitly adopting it, the Holocaust will have claimed its final victim: the Exodus master story and the people, god, and covenant of which it speaks.

Ironically, the so-called "religious" Zionists from whom we might expect the greatest sensitivity to the Torah's oft-repeated commandment about treatment of the stranger often seem the Jews most oblivious to it. They are frequently those Jews who, as settlers in the territories or as supporters of various religious parties, defend the use of terrorism and other acts of retribution against innocent Arabs. Some have even proposed expelling Arabs en masse through a policy of "transference," a code word reminiscent of another cold-blooded euphemism used not so long ago: "The Final Solution."[45]

To be sure, strangers, outsiders, that is, non-Jews living among Jews, must obey the laws Jews make for them. No one should romanticize the real threat some Palestinians and Arabs pose to the State of Israel. While pacifism is a Christian virtue, it is not a Jewish one. Self-defense is. Accordingly, non-Jews who commit acts of violence against a Jewish state should be punished, for they challenge the rule of Jewish law. But that law is even more plainly challenged, if not altogether undermined, when the state, the Jewish state, resorts to punishing the innocent together with the guilty. Those Israelis who fancy themselves "religious" while mouthing platitudes about entrusting the State's security to God would do well to remember the warning Jeremiah gave the first Jewish commonwealth right before its demise:

Thus said the Lord of Hosts, the God of Israel: "Mend your ways and your actions, and I will let you dwell in this place. Don't put your trust in illusions and say, 'The Temple of the Lord, the Temple of the Lord, the Temple of the Lord are these [buildings].' No, *if you really mend your ways and your actions; if you execute justice between one man and another; if you do not oppress the stranger, the orphan, and the widow, if you do not shed the blood of the innocent in this place, if you do not follow other gods, to your own hurt—then only will I let you dwell in this place, in the land that I gave to your fathers for all time."* (Jer. 7:3–7)[46]

Turning their backs on the stranger spells disaster for Jews and for their survival as Jews, for in turning away from the stranger, Jews turn their backs on their own story and, hence, on who they are themselves. But should Jews turn away nonetheless, then they can make no serious moral complaint about the world's indifference to their suffering as quintessential strangers, whether during the Holocaust or at other times in Jewish history, past, present, and future. Nor, for that matter, can Jews address any serious complaint to God should he dispossess them from the Land, for even in "their" land, their basic status as stranger, as outsider, remains unchanged, as the Lord himself reminds them: "The land is Mine; you are but resident aliens with Me" (Lev. 25:23). Though the Land may be promised to the Jewish People unconditionally throughout time, the People's ability to dwell in the Land at any particular time is always conditional on its behavior in the Land. Ultimately, Israel's Land belongs to God,[47] whose Torah spells out the provisions for Israel's tenancy.

That message—that God is the ultimate owner of the Land—is as hard to make heard in our time as it was in Jeremiah's. Part of what makes it so hard to hear is a phenomenon that faces us just as it faced Jeremiah: the false prophet. On staff at the royal court and temple, the false prophet, though purportedly "speaking for God," typically spoke only for the reward the (human) powers-that-be would provide when he told them what they wanted to hear. Thus, the false prophet Hananiah opposed Jeremiah, assuring the elite that everything would be fine in only a short time. Like other false prophets, his message was "All is well, all is well."[48] Unlike Jeremiah, Hananiah spoke not one word calling for reflection or repentance.

While the office of king has disappeared from among the Jewish People, the post of false prophet unfortunately has not. One such figure is Irving "Yitz" Greenberg, every non-Orthodox Jew's favorite Orthodox rabbi. Like the court prophets of old, he and his organization, CLAL,[49] are heavily dependent for funding on the major powers of the Jewish community, such as the Council of Jewish Federations and the United Jewish Appeal. Like his predecessors, Greenberg has fashioned words that are ready-made to turn aside any criticism of his masters. He has written, for instance, "I have come to see that anyone who insists that Israel be consistently judged by a higher standard of behavior than . . . others is an anti-Semite."[50] By Greenberg's standard, Jeremiah must have been an anti-Semite. So also must have been most of Israel's other prophets as well as most of the Bible's writers—including God. For God, Jeremiah, the other prophets, indeed Jewish tradition itself, all hold Israel, both the political entity and the people, to a higher standard. Certainly, the Jewish People were no worse than the Assyrians, the Babylonians, or the Romans. Nonetheless, Assyrians, Babylonians, and Romans were not picked as benchmarks of behavior, anymore than Palestinian terrorists or Syrian thugs ought to be. Instead, another yardstick was chosen—*Torah*.

What makes a state or people Jewish is adherence to the Sinai covenant and the Torah practices that stem from it. That is why, in the Exodus narrative, Israel's entry into the covenant precedes its entry into the Land. That is how that other sacred mountain in Jewish history, Zion, the symbol of Israel's political aspirations, can be invoked at the opening of the Torah service, which is Sinai re-enacted: "For Torah shall come forth from Zion, and the word of the Lord from Jerusalem; blessed be He who in his holiness gave Torah to his people Israel." Notice the first half of Isaiah 2:3 which precedes the vision of Torah issuing from Zion: "And the many peoples shall go and say, 'Let us go up to the Mount of the Lord, to the House of the God of Jacob, that He may instruct us in his ways, and that we may walk in his paths.' " The passage makes it clear that the politics of a Jewish state is not merely to be the politics of that state alone. The politics of a Jewish state ultimately must be the politics of God.

For a Jewish state, contra Herzlian Zionism, cannot be a state like any other state. It must be instead the embodiment of the Kingdom of Heaven on earth, with Jerusalem, from which the King's edicts emanate, not only as the Jewish state's capital city, but the world's. Thus, by its very nature, such a state, contra Revisionist Zionism, cannot be a fortress shut up against the non-Jewish world, but rather a place of pilgrimage whose guidance the world seeks. Finally, such a state, contra certain "religious" Zionists, must be a place that takes a special interest in safeguarding not only, for example, the sabbath, but also the strangers in its midst. For those who would truly be *k'doshim*, faithful witnesses to what the Jewish People claims as the truth about God, Torah, and itself, no testimony can be more powerful than that provided by Jews' conduct in conducting the affairs of the State of Israel. If Torah is instruction for the "real world," the whole world, and not just "religious" blather confined to pulpits and *kashrut* certificates, then its validity will be confirmed or negated by the communities and polities that Jews form. Now that peace seems to be breaking out in the Middle East, it will be revealing whether those who have claimed to be Israel's supporters in the past will continue to be so in the future as the military threat to her existence diminishes. Supporting and developing an Israel at peace is as or more significant to Jewish history than any number of victories in war.

Some have characterized American society as a "community of strangers" in which people encounter one another as potentially hostile adversaries—hence, the law court language of "persons" and "rights" so dominant in American moral and political discourse. Jews, however, are to form a community of former strangers which, for that very reason, is never to be estranged from strangers. In the end, the Household of Israel, like the Land of Israel, is to be home neither to prototypical victims nor to paradigmatic heroes. Its members must instead be former outsiders in possession of the most prized insider knowledge of all: There is no irredeemable class of "outsider," of stranger to be feared, if insiders will but realize it. If there is any redemptive, saving Torah to be learned from Jews' victimization through history, it is this: "The stranger who resides with you shall be to you as one of your home-born; you shall love him as yourself, for you were strangers in the land of Egypt: I the Lord am your God" (Lev. 19:34). For the House of Israel to legitimately occupy the Land of Israel, it must become home to just such wisdom. The House of Israel will then become like Isaiah's prophesied House of God—sought by outsiders on account of the wisdom it houses, a kind not attainable elsewhere in the world. Those who would be at home both in the House of Israel and the House of God must live by such wisdom as *k'doshim*, God's holy ones. In the last analysis, to be a member of the Household of Israel is to bear a family resemblance to its most venerated and beloved relation, God. To be a member of the Community of Israel means bearing a resemblance to no other community on earth.

Notes

1. Tom Segev, *The Seventh Million: The Israelis and the Holocaust*, trans. Haim Watzman (New York: Hill and Wang, 1993), p. 444.

2. Ibid., p. 183.

3. David Wyman, *The Abandonment of the Jews: American and the Holocaust, 1941–1945* (New York: Pantheon Books, 1984), p. 9.

4. *Encyclopedia Judaica*, s.v. "Frank, Anne," by Jozeph Michman.

5. Cf. David Biale, *Power and Powerlessness in Jewish History: The Jewish Tradition and the Myth of Passivity* (New York: Shocken Books, 1986), pp. 15, 59, 73–74.

6. Segev, p. 361.

7. Ibid., p. 516.

8. I first heard this story from Rachel Adler, who in turn heard it from many different people while living in a Chasidic community.

9. Again, I am indebted to Rachel Adler for helping me to see this point.

10. For a penetrating overview of the subject, see Joseph Amato, *Victims and Values: A History and Theory of Suffering*, with a Foreword by Eugen Weber (New York: Greenwood Press, 1990).

11. David Rieff, "Victims All?" *Harper's Magazine*, October 1991, p. 51.

12. David Blumenthal, *Facing the Abusing God: A Theology of Protest* (Philadelphia: Westminster/John Knox Press, 1993). If Blumenthal's calling God an abuser does not count as blasphemy, then we have no category of blasphemy.

13. Segev, p. 474.

14. Ibid, p. 399.

15. Amato, pp. 159–60.

16. Rieff, p. 53.

17. An observation made on C-Span, "Booknotes," 29 November 1992, by Charles J. Sykes, author of *A Nation of Victims* (New York: St. Martin's Press, 1992).

18. Cf. Thomas L. Friedman, *From Beirut to Jerusalem* (New York: Doubleday, 1990), pp. 357–59.

19. ABC, "This Week With David Brinkley," 7 February 1993.

20. Arthur Hertzberg, "An Open Letter to Elie Wiesel," *New York Times Book Review*, 18 August 1988, p. 14.

21. Josephus, *The Jewish War*, Book 7: Chapter 8, in *The Works of Josephus*, vol. 4, ed. and trans. William Whiston (Boston and New York: C. T. Brainard Publishing Co., n.d.), pp. 335, 336, 342.

22. In Chapters 1 and 3.

23. Segev, p. 424.

24. Ibid., p. 447.

25. See *Encyclopedia of Religion*, s.v. "Josephus, Flavius," by David Altshuler.

26. Cf. Yehoshafat Harkabi, *The Bar Kokhba Syndrome: Risk and Realism in International Politics*, trans. Max Ticktin and ed. David Altshuler (Chappaqua, NY: Rossel Books, 1983).

27. Yad, Hilchot Yesodei HaTorah, 5:1. Qualifications of the basic rule include, e.g., the specific transgressions to be committed (the prohibitions on idolatry, sexual impropriety, and murder must not be breached under any circumstances), the composition of the audience witnessing the transgression (otherwise permissible transgressions are barred in the presence of 10 or more Jews) and the intent of the non-Jew in requiring the transgression

(committing the transgression is forbidden if part of an overall policy to wipe out Judaism). Nonetheless, all these qualifications are just that—*qualifications of a more basic principle* that Jews are to show commitment to God and Torah by living, rather than dying, on their behalf.

28. What then about murder? For on Masada, a few were chosen to kill the others—including children—before killing themselves. Such stories are also told about the Jews of York, who killed their own children and themselves rather than fall victim to rampaging Christian mobs.

29. See Lucy S. Dawidowicz, *The War Against the Jews: 1933-1945* (New York: Holt, Rinehart, and Winston, 1975), pp. 196, 217.

30. As Jews from Eastern Europe did not choose suicide as a way of escape, neither did they attempt to elude their fate by abandoning other Jews to theirs. Said one survivor, "No one . . . dared escape and leave his father, mother, brother. Our solidarity was on religious and family grounds." By contrast, those relatively few who did attempt escape were typically young people without any close family ties. See Raul Hilberg, *Perpetrators, Victims, Bystanders: The Jewish Catastrophe, 1933–1945* (New York: Harper Collins, 1992), p. 176.

31. Irving J. Rosenbaum, *The Holocaust and Halakhah* (New York: KTAV Publishing House, Inc., 1976), p. 98.

32. Ibid., p. 99.

33. Yad, Hilchot Yesodei HaTorah, 5:11.

34. Cf., e.g., Ex. 4:10.

35. Cf. Chapter 4, pp. 73–74. See also the excellent discussions in Alasdair MacIntyre's *After Virtue: A Study in Moral Theory* (Notre Dame, IN: University of Notre Dame Press, 1981) and Stephen Toulmin's *Cosmopolis: The Hidden Agenda of Modernity* (Chicago: University of Chicago Press, 1990).

36. I have used the phrase "Judeo-American" in this section and "Judeo-Israeli" in the next to indicate that in these forms of Jewish identity—and of identification with the Exodus master story—Jewishness is a mere "add-on," a modifier at best, while the substance of identity comes from identification with and through the larger surrounding culture and its story. Historically, it has not always been that way, nor need it be that way today. Just as the previous eras could speak of "Babylonian Jews" and "French Jews"—rather than of "Jewish Babylonians" or "Jewish Frenchmen"—one can still find, despite the strength and allure of the broader culture, such people as "American Jews."

37. According to the 1990 National Jewish Population survey, only 41% of Jewish households currently affiliate with synagogues. See Barry A. Kosmin et al., *Highlights of the CJF National Jewish Population Survey* (New York: Council of Jewish Federations, [n.d.]), p. 53.

38. Attributed to Simon the Just in Avot 1:2.

39. Literally as well as figuratively!

40. The communal structure I am suggesting is no mere theoretical construct. It has existed at Congregation *Lev Chadash* in Indianapolis. *Lev Chadash*, which means "New Heart," was originally organized around a covenant among the members, who besides committing a certain amount of money annually to sustain the congregation also committed a specific amount of time each year to communal study, worship, and good deeds. I

am told that some *chavurot* also have been organized around such shared, nonfinancial commitments.

41. Cf. James A Sanders, *Torah and Canon* (Philadelphia: Fortress Press, 1972), Part I.

42. Wyman, pp. ix, 331.

43. Rabbi Arnold Jacob Wolf brought this irony to my attention.

44. Cf., e.g, Ex. 22:20, 23:9, and Deut.10:19. A brief scan of any biblical concordance will reveal at least 30 instances of the *ger*, i.e., the stranger, being singled out as a person who is to be *of special care and concern within the Israelite community*.

45. In reality, such purportedly religious Jews may not be totally oblivious to the obligations God and Torah ordained for the treatment of non-Jews in their midst. They have repeatedly tried to identify Arabs with those non-Jews whom Torah has marked for destruction, namely, Canaanites and Amalekites. But such attempts at identification, or better, at redefinition, will not work. Rabbinic tradition already ruled long ago that the Canaanites and Amalekites exist no more. Clearly, the Arabs, whether Christians or Muslims, can in no way be considered polytheistic pagans. Muslims in particular are notoriously monotheistic and iconoclastic, and hence not possibly identifiable with the idolatrous polytheists of ancient times.

46. NJPS translation.

47. As Rashi, the eleventh-century commentator, remarks on Gen. 1:1 in answer to the question of why the Torah, the "law book" of the Jewish People, begins with the account of Creation rather than with the first commandment given to the Jews during the Exodus: "Should the nations of the world say to Israel, 'You are brigands, for you took by conquest the land(s) of the seven [Canaanite] nations,' Israel can reply, 'The whole earth belongs to the Holy One Blessed be He. He created it, and he gave it to whomever he saw fit. When it pleased him, he gave it to [the Canaanites], and when it [later] pleased him, he took it from them and gave it to us.' "

48. Cf. Jeremiah 28 and 6:14, 8:11, 23:17.

49. The National Jewish Center for Learning and Leadership.

50. Irving Greenberg, *The Ethics of Jewish Power: A Series—The Ethics of Jewish Power I* (New York: National Jewish Resource Center [1983]), p. 2.

Chapter 7

Why Should Jews Survive?

The Jewish holiday preceding Passover is Purim. It celebrates one of the best-known stories in the Bible. Virtually every child with even a minimum of Jewish education knows the story, both because it is told each year (ad nauseam) in most religious schools and because practically every synagogue has some sort of Purim observance that children are expressly invited to attend.

In many respects, the Purim story rings true to Jews' historical experience. Implicit within the holiday's very name—*Purim*, meaning "lots"—is the notion that the Jewish People's existence is a dicey thing. What sets the Purim narrative into motion is the capriciousness of King Ahashverosh, ruler of Persia and Media, potentate over "a hundred and twenty-seven provinces from India to Nubia" (Esther 1:1). On a whim, during the seventh day of a drinking binge in his capital, Shushan, Ahashverosh decides to show off the beauty of his queen, Vashti. Vashti, who shows herself not to be very even-tempered or predictable either, refuses to appear. In response, the fickle king, following an advisor's suggestion, deposes Vashti and holds a beauty contest to find her replacement. The girl on whom fortune smiles is Esther, the ward of Mordechai the Jew. However, neither Esther nor Mordechai feels lucky enough, secure enough, to reveal to Ahashverosh Esther's Jewish background, including her Hebrew name, Hadassah. The name Esther may have seemed safer, derived as it is from "Ishtar," a fertility goddess worshiped by the Babylonians and Persians.[1]

In any case, more good fortune yet awaits the Jews in Ahashverosh's realm. While sitting by the city gate one day, Mordechai
overhears two disaffected royal officials plotting violence against
the throne. He tells Esther about the conspiracy, and she relays it to
her husband the king, who has the officials executed and Mordechai's name recorded for reward.

Suddenly, Mordechai's luck turns sour. As he sits by the city
gate on another day, Haman, the new chief advisor to the king,
strolls past. Everybody bows before him—except Mordechai. Haman, it turns out, is an Agagite, descended from the Jews' ancient
archenemy, Amalek, whom they had long ago been sworn to extir-
pate.[2] Haman is either unaware of this long-standing enmity or,
more likely, downright uninterested. The only thing that interests
him is Mordechai's refusal to bow before him.

Vowing vengeance, Haman intends to do away not only with
Mordechai, but also with all the Jews in Ahashverosh's empire. He
has the lot[3] cast to pick a propitious date for exterminating them.
Afterwards, he heads to the palace to seek the king's consent. He
describes the Jews as a people unlike any other in the realm; they
follow their own laws rather than the king's. Then Haman tells
Ahashverosh something that really gets his attention—and ultimate
approval. Haman will personally see to it that ten thousand silver
talents go to the royal treasury in exchange for the king's permission
to commit genocide. Ahashverosh gives Haman his signet ring to
seal the royal decree, which couriers then spread abroad throughout
the empire. Haman and the king sit down for (what else?) a drinking
feast. "But the city of Shushan was dumbfounded" (3:15).

Still, the odds against the Jews may not be all that bad. After all,
they have somebody "on the inside" near and dear to the king's heart.
But what rotten luck! As Esther explains to Mordechai, no one may
enter the king's presence without first having been summoned by
him, and, alas, he has not called for her in a month. How bitterly
ironic, and what a perverse twist of fortune. Esther became the queen
because her predecessor refused to go to Ahashverosh when summoned, and now she herself cannot go to him *unless* summoned.
Nevertheless, Mordechai refuses to take "No" for an answer. He sends
Esther word that if the plan for the Jews' extermination succeeds, her
rank will not save her—she will end up like all the other Jews in the
empire: dead. More ominously, he tells her that if she remains silent
in this crisis, "relief and deliverance will come to the Jews from another quarter, while you and your father's house will perish" (4:14).
And besides, who knows? Perhaps she has attained her present posi-

tion for this very purpose. Esther gives in and agrees to go to the king unsummoned. But her words make her appear far from confident, as though she is already resigned to her fate: "If I perish, I perish" (4:16). To Esther, the Jews' continued survival looks truly chancy.

Luckily, though, Esther knows her man. She goes to see Ahashverosh with an invitation for both him and Haman to come to a drinking party. In order to get the volatile king "in the mood," she cleverly waits until the bacchanalia's second day to make her case on her people's behalf. The previous night, however, the king had had trouble getting to sleep—too much partying that day perhaps? He had asked to be read the royal records concerning people to whom the throne owed a favor. When Mordechai's good deed was mentioned, Ahashverosh called in Haman for his advice on the proper way to honor such a man. Talk about a lucky break! And none too soon, because Haman, it turns out, had just finished having a gallows constructed for Mordechai's execution.

Next day, when Ahashverosh and Haman rejoin Esther to resume the festivities, she reveals to the king what Haman has in mind for her and for the other Jews of the realm. She quickly adds that she would not have even presumed on the king's valuable time if the Jews had been destined only for slavery. But genocide is, well, a bit more serious. Ahashverosh, as mercurial as ever, storms out of the room whereupon Haman throws himself on Esther's mercy by prostrating himself on her couch. Poor Haman, such lousy luck! For just then, Ahashverosh returns, only to discover Haman "lying prostrate on the couch on which Esther reclined"; enraged, the king cries out, "Does he mean . . . to ravish the queen in my own palace?" (7:8) Ahashverosh decrees that Haman be executed on the gallows meant for Mordechai and that Mordechai be installed in Haman's place as chief advisor.

As for the other Jews in the empire, they are on their own. Because a royal edict has previously gone out decreeing their deaths, only another royal edict can serve to save them—or at least permit them to take up arms to defend themselves against any assailants. In the end, Dame Fortune proves to be with the Jews, and they prevail over their enemies.

For Mordechai the Jew ranked next to King Ahashverosh and was highly regarded by the Jews and popular with the multitude of his brethren; he sought the good of his people and interceded for the welfare of his kindred. (10:3)

And they all lived happily ever after.

Though most would agree that the story of Esther is not historically true, many would say that it nonetheless rings true to Jewish
history. The fortunes of Jews throughout history have risen and
fallen depending on their having been in the right place at the right
time—or vice versa. Often, their welfare depended on the whims of
tyrants such as Ahashverosh, men of measly morals and avaricious
appetites. Ahashverosh is never concerned about the actual fate of
the Jews for good or ill. His only concern is how their continuation
or annihilation will affect his kingly cravings: He is willing to let the
Jews be killed for the sake of his pocketbook, and he is willing to let
them live for the sake of his passion. Near the story's end, he proves
to be, despite his pomp and bluster, so weak a figure that he cannot
even recall his own edict. Yet, his is precisely the kind of worldly
power on which Jews have had to rely and stake their lives throughout history.

And what about the others in the story? What about Haman,
for example? Like many of Jews' enemies over the centuries, he is
driven by a single-minded hatred that is anything but rational.
Because of some perceived personal slight by one Jew, he wants to
annihilate all Jews. Meanwhile, Haman's nemesis, Mordechai, is
the archetypal *stadtlan*, the Jewish community's intercessor with
the non-Jewish authorities. Mordechai's position depends on his
sechel, his savvy, for quickly sizing up and matching up the mutual
interests of Jews and non-Jews. And what of Esther? She is certainly
no Deborah. In the beginning, at least, she is neither candid about
her Jewish identity nor courageous in displaying it. Nor is she particular about her chastity. With a little prompting from Mordechai,
she voluntarily enters the beauty pageant, where the winner gets to
join the harem of a non-Jewish king. In the Purim story, as in other
instances throughout Jewish history, politics does indeed make
strange bedfellows.

Finally, in regard to the Purim story, there is one more character
to speak about. Only this character is notably absent from the story;
in the view of many contemporary Jews, this character has remained
absent from Jewish history as a whole. The character, of course, is
God. God is not even mentioned in the Purim story, not even in those
places where we might expect to find him mentioned. Thus, when
Mordechai tells Esther that if she refuses to come to the Jews' aid,
help would nevertheless come "from another place," the most that
can be said is that Mordechai *might* be alluding to God's interven-
tion. Later, in an episode where we would usually expect to hear of
God's presence, all we encounter is his absence. Typically, God sig-

nals non-Jewish rulers in their dreams.[4] By contrast in the Purim story, Ahashverosh receives the vital information which eventually leads to his saving Mordechai precisely because he cannot fall asleep.

The plain reading of the Purim narrative makes it clear that Jews' salvation does not depend on the "mighty hand and out-stretched arm" of God. For many Jews, the story of Purim could easily serve as a metaphor for the whole of Jewish history. Like the Jews in Shushan and in the rest of Ahashverosh's realm, these post-Holocaust Jews feel they can turn to no one for salvation but them-selves. From such a perspective, the Purim story is anything but a fairy tale. Instead, it is the all-too-true-to-life story of the Jewish People in the real world. In that world, Esther, Mordechai, and all other Jews need fear an Ahashverosh at least as much as a Haman, for the caprices of history always entail the chance that Jews will be doomed to death again. For such Jews, survival is assured only until next time.

And yet, before we set all of Jewish history within the context of the Purim story, we should consider the Jewish context within which that narrative receives its paradigmatic telling and hearing. For it is within the framework of the observance of Purim that *megillat Esther* is read by Jews amid much merrymaking, noisemaking, and making themselves so drunk that they "cannot tell the difference between 'cursed be Haman' and 'blessed be Mordechai.' "[5] In other words, the paradigmatic telling of the Purim story enjoins Jews not to take the story seriously! To those Jews who might view the story as an overarch-ing metaphor for Jewish history, Jewish tradition requires them in-stead to take it as a joke. Historically, Purim marked the one time during the year when Jews could dress up and pretend to be *goyim*, thereby making fun not only of those *goyim* but also more signifi-cantly of the world those *goyim* accounted powerful and real.

Traditional Jews could make a laughingstock of the Purim story's world, because they knew which holiday follows Purim: *Pesach*. On Passover, Jews tell another story, the Exodus from Egypt. During that narrative's paradigmatic telling (i.e., through the Hag-gadah at seder) the story is told with all the seriousness—and joy—the tellers can muster:

We were slaves to Pharaoh in Egypt, and God brought us out from there with a strong hand and an outstretched arm. Had the Holy One blessed be He not brought out our ancestors from Egypt, then, look! We and our children and our children's children would still be enslaved to Pharaoh in Egypt!

To be sure, some Jews who take their cue from Purim—and the Holocaust—might agree that parts of the Exodus narrative, like pieces of the Purim story, ring true to the misfortunes of later Jewish history. Just as Jacob's family trekked down to Egypt to escape the famine in Canaan, subsequent migrations of the Household of Israel have often been driven by dire economic necessity. Moreover, the ensuing harsh treatment of Jacob's descendants by the Egyptians has parallels with Jews' experience in countless other times and places. Though initially welcomed because of their economic know-how, Jews frequently found that when regimes changed, so did the host country's attitude toward them, with persecution invariably following.[6] Ultimately, though, for Jews whose history runs along a Purim/Holocaust axis, the story told on Pesach must sound utterly preposterous.

The Exodus narrative's vision of Jewish life, of life itself, is different from the Purim story's. While the Exodus story has an element of chance in it—Will Pharaoh's daughter spare the baby floating among the reeds? Will Moses turn aside to investigate the burning bush?—chance is not all there is in the world. Nor is a willful, Haman-like foe all there is in the world either. For there is also a God at work in the world, who is anything but capricious, who is more resolute in attaining his goals than any Haman, let alone any Ahashverosh, could ever imagine. In an Exodus-framed world, Jews do not have the luxury, like some Mordechai or Esther, of hiding their identities. Their being saved hinges neither on a Mordechai's shrewdness nor on an Esther's inventiveness. Instead, all depends on their identifying themselves as *God's*—lest the tenth plague destroy them along with the rest of Egypt. Perhaps most important, the Purim story comes to a close after the Jews' adversaries are vanquished throughout Ahashverosh's empire. But when the Jews' Egyptian pursuers meet their end at the Sea, the Exodus story is just beginning. From its perspective, Jewish history is about more than rescue. More fundamentally, it's about redemption.

The range of what redemption encompasses for Jews is best expressed through a practice the classical rabbis created for the seder, that ritual meal in which Jews are required to internalize and digest the meaning of the Exodus. The sages prescribed that four cups of wine be drunk, each corresponding to a Hebrew verb for redemption found in Exodus 6:6–7, a passage in which God previews for Moses the redemption story to unfold in Egypt:

Therefore, say to the children of Israel: I am the Lord. I will *free* [v'hotzati][7] you from the labors of the Egyptians, and I will *snatch* [v'hitzalti][8] you from their bondage. I will *redeem* [*v'ga'alti*] you with an outstretched arm and through great acts of judgment. I will *take* [*v'lakachti*] you for my People, and I will be your God, and you shall know that I, the Lord, am your God who freed[9] you from the labors of the Egyptians.

The first two verbs of deliverance, *hotzati* and *hitzalti*, have Purim-like overtones. There is rescue from suffering, hardship, enslavement, even perhaps from death itself. All the same, however, such deliverance remains only rescue *from*; it connotes no sense of preservation *for*, of salvation *for*, of survival *for*. Only the next two verbs, *ga'alti* and *lakachti*, point Jews' lives to a purpose beyond continued physical existence.

"And I will redeem you. . . ." In its various forms, the Hebrew root *g-'a-l* expresses the archetypal notion of redemption in Judaism.[10] One who practices redemption is called a *go'el*, whom the biblical scholar Nahum Sarna characterizes as "near kin who [has] primary responsibility for protecting or regaining persons and property for the extended family."[11] If an Israelite, to repay a debt, were forced to sell off his ancestral holding or, in the most dire case, himself and his family into servitude, a close kinsman had the obligation to come and redeem that which the relative had sold, whether land or persons.[12] Significantly, the Bible makes no moral judgment regarding the relative who had fallen into such impoverished circumstances. The Torah is not interested in whether the person was an irresponsible spendthrift who "deserved" what happened to him. Its only interest is the duty of that person's kinsman to serve as *go'el*.

But there was another way a kinsman could serve as *go'el*, and it, too, had to do with settling accounts. However, instead of money, blood was the currency of exchange. In the early stage of Israel's settlement of Canaan, there was no strong central authority, only a loose tribal confederation. When a member of one clan killed, even inadvertently, someone from a different clan, the deceased's kinsman had the obligation to play the role of *go'el ha'dam*, "the blood redeemer."[13] In this capacity, the kinsman, like a Fury from Greek tragedy, was obliged to pursue the manslayer relentlessly until he killed him or until the pursued gained admission to a city of refuge, a kind of "home base" where he was safe in this bloody game of tag.[14]

In either case, however, God stood as Israel's quintessential *go'el*, its redeemer par excellence. Thus, Israel, forced to go down to Egypt due to economic necessity and eventually enslaved because of it, has God, its *go'el*, to redeem it from servitude—and to return it to its ancestral holding, Canaan:

I established my covenant with [Israel's patriarchs], to give them the land of Canaan, the land in which they lived as sojourners. I have now heard the moaning of the Israelites because the Egyptians are holding them in bondage, and I have remembered my covenant. (Ex. 6:4–5)

Meanwhile, Ex. 4:22–23 explicitly depicts God as the blood redeemer who instructs Moses to say to Pharaoh: "Israel is my first-born son. I have said to you, 'Let my son go, that he may worship me,' but you refuse to let him go. So look! Now I will slay your first-born son."[15] Either way, whether God as *go'el* comes to Israel's aid to settle accounts in an economic sense or in a retributive one, the metaphorical implication is inescapable: God stands as close to Israel as kin, and like any other kinfolk among the community of Israel, he will honor his commitments to set things right for those near to him.

"And I will take you for my People, and I will become for you God." The image of God the redeemer who saves out of a sense of personal relationship and hence, of personal responsibility, is intensified by the use of a phrase that, in Sarna's words, "suggests the institution of marriage."[16] Like some hero in a classical romance or love story, God first rescues his beloved Israel from distress in Egypt, then enters into eternal union with her. Indeed, the wording here closely resembles that of ancient Israel's wedding vow: "I will take you for my wife, and I will become for you a husband."[17] As a result, Israel for her part will come to have close, intimate relations with God: "And you shall know [in the biblical sense, i.e., by first-hand, personal experience] that I am the Lord your God" (Ex. 6:7).

But the language of Ex. 6:6–7 suggests a relationship far broader than marriage. Coming at the beginning of the Exodus master story, it points to the story's denouement at Sinai. As Sarna correctly notes, the passage expresses God's intentions and hence "prefigures the covenant that is to be established at Sinai."[18] Sinai is the story's high point, because it is the place where the relationship between God and the Jewish People climaxes in a mutual covenant between the two. True, God had long before entered into a covenant with Abraham, Israel's venerable ancestor. But that covenant was of a different kind. There, God acted unilaterally, committing himself alone to perform certain deeds, while not requiring from Abraham the performance of any acts at all.[19] Freely, graciously, and unconditionally, God pledges himself to make Abraham "a great nation" by making Abraham's descendants as numerous "as the stars in the sky and as the grains of sand on the shore."[20] Starkly put, *God himself has assured Jewish survival for all time.*

Thus, contemporary Jews who obsess about "Jewish survival" may (not unreasonably) stew about how many Jews will survive, but that Jews will survive they need never doubt—unless they doubt that there is a God who makes and keeps his promises. But should they doubt that, then why care about Jewish survival at all? After all, the world has seen many ethnic groups come and go. If in the end, there is really no difference between Albanians and Jews except that Albanians eat shish kebob, while Jews eat matzo balls, then Jews should become Albanians—it's safer.[21]

Some "survivalist" Jews may try to counter here with the Jewish equivalent of a hellfire–and–brimstone sermon. Instead of keeping the rank and file in line with threats of eternal damnation, such Jews relentlessly raise the bogeyman of anti-Semitism to dissuade any of their co-religionists from straying from the flock. As if revamping the old James Whitcomb Riley children's poem, these Jews, in their very scariest voice, say to all huddled round them: "The *goyim* will get you if you don't watch out!"

Yet despite all the Jews-become-Christians caught by the Inquisition and all the half-Jews and quarter-Jews ensnared by the Nazis, numberless other Jews throughout history have left Jewish life—and survived. Ironically, survivalist Jews who promote the myth of inescapable anti-Semitism have themselves been bamboozled by a *bubemeise* about ineradicable Jewishness. They believe the bit of folklore claiming that until our time, Jews had no choice but to be Jewish. Thus, they (wrongly) regard American Jews as the first who have had the freedom to opt out. Accordingly, to keep them in, survivalist Jews resort to unsettling tales of implacable anti-Semitism on the loose. They recite a series of horror stories spanning ancient times to the present, a kind of Jewish *Friday the 13th, Part 5755*—with a new sequel due out each year until the end of time.

But to repeat: Throughout Jewish history, Jews have had the option to stop being Jewish—and to go on living. What was the point of the Babylonians' exiling the Jews if not to put them in a cosmopolitan environment so powerfully attractive that the exiles would voluntarily give up their Jewishness for the sake of assimilating into the larger non-Jewish population? I myself have seen a baptismal font at the entrance of the old Jewish ghetto in Rome that testifies to a similar strategy attempted by the Church. Above the font is the inscription "This is the way out"—which it was. Beginning in the late sixteenth century, Roman Jews were herded there to hear the Pope preach conversion sermons.[22] Any Jews so moved could step right up (or into) the font and get an immediate pass out of the ghetto. But the bulk of those Jews, like the mass of Babylonian Jews, like so many Jews throughout history who let themselves be martyred rather than converted, chose to remain Jews rather than to take on a way of life they believed to be profoundly false. Those Jews' primary concern was not "survival": It was truthfulness. God had guaranteed that the Jewish People would survive. That was not the issue. The issue instead was how to live truthfully with God, that is, true to the terms of the covenant made between God and their ancestors at Sinai.

Those Jews knew that the Jewish People's mere survival is never the point of its survival.[23] Doubtless, for Jews like those in the Purim story, survival is the point of the story; indeed, their surviving the danger posed to their lives is more or less the end of the story. But for the Jews of the Exodus narrative, surviving life-threatening danger is not the end, but only a means to an end, namely, living a truly redemptive way of life in covenant with God, a way of life first taken on at Sinai.

The Sinai covenant is different in kind from God's covenant with Abraham, because it is two-sided. No longer, says God, will he alone make commitments; Israel must now assume some obligations also: "Now therefore if you will obey me faithfully and keep my covenant, you shall be my treasured possession among all the peoples" (Ex. 19:5). As at the beginning of the Exodus narrative, so, too, at its climax, God's words hold out the possibility of Israel's joining him in a uniquely intimate relationship. Everything hinges on one particular word in God's proposal. But which one? Unfortunately, many Jews are conditioned to hearing about their God through Lutheran voices—even when those voices speak through allegedly Orthodox Jewish mouths. For these Jews, the only thing that matters is God's will. Accordingly, their choice is simple: The key word is *obey*.[24] But there is another word in God's offer just as crucial, and with respect to it, nothing matters more than human will: *if*.

Without that word, the Hebrews have merely traded one tyrant for another, in fact, for the worst tyrant possible, because this one is not simply the king of Egypt, but the King of the World. What sense does it make to exchange the burdens of Egypt for new, potentially heavier ones—unless there is a considerable difference between being a slave to Pharaoh and a servant of the Lord? By liberating the Israelites from Egyptian bondage and thereby setting them free for his service, God has *ipso facto* also left them free to decline it, should they so choose. Setting out on their own in the wilderness may not be a smart choice, but it is a real choice. Why should the Israelites ignore that option and instead consider God's offer of this new, bilateral covenant?

They should consider—and finally accept—God's offer, because they should take to heart the words preceding it: "You have seen what I did to the Egyptians, how I bore you on eagles' wings and brought you to me" (Ex. 19:4). This fugitive band should commit to God, neither out of blind fear nor blind faith, but due to what they have witnessed in Egypt. And what they have witnessed is a whole series of events leading to their deliverance, events that, as we've seen before, are characterized as *signs*:

The Lord said to Moses . . . "I will harden Pharaoh's heart, that I may multiply my signs and marvels in the land of Egypt. When Pharaoh does not heed you, I will lay my hand upon Egypt and deliver my troops, my people the Israelites, from the land of Egypt with extraordinary chastisements. Then the Egyptians shall know that I am the Lord, when I stretch out my hand over Egypt and bring out the Israelites from their midst." (Ex. 7:1, 3–5)

As signs, these events point to something beyond themselves, namely, God at work in Egypt to redeem the Israelites from slavery.

But as signs, they do not individually carry their own meaning; no one of them alone is readily intelligible as evidence of God's redemptive purpose or action.[25] Initially, the Egyptian magicians produce the same "wonders," the same "sign-events," as Moses and Aaron, and, as a result, Pharaoh not only refuses to let the Israelites go but makes their bondage even harsher. The Israelites, like the Egyptians, fail to interpret the signs correctly, mistakenly believing that the magicians' ability to reproduce them signifies that they cannot possibly be from God. The Israelites consequently trust neither Moses nor the God on whose behalf he claims to speak. And given what they had seen to that point, their lack of trust is justified.

However, even had the Egyptians been unable to duplicate the parlor tricks performed by Moses and Aaron, thus leading Pharaoh to let Israel go, the people still would have been unjustified—on the basis of that one event alone—putting their total trust in God. Having had one good experience with a used-car salesman might be enough to warrant going back and trusting that salesman on a subsequent deal. But no single experience, no one event or episode, justifies the kind of trust the Sinai covenant calls for from the fugitive Hebrews and turncoat Egyptians encircling the mountain's base:

staking their whole future on the trustworthiness of the one offering them the deal.

That kind of trust must rest on a pattern of experience over time. Hence, the Exodus' depiction of ten plagues[26] in a cycle of announcement-execution-cessation does what every story does. It makes us listen to the cumulative recounting of events to determine *the meaning of those events in that order.* For the Israelites, the significance of the series of events surrounding their liberation from Egypt justifies their entering into a pact with God at Sinai. Their own cumulative experience thus demonstrates that he is indeed trustworthy to deliver on the promises he makes. They therefore have good reason to believe that no matter what he promises them, he can be counted on to keep his promises. For he has proved himself to be their trusty *go'el*, their reliable redeemer, their close relation who will stand up for them and shield them, like a mother eagle who bears her fledglings on her wings, interposing herself between them and any who might attack them from below.[27]

As the story of the Jewish People has continued through time, similar patterns of experience have continued to display such sacred, redemptive meaning. While through the ages, individual Jewish persons have been brutally persecuted, even murdered, God's promise to sustain the Jewish People has not died. That promise and that People have managed to survive the worst the world could throw at them—including the Holocaust. One could of course attribute Jewish survival over the past three thousand years to "dumb luck." But considering what Jews have been through and considering how many other peoples have not made it through to the present, such a conclusion hardly seems warranted and certainly not self-evident. Or as Blaise Pascal, the seventeenth-century French-Catholic mathematician/physicist/theologian, argued:

In . . . considering [the] changeable and singular variety of morals and beliefs at different times, I find in one corner of the world a peculiar people, separated from all other peoples on earth, [among] the most ancient of all . . . a fact which seems to me to inspire a peculiar veneration for it . . . since if God had from all time revealed himself to men, it is to these we must turn for knowledge of the tradition.

This people is not eminent solely by its antiquity, but is also singular by its duration, which has always continued from its origin till now. For whereas the nations of Greece and of Italy . . . of Athens and of Rome, and others who came long after, have long since perished, [this people] ever remains—in spite of the endeavors of many powerful kings who have a hundred times tried to destroy it.[28]

For Pascal, the theologian cum scientist, the Jews' staying power is the physical evidence for drawing sensible conclusions about God's enduring power.

But looking at the Holocaust and drawing the "no-God" conclusion barely even qualifies as an argument; as the old Yiddish proverb reminds us, "One example doesn't make a proof." To focus on the Holocaust alone as the warrant for disbelief is to take up a very short-sighted perspective on Jewish history. First, it directs our view only to the Jewish People's sufferings in the past while blinding us to its triumphs—including its continued existence. Second, by fixating on life lost, a Holocaust-blinkered vision of Jewish history screens out Jewish life not merely saved, but revitalized, both in Israel and in the United States following the Holocaust. After virtually the whole world lent a hand in the attempt to drive the Jewish People out of the world, beholding a Jewish state's rebirth together with a Jewish Diaspora's revival is—dare one say it?—like witnessing the Jewish People's "Easter": raised up from the Good Friday of the Holocaust, brought back from the dead, made alive again by the power of God![29] Of all the "Lessons of the Holocaust," no one merits more serious attention than that one. Where was God during the Holocaust? With every Jew reading these words, *now*.

Part of the reason that many Jews view the Holocaust as *the* event in Jewish history that invalidates belief in God is that they frequently do not know very much Jewish history in the first place. And yet, as the Exodus master story repeatedly instructs us, it is Jews' cumulative experience through time that most distinctively points to or signifies God's active presence in the world. Consequently, lacking knowledge of their own historical experience, Jews will necessarily lack *the grounds* for belief in God. Thus, for such Jews to say that after the Holocaust, they don't see "how anyone can believe in God any more" is little more than a statement of their blind faith in unfaith, that is, their *ungrounded* belief in disbelief. And, tellingly, such Jews manifest the blindness of their faith in another way as well: They almost never raise the question of how, after the Holocaust, anyone can believe in humankind any more.

At a UJA fund-raising workshop, people were asked why they thought it was important for Jews to get involved in Jewish causes. After the typical answers had been given—"Jewish survival," "Israel's security," etc.—one man shyly stammered: "Why, to redeem the world."

The others in attendance giggled.

The devotees of civil Judaism and its Holocaust cult share the conviction that, ultimately, Jews can count neither on God nor on other, non-Jewish human beings to make Jewish existence safe in the world, a world that will never cease to be hostile to Jewish existence in it. So, in the last analysis, theirs is a triune faith: There is no God, humanity is incorrigible, and the world is irredeemable. But even supposing the cult's adherents could marshal support to ground any of those doctrines, a fundamental issue would still remain: Who would want to live with that faith? Indeed, who would want to live at all? The plainest answer to that question may be Jerzy Kosinski's suicide. If ever there were a story that accords with the cult's own articles of faith, *The Painted Bird* is it.

Even some children of the cult's adherents seem to have problems living with its creed. Lee Hendler is the daughter of Joseph Meyerhoff, one of the principal backers of the Holocaust museum in Washington. Hendler has said that her parents used to tell her, "You have to be Jewish, in part because you owe it to the six million." By her own testimony, she came to see that "that was not a good enough reason." Since then, she has taken up an increasingly traditional Jewish way of life, attracted to it perhaps precisely because it is a way of *life*.[30]

Jewish faith after the Holocaust calls for more than faith in God; it also calls for faith in humankind. Post-Holocaust, the former may be much easier to have than the latter. But without faith in humankind, belief in God is empty. The *go'el* of old, no matter how willing to perform his duty of redemption, could not successfully fulfill his obligation if the ones he sought to aid were unwilling to be redeemed. The Israelites were just such people from God's first attempt to rescue them from servitude to his later efforts to restore them to their ancestral home. Initially, no matter how much Moses told them of God's pledge to redeem them from the Egyptians' clutches, "they [would] not listen to [him] on account of their spirit crushed by cruel bondage" (Ex. 6:9). Later, in the wilderness, they were easily disheartened by the spies' report of the difficulties in conquering Canaan and immediately broke out into their old refrain of "Back to Egypt!"[31] Consequently, God gave up on that generation (save for Joshua and Caleb), condemning it to die before it reached its destination. Even a ready, willing, and able *go'el* such as God can be no true redeemer unless he can come to the rescue of a people, a humanity, and a world capable of being redeemed.

The Jews were the test case. In God's contest with Pharaoh, the Lord picked, as it were, the worst team he could find. To confront the world's most powerful (human) ruler, he selected as his spokesman someone who, by his own admission, had "never been a man of words . . . slow of speech and slow of tongue" (Ex. 4:10). Then, as the objective of his saving work in Egypt, one of the world's highest civilizations, God chose slaves who stood at the bottom of the social ladder. Those Hebrew slaves were anything but admirable—contrary, contentious, in the Bible's language, "stiff-necked." If there were ever any human beings who could make humanity seem hopelessly incorrigible, the children of Israel were just such people. In sum, they were chosen as the best example of the worst that God could find.

But somehow, by the story's climax at Sinai, some changes had begun to occur. Moses had become positively eloquent not only in exchanging ripostes with Pharaoh,[32] but at becoming God's own mouthpiece. Meantime, the Israelites had changed a little, too. They would not even listen to Moses when he had spoken to them early on about the possibility of their redemption from Egyptian bondage. Encamped before Sinai, however, they were "all ears" to hear God's proposal regarding a redemption even more transforming: "You shall be to me a kingdom of priests and a holy nation" (Ex. 19:6).[33] No longer in servitude to Pharaoh, the Israelites were offered the chance to enter into priestly service to God.

The image of the Jewish People as a whole nation of priests captivated the early Pharisees, the forerunners of rabbinic Judaism. Though they were certainly no fundamentalists, the Pharisees took God's proposal with a stunning literalness. They instituted the distinctive practice of laving their hands before partaking of a meal. By so doing, they imitated the priests' practice in the Temple before offering a sacrifice. They thus transformed their household tables into altars and thereby affirmed that what ordinary Jews did in their homes in their daily lives was every bit as precious, as pleasing to God, as holy, as what the priests did in the Temple precincts. With a kind of ripple effect, the Pharisees' program expanded the domain of holy service to God by bringing more and more Jews into that service.

That is exactly how it should be. The service priests perform has two sides: Priests serve the deity by serving those who would draw near to the deity. The priest is the enabler who makes it possible for others to come into the deity's presence. Such is the priestly, sacred service the Jewish People is to perform for God and for the world. Jews are to serve God by bringing others into his service also. The boundaries of that service, like the storyline and thematic thrust of the Exodus narrative, are to keep moving forever outward.

Jews, the world, and God all have a stake in maintaining the momentum of that story-powered process. Should that narrative-based dynamic of ever-expanding redemption come to a stop, Jews will lose hope of the world's redeemability and thus give up their unique mission in and to the world, leaving themselves open to serving powers in the world other than the Lord—perhaps even Pharonic ones. Not only will the world then go unredeemed, it will cease even to hear a story portraying it as a world capable of redemption. Finally, should the outcropping of redemption come to a grinding halt, then God's reputation will go unredeemed as well. For clearly then, he will not be *go'el*. But that will not be all. Because there will not be any kingdom of priests, much less any kingdom of Heaven on earth, he also will not be king. In short, lacking priests who serve him and worshippers who seek him, *God will not be God*.

Why should Jews survive? Whatever responses there may be, God's is the one that matters: *Jews should survive because they are the linchpin in his redemption of the world*. Bluntly put, *the Jewish People is* indispensable *to the redemption of the world and to the redemption of God's good name in that world*. At Sinai, God pledged that the people Israel would be his unique instrument of redemption. For better or worse, God must stand by that promise. For if God, like some fickle Ahashverosh, chooses some other people instead of Israel—or even in addition to it—he undermines his would-be reputation of faithful promise keeper. Hence, although God cut down most of the wilderness generation, he still stood by and sustained their children—and *their* children's children, even down to us. But should the Jewish People be unable or unwilling to function as God's promised instrument of redemption, that would break whatever hope the world would have of its redemption, for at least one highly visible, highly touted part of it—the Jews—would have shown itself to be utterly irredeemable, even by God himself. God may have assured the Jews' survival, but as to their redemptive mission, even he cannot guarantee their success.

Preserving "Jewish identity," maintaining "Jewish continuity," safeguarding "Jewish values"—all these aims, though not unimportant, pale beside Jews' true purpose in the world: *to serve as God's People upon whom the redemption of God's world and God's own name uniquely depends*. It is that purpose, that mission, that once empowered Jews to "walk through fire and water," and which can capture Jews' imagination again if Jews will dare speak it aloud once more—not merely to the world, but more fundamentally, to themselves. Unfortunately, those who serve at the altar of the Holocaust cult may have so deadened Jews' spirit and sense of hope that that mission to God and to world no longer stirs them. And yet, should Jews give up on Sinai, on the pact and purpose offered them there, they will revert to the same paltry rabble they were prior to entering the covenant. Instead of persevering in God's quest, they will have embarked on a life of endless wandering in a wilderness, always ready to re-enslave themselves to the oppressive powers that claim to rule this world.

Surely, there must be times when God wants to give up on the Jewish People, feeling that it might be easier to redeem the world than the Jews. However much we have changed since Egypt and Sinai, we are still often cantankerous and quarrelsome, mulish and rebellious. How can God bear us? Why does he bear with us? In part, the answer lies in God's concern for his good name, his desire to redeem his reputation in the world. Thus, by making a covenant with the Jewish People at Sinai, God in a sense bet on Israel as his own redeemer, and the worst thing he could do for his reputation would be to welsh on that bet now.

But God bears with the Jews for another reason. It, too, goes back to Sinai and the covenant, but it may be able to break through to the hearts of survivalist Jews even where grand purpose and pure self-interest have previously failed. Earlier, we saw how the language surrounding the covenanting of God and Israel richly suggested the metaphor of a marital union. Consequently, Israel's later deviating or straying from the covenant's clauses is often portrayed, especially by the prophets, as a kind of faithlessness akin to marital infidelity. Hosea, in fact, invokes that very image to describe what has become of the relationship between God and his people. More personally—and in true Israelite fashion—Hosea sees in that larger story his own individual story of his wife's betrayal of him. When Hosea's wayward wife, Gomer, is about to bear a son (who may or may not be his), God tells him to name the boy "Lo-ammi", explaining that "You [Israel] are not my people, and I will not be your God" (Hosea 1:9). With these words, God has negated those he used at Sinai to form the covenant with Israel, which entered God and Israel into an intimate union unique in all the world. With these words, therefore, God has divorced the Jewish People.

But God has even more bad news in store for Israel. Like a

cuckold, God is full of rage at Israel's act of betrayal and vows not to let her profit from it. The people have acted faithlessly by embracing the *ba'alim*, the local Canaanite fertility gods, as sources of prosperity. Significantly, the Hebrew word *ba'al* is not only the name for one of these deities, but also the common term for "husband" or "master." So Israel, in seeking out the *ba'alim*, had sought out new lovers as well as new lords, having thought to herself, "I will go after my lovers, who supply my bread and my water, my wool and my linen, my oil and my drink" (2:7). God, however, has a different scenario in mind:

> . . . I will hedge up [her] roads with thorns
> And raise walls against her,
> And she will not find her paths.
> Pursue her lovers as she will,
> She shall not overtake them;
> And seek them as she may,
> She will never find them. (2:8–9)

Thus frustrated, Israel will have a change of heart, away from the *ba'alim* and back to her true partner, God. Her change of heart, however, will not indicate any change of character, any sense of remorse or repentance over her faithlessness. Instead, it will reflect only a calculating mind: "I will go and return to my first husband, for then I fared better than now" (2:9).

Though Israel's infidelity may have made God seem like a cuckold, it has not made him a fool. When Israel, unrepentant, tries to return to him, he will remind her that *he* was the one who lavished gifts on her—grain, wine, oil, silver gold—which she then gave to *Ba'al* in adoration of him (2:10). Outraged, God will leave her to her own devices so that she can see just how well she fares. No more wine, wool, or linen; no more festive holiday rejoicings—there will be nothing to celebrate! He will strip Israel bare for all the world to see. In anger and heartbreak, God vows, "I will punish her for the days of the *ba'alim*, on which she brought them offerings; when decked with earrings and jewels, she would go after her lovers, *forgetting Me*" (2:15). It would seem that the relationship, the story, between God and Israel has come to an (unhappy) end.

And yet that story, like Hosea's prophecy, is not over. God will not let it be over. God, through Hosea, dramatically changes his tone, and the prophecy suddenly changes its thrust. Instead of concentrating on the dismal state of affairs at which their relationship has arrived, God thinks back—and asks Israel to think back—to the point where it all began:

> Therefore, behold I will allure her,
> And bring her into the wilderness,
> And speak tenderly unto her. . . .
> And she shall respond there, as in
>   the days of her youth,
> And as in the day when she came
>   up out of the land Egypt. (2:16–17)

God recalls—and wants Israel to recall—the intimacy of those days past so that such closeness might be present again.

If anything, God wants a closer relationship than before: "You shall call me *Ishi* [that is, 'my man'] and no longer call me *Ba'ali* [i.e., 'my master' or 'my husband']" (2:18). Everything associated with Israel's waywardness and estrangement from God, even the very name of her former paramour, *Ba'al*, will never be mentioned again. To ensure that the new relationship is new, and thus different from the old one, God has special engagement presents for Israel: "I will espouse you in justice and righteousness, in steadfastness, and in unflagging love; I will espouse you in faithfulness—and you shall know the Lord" (2:21-22).[34] Uprightness, fidelity—these are the virtues, the ongoing dispositions, that make lasting intimacy with God possible, and, as God's own gift, these will be the qualities that Israel will necessarily possess. Forgiveness has been granted, betrothal has been effected, and all that remains, therefore, is for the re-wedding to take place. It is God who renews the wedding vow: "And I will say to them that were not my people: 'You are my people,' and they shall say: 'You are my God' " (2:25). The covenant has been renewed, Israel and God have been reunited.

What moves God to renew the covenant and restore the relationship? His concern for the world's redemption? Certainly. His concern for his own name? Clearly. But it is also something else that moves him, something far more fundamental: God's love of the Jewish People. It is a love so expansive that it can overarch, overcome, Israel's covenantal breaches. God's love keeps God close to Israel by keeping the covenant intact. If God's covenant with the Jewish People remains unbroken and thus still in force, it is because a God still passionately in love with the Jewish People acts to keep it so—as he has been doing every day since Sinai and the Golden Calf, or whenever the Jewish People has turned its back on him in favor of directing its devotion somewhere else, whether to the *Ba'alim* in Hosea's time or toward the Holocaust, Israel, ethnicity, and survival in our own. In the end, God's love is the lodestar for redirecting Jews' commitment back to the covenant, the lodestone for drawing forth their desire to be *His*.

A young Jewish mother lies in a hospital bed with cancer. A passing Lubavitch rabbi making rounds to visit the hospital's Jewish patients comes into her room. She tells him that she does not want to know why God has given her cancer, only whether God cares about her and her cancer. The rabbi asks, "Which is more important, that God loves you or that you love God?" Before she can respond, the rabbi answers the question for her: "It is more important that we love God, and the way Jews show their love of God is by keeping the commandments. So maybe if you started keeping kosher, God might heal your cancer."

The rabbi is wrong. God's love is more important, more funda-mental, because God's love is what makes our love possible. It is God's love of the Jewish People that is the basis of our being able to love him back. The daily liturgy shows that. In the morning service, the prayer that immediately precedes the *Shema* concludes, "Praised are you, Adonai, who has chosen his people Israel out of love," while in the evening service, it ends more simply, "Praised are you, Adonai, who loves his people Israel." Only then, only after hearing of God's love for us, can we move to the *Shema*, which calls on each of us individually to love God back in kind: "And you shall love Adonai, your God, with all your mind, and with all your desire, and with all your substance."[35]

Yes, Jews should survive out of the hope of allying with God to redeem God's name and God's world. Yes, Jews should survive out of a sense of self-interest of working with God to redeem themselves. But if Jews finally follow God, and God alone, the basis for their lasting fidelity has to be a sense of loving gratitude for the devotion God first showed them long ago in Egypt. Or as the closing words of the *Shema* remind Jews twice each day, "Thus you shall be mindful to do all My commandments and so be holy to your God. I am Adonai your God, who liberated you from the land of Egypt to be your God. I, Adonai, am your God." Without such continuing demonstrations of God's love for the Jewish People, from his empowering it to survive Egyptian bondage to his enabling it to survive the Holocaust, God's support of the people Israel might be as iffy as Ahashverosh's while Israel's faithfulness to God, lacking any sure foundation, might be as inconstant as that of Gomer, Hosea's wife. Like Gomer, some Jews have sought out new gods, new powers, to sustain the Jewish People's existence—"Jewish continuity," "Jewish identity," "Jewish values." But also like Gomer, such Jews will discover that none of these provides what it is they seek, namely, the power to unequivocally sustain Jewish life. That is the gift of God alone.

Rabbi Hanina taught that "everything is in the power of Heaven except reverence for Heaven."[36] Although God may vividly demonstrate his powerful presence in the world, he cannot (*will not*) constrain human beings to recognize it. A fleeing Israelite who had just passed through the storm-tossed Reed Sea could, after all, have turned around and, seeing the drowning Egyptian host, responded not with the hymn of thanksgiving, "Who is like you among the gods, Adonai?" but with the nonchalant observation, "Gee, I listened to the weather report back in Goshen before we left, and they didn't predict rain today!" So, too, contemporary Jews can say that they do not see God's power manifest in the Jewish People's ultimately escaping the crematoria, in its rising from the ashes to establish the first Jewish commonwealth in two millennia, and in its re-enkindled communal life in so many places around the world. Nevertheless, even God, especially God, cannot force the Jewish People to see his hand in such events. For this is the God who first reached out to Israel by offering its father Abraham a covenant that asked nothing in return. Israel's love of God, like his for Israel, cannot be coerced but must be freely given.

One thing is certain, though. Jews will never have even the possibility of seeing God's power at work in the world unless they recant the dogma that the Holocaust proves there is no God, unless they foreswear the idolatrous belief that only the State of Israel can ensure Jewish survival, and unless they give up looking for God in the narrow, private realm of ethnicity and "psycho-Judaism" on the one hand, and of a sham spirituality on the other, be it *ersatz* Chasidism or "Jewish meditation workshops."

Without a corrected, truer vision of God's presence in the world, Jews' outlook on the world cannot help becoming bleak. In such a world, Jews will not be able to see any "light at the end of the tunnel," because history, whether Jews' or anybody else's, will have no end, that is, no point or purpose, and because looming over such a world, eclipsing any hope or promise in it, will be the shadow of the Holocaust. Many young Jews have clearly chosen to leave that dark, forbidding, joyless world, as each year more and more of them inter-

marry, assimilate, and turn their backs on a people—and a story—of
such ceaseless and pointless suffering.

The dominance of such a story over much of contemporary Jewish life is reflected in the fact that next to the *Shema*, the prayer
known by even the most unlearned Jew is *Kaddish*. Though the
synagogue service contains many forms of *Kaddish*, the best-known
is the so-called "Mourner's *Kaddish*":

Yit-gadal ve-yit-kadash shemei raba b'alma divra khri'uta ve-yamlikh mal-
khutei be-chayei-khon uve-yomei-khon uve-chayei di-khol beit yisrael be-
agala u-vizman kariv v-imru amen. . . .

These Aramaic words, rendered into English, read: "Magnified and
sanctified be God's great name in the world which he has created
according to his will. May he establish his kingdom soon, in our
lifetime. Let us say: Amen." Recited by mourners immediately following a death and at other times throughout the year, *Kaddish*
with its staccato Aramaic has a powerful effect on those who recite
and hear it. So powerful, in fact, is its mood and aura that a special
"Holocaust-*Kaddish*" was written for recitation during Yom Hashoah
observances:

> *Yit-gadal*
>   Lodz
> *ve-yit-kadash*
>   Gurs
> *shemei raba*
>   Warsaw
> *b'alma divra khri'uta*
>   Bogdanovka
> *ve-yamlikh mal-khutei*
>   Ravensbruck
> *be-chayei-khon uve-yomei-khon*
>   Vilna
> *uve-chayei di-khol beit yisrael*
>   Treblinka
> *be-agala u-vizman kariv*
>   Chelmno
> *v-imru amen.* . . .

Originally, however, the locus for reciting *Kaddish* was not, for
example, the house of mourning, but the schoolhouse, the *beit mid-*
rash. After one of the rabbinic masters had delivered his *d'var Torah*
(his interpretative discourse on some sacred text), all present would

recite *Kaddish*, appropriate after hearing about God's unfolding story with the Jewish People, not because it had anything to do with death or grieving, but because it had everything to do with hope: "May He establish his kingdom in your life and during your days and in the life of the whole household of Israel, speedily and soon." Later, *Kaddish* moved beyond the schoolhouse to the synagogue and in a somewhat reformulated fashion became a prayer for those who had suffered the loss of a close relative. The cliché, of course, is that this prayer recited in the face of death never once mentions death. Exactly! For what it asserts in the face of death is God's living presence; even at that most broken of times, of broken hearts, broken lives, and broken worlds, the mourner stands up and declares aloud, publicly, before friends, relatives, and God, the hope that there may yet be "great peace from Heaven, *life* for us and for all Israel."

Kaddish gives voice to why Jews *should* survive: They are the hope of the world. They embody such hope. If ever any people had a right to feel the world is a hopeless place, it is surely the Jewish People. In that sense, Jews who have taken up a Holocaust master story are right in what they have done. They are wrong, however, in thinking that they can remain Jews while holding such a story. For even as they recite their Holocaust-*Kaddish*, they must scrupulously ignore the One to whom the prayer refers and the hope which it articulates. They must assiduously push into the background the Lord of Heaven and Earth, being mindful only of a litany of inhuman violence, cruelty, and death. Just as Jews cannot long remain Jews while holding a Holocaust-shaped story—after all, given such a story, why should they?—neither can humankind stay human if such a narrative becomes the paradigm of human existence in this world. If the Jewish People would continue to be the bearer of a master story about redemption—not only theirs, but the world's, not only humanity's, but God's—Jews must come to recite *Kaddish* once more not as a doleful lament, but as a joyous affirmation, proclaiming the hope of its closing line, "He who makes peace in his heavens, he *will* make peace for us and for all Israel."

Oseh shalom bimromav, hu ya'ase shalom aleynu v'al kol yisrael. . . .
Amen.

Notes

1. Similarly, "Mordechai" name may be derived from the name of another pagan god, Marduk.

2. Cf. Ex. 17: 14–16, Deut. 25:17–19, and I Sam. 15.

3. Hebrew, singular: *pur*; see Esther 3:7.

4. Cf., e.g., Gen. 41, which relates Pharaoh's various dreams of cows and ears of grain, the meaning of which Joseph deciphers.

5. Megillah 7b.

6. Another uncanny—and disturbing—parallel also exists between the Exodus narrative and later Jewish history. When the famine breaks out, Joseph sells the stored food to the starving Egyptians: when they run out of money, he takes their cattle; when they run out of cattle, he takes their land and them. (Cf. Gen. 47:12–27.) Thus, Joseph, in the role of Pharaoh's middleman—the only role in which he could have saved himself and his brethren—ends up being the oppressor of the native Egyptian population (an oppression even more pronounced if the Pharaoh, as some scholars think, was himself also a non-Egyptian). Perhaps when that Pharaoh died, his successor and the rest of the Egyptian populace ignored the good Joseph had done, focusing instead on the hardship he had caused. The same storyline goes throughout later Jewish history, when Jews, forced to become moneylenders in medieval Christendom and, later, tax-farmers in Eastern Europe, found themselves in an untenable interstice between distant overlords and local peasants living at the margins of existence. The classical rabbis were themselves not unaware of such eerie historical parallels; hence, their dictum, *Ma'aseh avot, siman l'vanim*: "an incident involving the patriarchs, a signal to their descendants."

7. Literally, "to bring out"; here, as in, e.g., Ex. 21:1, used for the emancipation of slaves. Cf. *A Hebrew and English Lexicon of the Old Testament*, s.v., "*yatza*."

8. Ibid., s.v., "*natzal*,"; cf. also Ex. 12:36.

9. Once more the Hebrew verb *hamotzi*. The classical rabbinic sages disagreed whether this mention of redemption should be counted along with the other four and thus occasion the drinking of another cup of wine. As with all unresolved halachic disputes, the rabbis set this one aside for Elijah to resolve when the Messiah comes. Hence, a fifth cup is poured at the seder, not for the participants, but for Elijah—and the messianic age.

10. Alluding to the redemption in Egypt in the past as well as to the redemption to come in the future, it appears as a verb in several key benedictions: immediately following the *Shema* in both the morning and evening services; as one of the so-called "Eighteen Benedictions" recited thrice-daily; and, significantly, at the seder in the blessing over the second cup of wine, "the cup of redemption," which immediately precedes the meal itself.

11. Nahum Sarna, *The JPS Torah Commentary: Exodus* (Philadelphia: Jewish Publication Society, 1991), p. 32.

12. Cf., e.g., Lev. 25:24–26, 47–49, 51, and 54.

13. Some refer to this person in English as "the blood avenger."

14. Cf. Num. 35:9–28.

15. Surely, this image of God-the-redeemer-who-settles-scores is present in the words recited at the seder immediately following the cup poured for Elijah, herald of the Messiah and the coming Final Redemption:

Pour Your anger on the nations who do not know You and on the kingdoms that do not invoke Your name, for they have devoured Jacob and laid waste his dwelling place. Pour out on them Your indignation and let Your blazing wrath catch up with them; pursue them in anger and obliterate them from under the heavens of the Lord.

Interestingly, the root, *g-'a-l*, which always carries with it the connotation of personal relationship and responsibility, has no parallels in other Semitic languages. It is different from another term for redemption, *pdh*, which has strictly commercial connotations referring to "the payment of an equivalent for what is to be released or secured," and which has cognates in Akkadian, Arabic, and Ethiopic. (*Encyclopedia Judaica*, s.v. "Redemption," by Donald Daniel Leslie.) Thus, when Job in his anguish cries out, "I know my redeemer lives!" (19:25), it is more than a howl of pain; it is an affirmation of conviction that his personal relation is on the way to deliver him— or soon will be.

16. Sarna, p. 32. Sarna cites parallel usages in Gen. 4:19, 6:2, 11:29 "and over seventy other biblical occurrences." See p. 242, n. 14.

17. Compare the divorce formula in Hosea 1:9 after Israel has been unfaithful by "whoring after" other gods: "You are *not* my people, and I will *not* be for you [God]." See the discussion *infra* on pp. 169–71.

18. Sarna, p. 32.

19. This kind of unilateral pledge is called a covenant of grant. See M. Weinfeld, "The Covenant of Grant in the Old Testament and in the Ancient Near East," *Journal of the American Oriental Society*, vol. 90 (1970).

20. Cf., e.g., Gen. 12:1–3; 15:5; 22:17.

21. Cf. Eugene B. Borowitz, *A New Jewish Theology in the Making* (Philadelphia: The Westminster Press, 1968), Chapter 5, "Mordecai Kaplan: The Limits of Naturalism," pp. 99–122, esp. p. 120.

22. *Encyclopedia Judaica*, s.v. "Rome" and "Sermons to the Jews," both by Cecil Roth.

23. In the face of those who would claim that Auschwitz justifies a "survival ethic" in a meaningless world, the late Christopher Lasch contended that "the only lessons Auschwitz has to offer [are] the need for a renewal of religious faith, the need for a collective commitment to decent social conditions." Quoted in James Seaton, *First Things*, 45 (August/ September 1994): 12. I am indebted to Ms. Cynthia Read for bringing this passage to my attention.

24. Very briefly, the genealogy of a mistake goes like this: Classically, both Jews and Christians believed that God's commandments ought to be obeyed, because the God who commanded you had created you and, moreover, had redeemed you, thus knowing you better than you knew yourself and loving you more than you could imagine. Hence, God's commandments were to be followed, because (1) they were in themselves good for you, and (2) you owed it to God out of gratitude and love.

However, Martin Luther and certain varieties of Protestantism brought an end to all that. Luther, following a medieval scholastic named Duns Scotus, taught that human nature, including human reason, was corrupt. Thus, the very attempt to find some rationale for obeying God's commandment was a sign of just such corruption and sinfulness. The only thing that mattered was that God willed it.

The notion that a perfect will is the center not only of the religious life, but also of the moral life was eventually taken over from Luther by another

German, Immanuel Kant—whose parents were, by the way, Christian pi-etists. Finally, a half-century later, the notion that one obeys the command-ments primarily because they are God's will makes its way into Judaism when it is picked out of the German cultural stew of the time by the founder of "neo-Orthodoxy," Samson Raphael Hirsch. As the old Yiddish maxim puts it, *vie christl't sich, judel't sich*; very loosely translated, it means: "The more something spreads in the non-Jewish culture, the more it also spreads among the Jews." (Cf. Alasdair MacIntyre, *Against the Self-Images of the Age* [New York: Schocken, 1971], pp. 123–69.)

25. See Chapter 4, pp. 72–73.

26. Plus one more if we count the Egyptians' drowning at the Sea! In any event, the biblical text typically refers to these events not as "plagues," but as "signs" or "wonders."

27. See Rashi *ad loc.*

28. Blaise Pascal, *Pensees*, trans. W.F. Trotter (New York: Modern Li-brary, 1941), pp. 618–19.

29. Ezekiel certainly said something very much like this in his "dry bones" prophecy; cf. Ez. 37. As Professor Jo Milgrom once insightfully pointed out to me, the rabbis' selection of this prophecy for the Haftarah on the intermediate Sabbath of Pesach may have been a conscious attempt to give a Jewish "answer" to a Christian holiday always celebrated about the same time: Easter.

30. PBS, "MacNeil-Lehrer News Hour," 5 May 1994.

31. Cf. Num. 13–14.

32. See, for instance, Ex. 10:28–29 and Moses' parting shot to Pharaoh before the advent of the tenth plague.

33. Cf. also 19:1–8.

34. Strictly speaking, what God gives Israel is the bride-price.

35. Usually translated as "with all your heart, and with all your soul, and with all your might." The translation I have given more clearly identi-fies the force and point of the words. In any case, in a liturgy cast almost entirely in the plural—"we," "us," "our," "their"—the first paragraph of the *Shema* stands out as the only place in the service where God addresses each worshipper in the second person *singular*.

36. Niddah 16b.

Glossary

AIPAC.   American Israel Political Affairs Committee.

'al cheyt.   Literally, "For the sin of. . . ."; these words begin each line of the lengthy confessional recited several times on Yom Kippur, the Day of Atonement.

Amidah.   The collection of benedictions of praise, petition, and thanks recited three times daily.

Ba'al.   The Canaanite fertility god; in addition, there were many *ba'alim*, or local fertility gods.

bamot.   The "high places" that various biblical texts condemn as sites where improper sacrifices are offered.

bimah.   A stage; in a synagogue, the general area from which the Torah is read and the sermon is given.

brit.   Covenant.

bubemeise.   Literally, "a grandma story"; an old wives' tale.

chametz.   Leaven forbidden during Passover.

Chasidism.   A Jewish religious movement founded in the eighteenth century emphasizing ecstasy and charismatic leadership.

chavurah/ot.   Small-group fellowship(s).

chesed.   Technically, "covenantal loyalty," but, more broadly, fidelity or steadfastness; hence, by extension, *gemilut chesed* is a "deed of lovingkindness."

churban.   "Destruction"; often refers to the respective destructions of the first and second Temples.

chutzpah.   Cheekiness; nerve.

go'el.   Redeemer.

goy; pl. goyim; adj. goyisch.   Originally, a biblical term for "nation," of which the descendants of Abraham constitute one example (see, e.g., Gen. 12:2); in rabbinic literature, however, the term comes to refer to nations or peoples *other than* the Jews, and in time, it takes on an extremely pejorative connotation.

Haggadah.   Literally: "telling"; the paradigmatic narration of Israel's Exodus from Egypt recounted through various blessings, psalms, hymns, and *midrashim* recited during the Passover seder.

halacha; adj. *"halachic."*   Jewish law.

hechal.   The main hall or chamber in which the ancient Temple service was performed.

kabbalah.   Broadly, the Jewish mystical tradition.

Kaddish.   Various prayers in which worshippers proclaim God's holiness and their hope to see the advent of his kingdom.

kadosh.   "Holy," "separate," "special."

kashrut.   The Jewish dietary laws.

k'doshim.   Literally, "holy ones"; typically refers to Jewish martyrs.

Kedusha.   Part of the *Amidah* in which the community of the Jewish People, symbolized by the presence of a *minyan*, declares God's holiness.

kibbutz. An Israeli communal farm.

kiddush haShem. Literally, "the sanctification of the Name"; refers to human acts that enhance God's reputation, often through martyrdom, but also through less dramatic behavior such as uprightness in business dealings.

kitzur Shulchan Aruch. A nineteenth-century abridgment of an earlier classical code of Jewish law; it has become the main handbook of Jewish practice for many Orthodox Jews.

landsman. Yiddish for countrymen.

Lubavitch. Chasidic sect known for its devotion to joyousness, study, and outreach to non-observant Jews.

macher. Yiddish for "big shot"; can be used pejoratively or non-pejoratively

matan Torah. The giving of Torah to Israel at Sinai.

matza. Unleavened bread eating during Passover.

megillat Esther. The scroll (i.e., biblical book) of Esther.

midrash. Literally, "to draw from"; narrowly, rabbinic exegesis of biblical texts, but, more broadly, textual interpretation in general.

minyan. The quorum of ten adult Jews needed to perform certain parts of the liturgy.

Mishnah. Initiated under the auspices of Rabbi Yehuda HaNasi in the third century in Israel, it is a compendium of early Pharisaic and rabbinic teachings.

Mishnah Torah. Maimonides' twelfth-century code of Jewish law.

mitzvah. "Commandment"; pl. *"mitzvot."*

nebisch. Yiddish for "wimp."

Pesach. Passover.

sabra.   A native-born Israeli.

seder.   The ritual "talk-feast" of Passover where participants try to "digest" the story of the Exodus.

Shabbat.   The Sabbath.

Shavuot.   "The Feast of Weeks" commemorating God's giving Torah to Israel at Sinai, and the bringing of the "first fruits" to the Temple.

Shema.   A core, if not *the* core, prayer recited twice daily; beginning with the words, "Hear O Israel," it consists of three biblical passages: Deut. 6:4–9, 11:13–21, and Num. 15:37–41.

Shoah.   "Catastrophe"; increasingly the accepted term for the Nazis' murder of six million Jews.

shul.   Yiddish for "synagogue."

talit.   A prayer shawl.

Talmud.   "Learning"; *generally*, the collection of rabbinic teaching ranging from the first century through the sixth.

talmud Torah.   Sacred study of traditional Jewish texts.

Tanach.   An acronym for the Hebrew Bible, stemming from its three major divisions: *Torah* (the Pentateuch), *Nevi'im* (Prophets), *Chetuvim* (Writings, e.g., Psalms, Job, Chronicles).

tefilla.   Prayer.

Torah.   Literally, the term means "teaching" and can refer to the whole of the Five Books of Moses or to any individual instruction contained within them; more broadly, it encompasses the whole corpus of rabbinic interpretation and generally alludes to the covenant between God and the Jewish People.

tzedakah.   "Justice," "righteousness"; the *obligation* to assist those in need or peril.

UJA.   United Jewish Appeal; an organization that raises money for the humanitarian needs of Jews in Israel and other countries around the world.

yahrzeit.   Yiddish, literally: "year time"; the commemoration of the anniversary of an immediate family member's death.

yeshiva.   The traditional academy at which rabbinic texts such as the Talmud are studied.

yizkor.   Literally, "He [i.e., God] shall remember"; a memorial service recited on the Day of Atonement as well as on the last day of the three pilgrimage festivals.

Yom Hashoah.   Holocaust Memorial Day.

Index